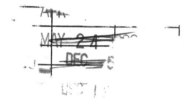

SEARS, ROEBUCK, U.S.A.

Other books by Gordon L. Weil

A Handbook on the European Economic Community
A Foreign Policy for Europe
Trade Policy in the 70's
The Gold War (with Ian Davidson)
The Long Shot: George McGovern Runs for President
American Trade Policy:
    A New Round
The Consumer's Guide to Banks
Election '76

SEARS,

☆☆☆☆☆☆☆☆☆☆☆☆☆☆☆☆☆☆

THE GREAT AMERICAN

ROEBUCK, U.S.A.

CATALOG STORE AND HOW IT GREW

Gordon L. Weil

STEIN AND DAY/*Publishers*/New York

First published in 1977
Copyright © 1977 by Gordon L. Weil
All rights reserved
Printed in the United States of America
Stein and Day/*Publishers*/Scarborough House
Briarcliff Manor, N.Y. 10510

Library of Congress Cataloging in Publication Data

Weil, Gordon Lee.
    Sears, Roebuck, U. S. A.

    Includes index.
    1. Sears, Roebuck and Company—History. I. Title.
HF5467.S4W44   381'.45'0006573   77–8758
ISBN 0–8128–2314–1

To the Commissioner
and to the memory of
Mary G. Wilson

CONTENTS

List of Illustrations

PREFACE

Writing a profile of a corporation has its risks. The idea for a book about Sears came from Sol Stein. I had had no previous contact with Sears, Roebuck and Company except as a customer, a reasonably well-satisfied one. But the risk remained that whatever favorable comments I might write would make it appear that somehow the book was a piece of corporate promotion. Yet, if I approached the story in the belief that "something has to be wrong here," I could eliminate any cooperation that might be vital for doing a balanced profile.

When I contacted Sears, I was told that the company would prefer not to have a book done about it. When I persisted, the company agreed to limited cooperation. Interviews and visits to Sears units were arranged at my request. I was accompanied to all of them by representatives of the company's public relations department. In almost all cases, it was agreed that I could not quote sources directly. A handful of the highest corporate officers were not available for interviews. No confidential corporate records were opened to my inspection, and no information that might be of use to competitors was provided.

Within these limits the company was most helpful. In Sears's archives, I found numerous critical articles about the company, and they were cheerfully copied and given to me. All of the people I interviewed appeared to make a sincere effort at open and full replies.

Of course, a great many people outside the company were most helpful in providing their views, recounting their experiences and opening their research resources.

As it approaches its centennial, Sears is a vast corporation. It is impossible to cover its history in detail or all phases of its operations. Instead, this book represents my impressions of the largest retailing organization in the world. I have tried to extend my curiosity to those areas where people who have some contact with Sears—almost everybody—might have some interest.

The strengths and weaknesses of Sears are almost the same as those of the United States itself. To have achieved and held its imposing position, it must have done something right, but no institution of its size and history could be free of errors and shortcomings. I have tried to put the successes and failings in a proper perspective, one I have developed independently of both the publisher and the subject.

A great many people have helped me learn about the retail business and about Sears. They all have my most sincere appreciation.

Special mention should be made of *Catalogues and Counters: A History of Sears, Roebuck and Company* by Boris Emmet and John E. Jeuck, published by the University of Chicago Press in 1950. This book is the corporate biography of Sears to that time and is based on access to a considerable amount of confidential data. It was most useful to me as a source of background data and of ideas for orienting my own research. It is a tribute to this book that, after 27 years, it is now in its fifth printing.

I also thank four people who were particularly helpful. Ernest Arms, Sears's national news director, was unfailingly helpful and completely frank about what information he could or could not provide. Thanks to his help, Sears, Roebuck provided the photographs used in this book. I greatly appreciate his excellent cooperation. Roberta M. Weil served, as usual, as a sounding board for ideas and as a critic. Without her help on this and other projects, this book could not have been completed. Patricia Day helped me improve the manuscript considerably by her careful and judicious editing. Finally, Mary Ellen Cooper was a most reliable and cooperative typist.

Obviously, the usual disclaimer applies. I alone am responsible for all research findings, analyses, and errors.

Harpswell, Maine
June 1977   G.L.W.

CHAPTER 1

SEARS, ROEBUCK AND THE AMERICAN WAY OF LIFE

Some years ago, an order clerk opened an unusual letter from a Sears catalog customer. A man in Portland, Oregon, had written to complain about his daughter.

"She has decamped for parts unknown with a low-down, no-account bum," he wrote, "and I would be very much obliged if you would be on the lookout for him when he sends in an order, as I know he will do just that sooner or later."

The clerk made a note of the young man's name although the chance that he would receive his order was slight. To his surprise, several months later, in came the order. The clerk wanted to avoid getting entangled in a family squabble, but he was able to write back to the harried papa that his son-in-law was turning out better than expected. He told the Portland man that the young fellow was taking good care of his daughter and seemed ready to buckle down to some honest toil. He had gleaned this intelligence from the order, which read, "2 pairs of silk stockings for wife; one machinist kit for self."

The story, which the folks at Sears, Roebuck love to tell, reveals a lot about the company. Its product line extends to silk stockings and machinist's tools, and well beyond. Its customers are so faithful they can be counted on to come back again and again—even if they are "low-down, no-account bums." Many customers look upon the company more as a public utility than as a profit-making corporation. It has been around for a long time, so people do not consider it an impersonal outfit. They do not hesitate to ask it to help them out with their personal problems. They look upon it as a friendly neighbor.

But the story also fails to reveal much about Sears. For the friendly neighbor is also a giant. Almost any way you look at Sears, Roebuck today, it is the biggest, the most, the richest.

It is tempting to say that Sears touches every part of American life simply because it is everybody's neighbor. But Sears is actually more than that; it is itself a slice of American life. No single institution, including perhaps the government itself, so nearly reflects so many aspects of the daily lives of the American people.

Listen to *Cosmopolitan* magazine. "Which company do you think has the most stores, the most customers, the most sales, the most profits—and at the same time is the most loved, the most far-flung, the most legendary, the most *American* institution ever to charge two bucks for a bottle of snake oil?" Sears, of course.

The very bigness of the outfit is all-American. Sears Tower, its headquarters in Chicago, is, not surprisingly, the tallest building in the world. Also, not surprisingly, it is no architectural gem; it is your average, run-of-the-mill office building on a Brobdingnagian scale. Sears, Roebuck turns out more than 15 million copies of its "big book" five times a year, to say nothing of the specialty and tabloid catalog, which brings total production to 315 million a year. That makes Sears the biggest publisher in the United States.

The economic impact of this 90-year-old firm may be the most significant aspect of its bigness. It is a customer, often the prime customer, of thousands of American firms. Out of every 204 working people in the United States, one works for Sears. And its sales represent 1 percent of the entire gross national product (G.N.P.) of the United States. (The G.N.P. is the sum total of all the goods and services sold in a country in a given year.)

At one time all of Sears's sales were made through mail orders out of the catalog. Now, those sales are just a tiny fraction of the total. In 1975 the company had 858 stores plus 2918 other catalog sales outlets, many in rural areas. The retail store is where the big money is.

Sears does not sell everything although the catalog may make it seem that way. It does not sell perishable goods. Nor does it now sell whiskey, handguns, cigarettes, automobiles, or houses. (It has in the past sold both cars and houses—out of the catalog.) But all that it does sell—from maternity bras to muffin pans, from lambskin coats (the first article in a recent catalog) to comforters (the last), from motor oil to dish cloths—comes with the original Sears pledge: "Satisfaction guaranteed or your money back." And if you try to take advantage of the guarantee, you will find that it works.

To finance all those purchases, you may rely on another typically American institution: credit. According to the company, one out of every three adult Americans is a card-carrying Sears customer.

Like many other corporate giants, Sears bears the imprint of just a few people who shaped its development. Richard Sears, the founder, was a swashbuckling salesman. He loved to sell, even products he did not have. His boldness made the company. In fact, it was his willingness to take risks that finally convinced Alvah Roebuck to sell his share of the company and seek a more tranquil life. His place was taken by Julius Rosenwald, a man whose administrative and business skill struck the proper counterbalance to Sears's dynamism. The third of the Sears greats was General Robert Wood, who took the firm from mail order into retail sales.

While all three were obviously superb businessmen, Rosenwald was exceptional, because he was also a moralist. He set standards for dealing with the public that dictated that Sears would not cut corners and would keep its promises. Although he left the company 50 years ago, he is continually quoted at the Sears Tower, and his old desk is enshrined there as something of a monument and a reminder.

For all of its riches and glory, Sears also reflects the weaknesses of American society. It had to be pushed by the federal government into a policy of hiring and promoting women and members of minority groups. In typical Sears fashion, too, once pushed, it set up just about the best affirmative action program in private industry. But still there is no woman, no black, and, despite Rosenwald, no Jew at the highest levels of the company.

Fly-by-night outfits use "bait and switch" techniques. They encourage you to come into the store to purchase a sale item, then they try to get you to buy a more expensive product by pointing out the defects of the product they had touted to get you there in the first place. So did Sears. The Federal Trade Commission had to order it to halt this practice, a throwback to the days of Richard Sears.

"Disclosure" and "openness" are key words these days in both business and government. It is sound policy to keep people happy by revealing a lot about how you operate. And Uncle Sam has all kinds of requirements to help make sure you do. But retail stores are subject to less regulation than most businesses. So Sears is open about only one thing: its worry about what outsiders will discover about the company. Sears has few skeletons to hide and no truly unique merchandising methods that have to be kept from the prying eyes of competitors. Sears simply does not like to make news. It has no problem making its name known, so many officials believe that the only news about Sears, Roebuck is likely to be bad news.

Sears is a particularly human institution, with the strengths and weaknesses that all people have. Its corporate idealism sets it apart from many other businesses. It has established a higher standard for itself and must be measured by that standard.

Sears has not merely survived for more than nine decades; it has been king of the mountain for most of that time. That is a dangerous and difficult place to be. Competitors and regulators, consumers and the media, all look for signs of weakness or poor judgment. To stay ahead of the pack for so long requires remarkable continuity of management, a continuity that looks not to the successes of the past but rather to the changing market of the future. Indeed, the only constant appears to be an overriding concern for staying in touch with the needs of its customers.

In the process, the company has become a part of American folklore. Recently, Senator Robert Byrd, the majority leader, said, "I always tell the people of West Virginia [his state] that they have always had five friends: God Almighty, Sears, Roebuck, Carter's Little Liver Pills, the Democratic Party, and Robert C. Byrd." That is a pretty high rating—right after God Almighty and well ahead of the Democratic Party.

But for all that we may revere it, and for all it may know about us, we know little about this giant neighbor of ours.

CHAPTER 2

MR. SEARS AND MR. ROEBUCK

Richard Sears was a visionary, but even he would not believe what he saw if he visited the Sears Tower today. Huge block numbers hang on the walls on every floor identifying nameless departments. Quotations on Sears stock are posted hourly at locations throughout the building. Messengers have been replaced by robot carts, which carry interoffice communications along an invisible track that has been sprayed onto the carpet. At four P.M., an otherworldly voice—Big Brother?—brings all work to a brief halt to provide the weather forecast for the thousands who will soon be on their way home. The firm is so big that work hours must be staggered to prevent enormous traffic jams at the high-speed elevators. Pistol-packing guards patrol.

It is 2001.

Quite unlike 1886, when Richard Warren Sears, a freight agent in North Redwood, Minnesota, first discovered his incredible knack for selling things. Hunger will spur you to try almost anything, and Richard Sears was hungry.

His father had led an unhappy life. He had failed in his quest for gold in California in 1849. He had been a bitter soldier in the Civil War, which he blamed on politicians and in which he had suffered a leg wound. He had made some money as a blacksmith only to lose it in a stock-farm venture. Finally, he gave up, and at 15 Richard had to become the family breadwinner. He had to give up his hobby of answering any and all advertisements for mail-order goods, which he then promptly traded to other boys in Spring Valley, Minnesota. He learned telegraphy and then went to work for the Minneapolis and

St. Louis Railroad. He soon found himself in St. Paul, working in the auditing department. That put bread on the table, but he was restive.

Richard Sears was hungry not only in the literal sense, but also for independence. He did not like working for somebody else. So he asked for an assignment in the field and was given the North Redwood station. There, he learned how the mail-order business worked. Watches would arrive for local people, shipped from outfits in the East. He studied their catalogs and worked out the mark-up between the wholesale and retail prices. Then, in 1886, at the age of 23, he got—or, rather, made—his chance to get a piece of the action.

A jeweler in the nearby town of Redwood Falls had refused a shipment of "yellow watches" sent by a Chicago outfit. It had been sent on consignment or possibly without even having been ordered by the jeweler, a common practice at the time. Sometimes, mail-order houses would make shipments to merchants who did not exist in hopes of getting the local station agent to take delivery and sell the goods himself.

The Chicago house told Sears he could have the watches for $12 each. These were gold-filled pocket watches, very much in vogue at the time. Sears took up the offer, although he had no intention of going into the retail business himself. Instead, he proposed to ship the watches back down the line toward Chicago. He offered each freight agent along the way some of the watches at $14 each. Anything they made over that amount they could keep. Similar timepieces were bringing $25 in local stores, so the other agents stood to make a nice profit by underselling the competition. There was also a profit in it for Sears, with no risk.

The young man was seduced by the mail-order business. He ordered more watches C.O.D. and offered them to other agents on the same terms, subject to their refusal if they were not satisfied. When he received their payments, he settled his own account. As a freight agent, he had not been required to pay in order to take delivery. Both Sears and the other agents were bonded, so the watch company must have calculated that they were reliable and would eventually pay their bills. The Chicago company took only a slight risk. Sears took none. Then, he began the game of sending watches to fictitious names, expanding his network of station agent–salesmen.

Richard Sears struck it rich as his father never had. Within six months he had netted more than $5,000, a sizable fortune at the time. That was enough to get him out of the railroad business. He was rich, and he intended to stay rich. He moved to Minneapolis, the biggest city he knew, and founded the R. W. Sears Watch Company. It was still 1886.

So far Sears had played the conventional game, although with great skill. Now, he took a risk. He began advertising the Chicago-made watches in newspapers, unheard of until that time. The station agent had found his métier. He was a natural-born advertising copy-writer. Orders poured in, and within a matter of months he had outgrown Minneapolis. He needed a better communications and shipping center, and then, as now, the answer was Chicago.

On March 1, 1887, Sears set up shop on Dearborn Street. He started writing newspaper ads immediately, offering watches for a deposit of fifty cents or a dollar. His staff included a man to handle the bookkeeping and correspondence and two stenographers. Nobody, including Sears, knew anything about watches. Yet he had already made such a name in the business that letters began to arrive asking him to repair timepieces, many of them bought from other mail-order houses. Sears sensed an opportunity for more profit.

In Hammond, Indiana, Alvah Curtis Roebuck was earning $3.50 a week repairing watches. Like Sears, he had gone to work at 16, fixing everything from watches to sewing machines. He was a tinkerer. He, too, learned telegraphy and even became a small-time printer. But he was happiest fixing watches. Then, he read an ad in the April 1, 1887, edition of the Chicago Daily News:

WANTED—Watchmaker with reference who can furnish tools. State age, experience and salary required.
ADDRESS T39, Daily News.

Should he move, pull up stakes? Roebuck thought about it for only a few hours and then mailed his answer to the ad. Two days later, Sears wrote him and asked him to come for an interview.

A tall, thin man wearing a black bow tie shambled into the office on Dearborn Street. He had brought with him an example of his best work. Sears took the timepiece and examined it, much as an illiterate "reads" a letter. Finally, he dropped all pretense. "I don't know anything about watchmaking, but I presume this is good, otherwise you wouldn't have submitted it to me. You look all right and you may have the position."

Sears had moved and expanded his business faster than was justified by new orders. So he had to devise better ways of promoting his product. He continued to try to undersell the market. The major watch manufacturers had used every method, legal and illegal, to drive out the smaller producers. A trade association was created to regulate competition, thus making it difficult for Sears to obtain watches at cut rates. But manufacturers were allowed to reduce prices on discontinued lines, and Sears gobbled these up. He was a popular customer because he always paid his bills promptly. He began selling watches to freight agents on the installment plan. He "borrowed" the idea of clubs, in which members would contribute a fixed sum each week and one member would receive a watch each week.

In the United States, the nineteenth century was the era of the farmer. History was proving Thomas Jefferson right. He had claimed that farmers were "the chosen people of God, if ever He had a chosen people," while cities were "essentially evil" and "ulcers on the body politic." As late as 1880, the United States was 72 percent rural, and agriculture was the biggest single source of the national wealth. The real American economic force was still in the countryside, with much of its potential for consumption still untapped. The numbers and the economic power on the farms were well known to the politicians, who never forgot how to cater to the agrarians. Then, industry began to recognize this enormous market and so did the mail-order houses.

The wealth of rural America was hard won. Farmers and their families toiled long hours to clear and cultivate the land and harvest their crops. There was an obvious need for mechanical help, and the tide of the industrial revolution swept across the prairies. The spring-tooth harrow and the gang plow were followed by corn shuckers and fodder shredders and the giant combine harvest thresher. The cream separator was invented in 1879, and, by the turn of the century, no dairy farm could be without one. Commercial fertilizer helped make growth, both agricultural and economic, possible.

All of this came pretty fast to farmers who had been doing things much the same old way for centuries. So they were careful how they spent their money, although anxious to acquire the labor-savers.

Mechanization meant more land under cultivation, bigger crops, and a growing farm market. The output of corn tripled between 1860 and 1900. Often, supply exceeded demand or at least the ability of the distribution system to get the produce to market, and farmers suffered serious losses. Yet, overall, farm income grew as rapidly as national income. And, of course, a lot of industrial profit was derived from making and selling the plows and baling wire that the farmers needed.

Commercially, opening up the rural areas was like exploring an unknown land. First came the peddlers. Then came the local merchant, the man who ran the general store. Next, the mail-order house, the first to link the growing Midwest and the industrial East for a whole range of products, not just the essentials of life.

Richard Sears's advertising was aimed at the farmer. The independent tiller of soil had little use for big companies or trade associations, and Sears stressed that he, too, was an independent. His lower prices were the proof. So was his willingness to send watches on approval for just the payment of a deposit.

It was a successful formula. By the end of 1888, he had established a branch office in Toronto to handle Canadian orders. But his formula was easily copied by competitors, and Sears wondered how he could keep ahead of the competition. The answer turned out to be a guarantee, hardly a new idea. But, if low prices were his chief selling advantage, it also made farmers wonder about quality. The guarantee was the best reassurance he could give, and with each new catalog he issued in 1887, he made the pledge stronger.

Although he seemed to thrive on the business, Sears longed for a more bucolic life. The dual pull of commercial success and the desire to sit back and enjoy his life would always be present in him. He was able to succeed with farmers because he remembered life in small towns with great affection. Within six weeks of Roebuck's having joined him, Sears told the Indiana watchmaker, "We will not stay here much more than a year. I'll sell out. We'll go to some town in Iowa and start a big retail store, and you will be my best and first man."

Just one year after coming to Chicago, Sears sold out. Some 15 months earlier, he had been a poor freight agent in North Redwood. Now, he was paid $72,000 for the R. W. Sears Watch Company. Roebuck and the original bookkeeper bought a half interest in the Toronto branch for the sum of $1475, one-half the value of the inventory. Sears remained alive commercially through his remaining half-interest there.

But Sears did not go Iowa. His money did. He invested some $60,000 in farm mortgages in that state. Realizing the risk in such an investment, he decided he had better get back to work. He also decided to get back to Minneapolis because his family, who had become his employees, did not like Chicago. In 1889, he was back in business again under the name of the Warren Company, using his middle name because he had agreed not to use the name of Sears for three years. He was selling watches again. At times the market was tough, as the economy slowed down. A year later, he sold his half-interest in the Toronto Sears to Roebuck for $5,190.18. In 1891, he sold the Warren company to Roebuck who promptly changed its name to his own. Sears, again dreaming of the bucolic life, had retired again, and Roebuck, who was more interested in fixing watches than running a business, now owned all that Sears had created.

It did not last long. Within a week, Sears was restless and asked Roebuck for half of the business, which was readily given. As the corporate biographers later noted, "Persuading Roebuck seems to have been among Sears' most easily come-by accomplishments. . . ." In a few more weeks, Sears had two-thirds of the company in return for the promise that he would invest more capital. Roebuck later maintained that Sears never had invested any more funds in the Roebuck Company, despite a critical need.

Soon after Sears rejoined Roebuck, they published a catalog with 52 pages devoted to watches. Just a year later, the book had gone to well over 100 pages, still dominated by watches and watch chains. But now, other products had been added: diamonds, charms, rings, silverware, a scattering of smaller items, and even revolvers. As new products would strike Sears's fancy, he would include them in the plans for the next catalog. In late 1893, the book had expanded to 322 pages and included sewing machines and bicycles, organs and pianos, and men's and boys' clothing. Sears seemed to have an almost unerring genius for judging his market. As the catalog grew, so did sales. Of course, not all of his schemes succeeded. A toilet soap subsidiary failed, but other lines were doing so well that the loss was easily absorbed.

The guarantee remained, and to back it up came a story that traveled by word of mouth through the Midwest. A customer had once come to Sears in Chicago with a watch that he had dropped on a rock in the mud. It was a mess. Without hesitating, Sears handed the man a new watch. When the customer protested that the damage was his own fault, Sears is said to have replied, "We guarantee our watches not to fall out of people's pockets and bounce in the mud."

Not everything Sears did was that reassuring. He had once published an ad for a "beautiful miniature UPHOLSTERED PARLOR SET of three pieces," complete with a picture of the furniture. The price was an amazingly low ninety-five cents. What the farmers got was doll furniture. Of course, the ad had included the word "miniature," but had also mentioned the need to box and ship the merchandise, which could have given the purchaser the impression that he would get something on which he could actually sit.

On September 16, 1893, the firm became Sears, Roebuck and Company, the name that would stick whatever happened to Richard Sears and Alvah Roebuck. Again came the pull of Chicago with its superior location for filling orders from the company's main markets in Pennsylvania, Georgia, Texas, and Iowa—areas where farmers had seen Sears magazine ads and had sent for the catalog. A branch office was opened in Chicago, and it was inevitable that Minneapolis would again be abandoned.

Late that year came the first of the Sears, Roebuck catalogs that have become so familiar. The cover was anything but modest, reflecting Sears's belief in the hard sell. "Cheapest Supply House on Earth," it proclaimed. "Our trade reaches around the world" was the subtitle. But, perhaps most perceptively, along the bottom were the words "Consumer's Guide for 1894." The catalog was that above all else, a guide to most of the merchandise then available by mail order.

The catalog was the key to Sears's success. He talked to farmers in their own language, which was simple, earthy, and direct. Even the hyperbole was designed to cater to their dreams of the greater world that most of them would never see. Sears did not hesitate to claim that his goods were "the best in the world" because he knew that his customers would never be able to judge them by that standard. (Of course, he could not either.)

Sears was no more honest than the other "snake oil" salesmen of his time. But he was a lot better at writing advertising copy. Where others failed to overcome the skepticism of the farmers, Sears managed to sell them by a combination of aggressiveness and apparent simplicity. As the corporate biographers note, "He was convinced that the mail-order pot could be kept boiling only with a red-hot fire." During the depression of 1893–1894, Sears stepped up his advertising. At the same time he drove his company further into debt and boosted its sales. Increasingly, he kept the company going by a kind of levitation, known as pyramiding. It could only succeed so long as orders continued to grow. If he faltered, even for a short while, the company would fail, because its net worth was $54,570.76, far less than its liabilities of $78,163.78.

It was too much for Alvah Roebuck. He knew he owed a lot to Sears and greatly admired the Minnesota man's ability to bring in new business. But Roebuck was no swashbuckler; at heart he was still a tinkerer. He was not comfortable with the problems of a rapidly growing company. Orders poured in, thanks to the compelling advertising, but the problem, one that seemed to escape Sears, was in meeting them. Often the two would put in seven-day weeks, sixteen hours a day. The watchmaker might have been able to stand the hard work, but he could not bear the strain of what he believed to be impending financial collapse. He was more like a parson than a gambler, and everything Sears did was a gamble. Richard always seemed to look ahead to new markets to be conquered, sustained by his optimistic belief that more sales were the solution to the company's problems.

The long-term future was indeed promising. But it was chancy. In the meantime, the short-term problems, especially the threat of bankruptcy and personal liability, were more than Roebuck could take. On August 17, 1895, he went to Sears to say he was quitting. He was worried about his health and his ability to keep up the pace. Sears agreed to pay him $25,000 for his one-third interest in the company.

The decision seemed right at the time, and no doubt Roebuck was relieved to be free of Richard Sears. Yet it was a decision that he must frequently have regretted in later years. If he had hung on for just a few more years, his interest in the firm would have been worth millions of dollars.

His partner now gave no thought to selling out and seeking a quieter life. On June 20 he had married Anna Lydia Meckstroth of Minneapolis. However busy he might be with the business, he would always remain devoted to her. She would present him with two sons and two daughters. First his marriage and then his growing family would drive him to keep building his company.

Richard Sears was a lucky fellow. He needed somebody to run the company in a businesslike way. He had hoped that solid Alvah Roebuck would be the man. When the hope was disappointed, a new prospect had already entered the scene.

Aaron Nusbaum was himself something of a gambler. When the 1893 Chicago Columbian Exposition, the equivalent of a World's Fair, was announced, he decided that what visitors would need above all was refreshment. So he bid for and received the soda-pop and ice-cream concession. From selling crushed ice doused with syrup, he had made a profit of $150,000, an incredible sum at the time.

With his new-found wealth, Nusbaum went into the business of selling pneumatic tubes systems, those labyrinths of pipes that used to carry cash and vouchers through department stores. Early in the summer of 1895 he had approached Sears. He could make no sale, but he was fascinated by the budding mail-order mogul. On August 7, Sears offered him a half-interest in the company for $75,000. The offer would remain open for just ten days, until the very day that Roebuck, who may have known nothing about the arrangement, was to take his leave.

Nusbaum wanted in. But he did not have all of the cash in hand. He began asking around among his relatives, but none wanted anything to do with the new venture. Finally, he went to his brother-in-law Julius Rosenwald, then a successful merchant of men's suits.

Rosenwald already knew something about Sears. One day, Richard had come to his offices. He had wanted to buy some suits. A salesman offered to show him a selection, to explain the quality of the fabrics. Sears had brushed him aside and had given the stock a quick glance. The quality was adequate. He would take 50 suits. The salesman suggested a more modest order. How could he be sure to sell so many suits? Sears insisted on the 50; he had already sold them. He would be back for more.

If Richard Sears could sell suits at that pace, Rosenwald was already convinced that the mail-order business would work. He was willing to invest. Fortunately, he did not have to come up with a single penny in cash. Sears already owed Rosenwald and Company quite a bit for suits it had delivered to him; so Rosenwald simply reduced the liabilities of the mail-order house. On August 23, new corporation papers were drawn up. Sears held 800 shares; Nusbaum and Rosenwald each were given 350. The capital was set at $150,000. Soon, Sears would sell each of them some of his shares, so that each would hold 500.

Roebuck seems not to have been perturbed by the speed with which he was replaced. He became the firm's merchandise trouble-shooter and eventually the head of the watch and jewelry department. Every so often, Sears would come to him, complaining about his new associate Nusbaum, and together they would daydream about giving it all up and starting another business of their own. Roebuck would always agree, knowing that nothing would come of it.

What the company needed was a good manager, and that is just what Aaron Nusbaum was. Sears, Roebuck paid its bills. But Nusbaum lacked the human touch that was so important to Richard Sears. He was forever saying "I told you so," a phrase not designed to endear him either to Sears or to the employees. He was rough on the people who worked for the company, not hesitating to furlough them when he needed their paychecks to meet overdue bills. There was a classic personality clash between Sears and Nusbaum and then with Rosenwald, who had sold his business to devote his full attention to the company.

Finally, Sears resolved to pursue his daydream of going back into business with Roebuck, who at least shared his small-town values. In 1901, he walked into Rosenwald's office and is reputed to have said: "Someone's got to go. Either you and Nusbaum buy me out, or you and I buy him out." Without pausing, Sears strode from the office. He closed his desk and went to Roebuck's office to await the answer.

Here was the biggest gamble for the big gambler. After all, Nusbaum was married to Rosenwald's sister, and Julius did not like to cause family friction. What's more, Nusbaum had brought him into the business. Rosenwald was well aware of the maverick in Sears, which meant that, if the business was to succeed, he would have to keep Richard under some constraints. But Rosenwald was now deeply involved in the business, and he did want it to succeed. Neither Aaron nor he knew anything about farmers or rural America. The essence of the business was selling to farmers, and there Sears was the past master.

By his action, Sears had placed Rosenwald in the pivotal position. If he opted for Richard, he would gain complete control over Sears, Roebuck's internal operations. Sears would be "Mr. Outside," but he would become "Mr. Inside." Rosenwald was ready to bid for the big time. He sent word to Sears that they would buy out Aaron Nusbaum. They agreed to pay him $1 million for an interest that had cost him only $37,500. When Nusbaum upped the ante to $1.25 million, Rosenwald and Sears were united in their outrage and glad to be rid of the stiff-necked brother-in-law.

The incredible amount of the purchase price and that it was fully paid in just two years, signified the success of Sears, Roebuck. Rosenwald had made a sound judgment in opting for Sears.

At the turn of the century, the United States was still essentially rural. The frontier, at least for the farmer and rancher, was in the process of opening. The plains states were growing rapidly in population. The rail network, which Sears knew so well, was spreading rapidly into the hamlets of the West. Chicago was at the hub. In addition, post offices were opening everywhere.

The farmers moved rapidly from subsistence and barter to a cash economy. But they did not like what they found at the general store. Prices were high because so many middlemen took their share as goods moved from the manufacturer to the small retailer. The Grange and other farm organizations gained strength as they became the vehicles of protest against the middlemen.

Sears, Roebuck was a big part of the answer. Of course, Sears was also a middleman, but the only one between the manufacturer and the purchaser. And Richard understood that if you gouged the customer one year, you would lose him the next. So, much like the latter-day discount stores, Sears, Roebuck bargained for lower prices from suppliers in return for making volume purchases. Then, the company passed the savings on to the farmer. The only people who were left unhappy in rural America were the owners of general stores for whom the mail-order houses were the arch enemy.

If you were to succeed in selling to the farmer, you had to know what he wanted and how to tell him you had it at the best price. Richard Sears did it all by a kind of informed intuition.

In 1902, he went to North Dakota on a hunting trip with a couple of company officials. He stopped at a dairy farm and noticed a man using a centrifugal cream separator. How well did it work? How much had it cost? When the farmer told him that he had paid over $100 for the machine, Sears knew he had found a new promotional item. That ended the hunting season for Sears and his friends. He rushed back to Chicago. It took him some time to find a manufacturer who would meet his demands; then he placed a large order for the separators, in the firm belief that he would be able to stir up a sizable sales volume. Until that time, the cream separator had not been sold by direct mail.

Now, Sears the salesman went to work. He labeled his model "The Economy" and offered the smallest one for $24.95, about $35.00 less than any competing separator. The advertising copy poured from his pen. "We will give $1,000.00 in Gold to the separator manufacturer who can produce a machine that will outskim the Improved Economy. . . . We make this offer to makers of the DeLaval, the Sharples, the Empire, the United States and every other machine sold in the United States. We have tested them all and we know what we are talking about. The Improved Economy ranks first. The others a poor second."

The company could barely keep up with the orders. Sears had gambled that if he spent as much as $2 in securing each order he could make money. He was right.

Sears was churning out his extravagant ads at a time when there was no Federal Trade Commission or consumer movement. But some of the people in his office were uneasy. One day a catalog editor got up his nerve to take on the great man. He was disturbed by an ad for cooking ranges. It showed one of the company's best with the price of $4.38 superimposed. The actual price of that particular range was several times higher. The copy read: "Why stoves can be sold for ridiculously low prices. . . . Why we can undersell all others in stoves." The potential customer was asked to send for a free catalog. The editor asked Sears "if it would not be better to tone down the statements in our ads to avoid overselling our customers. I figure they would be sure in many cases to believe they had been duped."

Sears explained his approach.

"Now," he said, "who would answer that ad?"

"Someone who wants a stove," the editor replied.

"Right. A man who wanted a saddle wouldn't answer the ad, would he?"

"No."

Then Sears launched into a tirade, explaining that he wanted to get anybody who had the faintest idea of buying a stove sufficiently "wrought up" to send for the catalog. Once he received it, he would see that Sears was really selling stoves below the competition and would forget all about the "strong language" in the ad. Without such exaggeration, Sears explained, 90 percent of the prospects would not even ask for a catalog. The editor gave up, because "we were selling an enormous number of stoves at that time."

Sears knew no limits. In one issue of *Comfort* magazine, he placed no less than 70 different ads. He was no believer in "white space." Instead he filled every available inch with copy and illustrations. In the 1904 catalog, Sears devoted 16 solid pages of type to touting Customers' Profit-Sharing. What it boiled down to was a detailed explanation of the simple fact that volume buying allowed the company to sell at lower prices. But he did not hesitate to proclaim that Sears's profits were "no doubt much smaller than any other house in the world selling merchandise to the customer." Then, Sears suggested that customers pool their orders under a single name in order to save on freight charges.

The super salesman was forever coming up with new ideas. Some of them were outright flops. He started a banking department where he urged customers to deposit their savings at 5 percent interest. The only trouble was that this violated state banking laws. He offered a premium certificate plan; a certificate in the amount of purchases was sent and could be redeemed for certain catalog items. The cost of administering the plan ate dangerously into profits, and it was dropped. But just as soon as one idea failed, Sears had another to replace it. Installment purchasing was started simply on the strength of a letter Sears had written to Rosenwald. He forecast branch mail-order operations, warehouses much like the main one in Chicago, years before they came into service as a way of speeding merchandise to customers. He was irrepressible.

The result of Sears's efforts was phenomenal growth. On December 31, 1903, Sears, Roebuck could pay a special dividend of almost $2.5 million to Rosenwald and Sears. But that kind of success entailed serious problems for the company. It needed more space and more money and, according to Richard Sears, more markets.

From 1896 on, the company expanded across the face of Chicago, gobbling up offices and warehouses and building new ones whenever necessary. By 1904, it was obvious that the operations of the company should be brought under one roof—a large one—and plans were made to build a new plant in the next year on the western edge of the city.

The new headquarters would allow Rosenwald to bring order out of chaos, to establish a system for dealing with orders promptly and for coordinating what Sears was selling with what Rosenwald and others were buying. Richard Sears had little interest in such problems, so Rosenwald plunged ahead with considerable success. After all, he had the full support of a disastrously overworked staff.

Meanwhile, the company was running into serious capital problems. A sizable sum was required to finance increasing sales. Working capital shrank from over $4 million in 1904 to just $700,000 a year later. In addition, building the new West Side plant would take major financing.

Again, it was Rosenwald who acted. His boyhood friend Henry Goldman was now a principal of the New York investment house of Goldman, Sachs. He asked Henry for a $5 million loan. Instead, Goldman suggested that the company offer its stock to the public as a way of raising capital. He argued that the company's good will, the name that Sears had given it, was of great value and would certainly be sufficient to attract the needed funds. Rosenwald agreed.

In August 1906, a syndicate headed by Goldman, Sachs and Lehman Brothers offered some $9 million of Sears preferred stock. With a booming stock market, the public went for the issue eagerly. The move had come at just the right time, for one year later a depression would strike, panicking the market.

While Rosenwald was putting the house in order, Sears was seeking new markets. He worried about leaving the cities to Montgomery, Ward while his company worked rural America. Although it would take two decades for Sears, Roebuck to begin retail operations in the growing cities, Richard Sears spurred it to step up mail-order activities there as early as 1906.

Even more significant, at least at the time, was Richard Sears's decision to open a branch mail-order plant. This was his project alone; Rosenwald bitterly disagreed. Sears did not wander from his beloved Midwest, but he located the new mail operation closer to a large part of the company's market—in Dallas. At first, this office was merely a promotional scheme to appeal to Texas chauvinism. But Sears quickly realized that the company could save money by purchasing from local suppliers and avoiding considerable freight costs. Rosenwald did not take to the idea of stocking goods anywhere but in Chicago, so Sears's man in Dallas had to start the operation almost surreptitiously. Elmer Scott, whom Sears had sent to Dallas with the idea of creating a strong mail-order operation, actually purchased the land for a Dallas plant out of his own pocket. Rosenwald ordered him to sell it and take the loss himself. But Scott held on, and when the Dallas idea proved itself, Rosenwald grudgingly reimbursed him for the precise amount he had paid.

Richard Sears had again demonstrated amazing foresight. Pushing the Dallas operation, he had written: "If with this trial we can get any success, the next place will get the kind of preparation that will insure success, and encourage us to cover the United States rapidly with ten or more branches. . . ." Today, Sears has 14 catalog distribution centers.

Scott also took the first step toward making Sears, Roebuck an international merchandiser. He saw that Mexico was developing rapidly, and, in 1909, sent a carload of sewing machines to Mexico City. Although political conditions there discouraged him from going further, this shipment was the precursor of the company's major expansion into Latin America. And it sowed the seeds of the corporate approach of treating Latin American operations as just another part of the overall retailing program.

Richard Sears himself was spending more and more time away from Chicago. He traveled to the major cities of Europe in search of medical care for his ailing wife. But he never stopped working for the company, and almost every day letters would arrive with new suggestions for boosting sales. His views, even sent from exotic places like Vienna and Strasbourg, were always considered and frequently adopted.

By staying away, Sears avoided what seemed to be inevitable conflict with Rosenwald. While they always respected each other personally, their views of how to conduct the business of Sears, Roebuck sharply differed. Richard Sears had thrived on expansion, and he devoutly believed that the way to maintain corporate health was to keep selling more and more, to keep opening markets. Rosenwald was determined to bring the company into the twentieth century. He worried that setbacks to the national economy could topple a company, even one as successful as Sears, Roebuck, which depended on sales growth and huge advertising budgets to survive. Sears wanted to expand; Rosenwald preferred to consolidate.

On one point, Rosenwald had his way. Sears pulled back from his extravagant advertising. Just as he recognized the growing market in the cities, so, too, he accepted the growing sophistication of urban customers. "That the old way was not *bad for the time* we have proof in at least a fairly successful career to date," he wrote. "Our future will rest largely *on the kind of goods and service we give.*"

The conflict between Sears and Rosenwald remained dormant so long as sales continued to increase. But the depression of 1907, caused by the failure of the Knickerbocker Trust Company and other New York banks, brought a sudden halt to unbridled expansion. Although the rural economy continued to thrive, farmers as well as urbanites worried about "liquidity," whether or not they would have cash when they needed it. So they tended to hold on to what they had. Profits in 1907 were almost a half million dollars less than in the year before, a shock to a company that had never experienced any drop in sales or profits.

Company officials worried that they would not be able to sell the vast quantities of merchandise they had on order. At Sears's urging, they asked farmers who had purchased the cream separator to send in the names of others in their communities who might be interested in the machine. If some of these prospects became customers, those suggesting their names were given merchandise premiums. The ploy worked, and the separator provided about one-third of the entire profit of Sears, Roebuck in 1908.

Writing from abroad with increased urgency, Sears argued that the plan should apply to other products. He wanted orders pouring in, even if the company fell behind in filling them. He favored drastic merchandising techniques because he was openly worried that the downturn in sales was not a temporary reflection of generally deteriorating economic conditions, but a sign that the market was not being vigorously enough exploited.

Rosenwald balked. He believed that the company could only weather the storm if it trimmed expenses, particularly for advertising and promotion. He was content to wait for the improvement in the economy that he felt was inevitable.

The result was stalemate between the two prime movers of Sears, Roebuck. The balance was finally tipped by the very corporate executives most loyal to Richard Sears. They reckoned that advertising costs were outstripping profits, which would have a disastrous effect on cash flow and, now that the company was publicly held, on investor confidence. In short, Henry Goldman had to be kept happy, and he agreed with Rosenwald.

Sears was not persuaded, but he was absent from headquarters, and Rosenwald and the staff refused to follow his advice. What is more, the Rosenwald approach worked. Sales remained steady and profits grew. Sears returned from Europe in the fall of 1908. The corporate biographers were later to write: "For the first time, Sears was estopped; he had lost the momentum of initiative he had held in the firm ever since there had been a Sears, Roebuck and Company."

He had gone too far in life to rekindle his plan for retiring to a retail store in Iowa. His chief satisfaction had not been in making money, but in making the company grow. But times had changed, and Sears was unable to accept the changes. He was much like the firebrand who thrives on making a revolution but quickly becomes disenchanted when it has succeeded and he is forced to become an administrator. If you took away Sears's right to be such a firebrand, you denied him the very breath of life.

Having made his fortune, Sears became increasingly consumed with personal concerns. His wife had been ill for years, and she was only slowly recovering from the amputation of her leg. His own health had suffered from his total devotion to the company.

On November 21, he again went to Rosenwald's office and closed the door. They talked about the company; they did not argue. When he emerged two hours later, it was all over. He had formally resigned as president of Sears, Roebuck and Company. He was named chairman of the board, and Rosenwald became president. Yet the form meant nothing to Sears, and he soon resigned the chairmanship. He never attended a meeting of the board, from which he finally resigned in 1913.

He was not bitter, but he was consumed by an obvious sadness. A few months after his resignation as president, he wrote:

> I have been selfish enough to feel that a good part of a life's work devoted to the effort of helping, perhaps in a feeble way, to bring about the conditions of the present, and the promise for the future, in this line has earned for me something besides money, namely a little relaxation and a little time for my family; and perhaps some of the time that would otherwise go to merchandising will go to my dear old mother in her last years.

On September 28, 1914, he died at the age of 50, survived by his wife. His epitaph was written by *Printers' Ink,* the magazine of the advertising business.

> R. W. Sears was a mail-order man, had the mail-order viewpoint, knew how to use advertising space, knew the value of copy, knew the conditions surrounding mail-order publications, and he succeeded in a big way because he possessed those qualities to a greater degree than any other mail-order man who ever lived.

This memorial would have suited Sears. He had no pretentions about the "better things in life." All of life for him was Sears, Roebuck and Company.

Sears "succeeded in a big way," but he was also disappointed in a big way. Not so Alvah Roebuck, the Indiana watchmaker, who never wanted to dream the big dreams.

Roebuck, after leaving the company, had amassed a modest fortune by developing equipment for yet another new industry: motion pictures. Once again, he sold out early, and in 1925 he moved to Florida and invested in land. The 1929 crash wiped out his investment. Broke, he returned to Chicago and, in 1933, sought work with the company that bore his name. A year later, he casually stopped by a retail store. The manager asked if he could publicize the visit of one of the founders. After Roebuck agreed, the crowds came. The advertising ploy was so successful in pulling customers that Roebuck went on tour for several years. Yet his prime task was writing a personal history of the company's early days. He died in 1948 at age 84, once again a shareholder in Sears, Roebuck and Company, by virtue of his holdings in the firm's profit-sharing plan.

CHAPTER 3

THE GREAT WISH BOOK

If you were a book publisher, would you dig up a volume 76 years old, all of whose contents are hopelessly out of date, not actually a very rare item, and republish it at $15 a copy? You might, if the book was the 1897 Sears catalog. In fact, a few years ago, somebody did just that and sold 150,000 copies.

The American people are fascinated by the Sears catalog. As someone once wrote in *Esquire* magazine, "It may very well be that mail-order catalogs in general, and the Sears, Roebuck catalog in particular, are the greatest inventions in the interest of pure fantasy since the discovery of hard-core pornography."

The Sears catalog seems to be talking to each individual reader, so you do not just read it; you relate to it. You can go on a "shopping spree" without leaving home and often without spending a penny. You can pick out a bicycle to save for or a hair dryer for your Christmas list (the Christmas book is actually called the "Wish Book"). The whole family can go shopping together even when the stores are closed.

Face it. We are all materialistic. And the Sears catalog is the horn of plenty, designed to satisfy almost all of our secret and not-so-secret cravings for the better things in life—and more of them. Best of all there is no salesman standing over our shoulder, no reason why we cannot indulge our fantasy over a second cup of coffee, or debate the virtues of one product against another with our spouse. And in an inflationary world, where we are forced to do a whole lot more comparison shopping, the catalog becomes the standard of measure for millions of American families.

The message of the catalog is direct, and the products seem real. Take the case of a rural boy who needed a new bike. His dad studied the catalog and then visited local stores. When he found that none of them could match Sears for quality and price, he decided to order one from the catalog. The boy sat by as his father phoned in the order. When his father hung up, the boy's eyes were shining. "That bike's mine now," he said, with obvious pride. Then, he went back to the catalog and slowly wrote his name under the picture of a bike he would not see for many weeks. From that moment on, although Sears did not know it, they had a bike that belonged to a happy boy.

If you grew up in rural America, you probably remember the Sears catalog with affection. The old edition of the big book frequently was hung in the outhouse, where it would provide essential reading material and where its pages could serve a more mundane but not less vital function.

Richard Sears called his catalog "the farmer's friend." In the early years, the catalog was almost a letter from Sears to each of his potential customers. Its first job was to build up the farmer's confidence to the point where he would write off to the big city. "Don't be afraid that you will make a mistake," Sears wrote on the first page of the book. "We receive hundreds of orders every day from young and old who never before sent away for goods. We are accustomed to handling all kinds of orders. Tell us what you want in your own way, written in any language, no matter whether good or poor writing, and the goods will promptly be sent to you."

This friendly folksiness was the hallmark of the early catalog. Customers were even invited to drop into the Chicago plant and use it as a home away from home.

That Sears would go to great lengths to prove the company a good neighbor was also indicated by the many references and testimonials included in the catalog. He even persuaded public officials to testify to his honesty, a measure that might seem somewhat misplaced these days.

Then, even more often than now, shipments would go astray because of either the chaos at Sears, Roebuck or shipping delays en route. For that reason, the guarantee was of prime importance. "We Guarantee Satisfaction and Safe Delivery on Everything You Order" was Sears's original pledge, which gradually evolved into today's "Satisfaction Guaranteed or Your Money Back."

Of course, some people took advantage of this guarantee. Once a customer returned a coat, so worn that it was impossible to tell when it had been purchased. "I have never been fully satisfied with this coat," read the accompanying note. "Please refund original price of $32.50." Another customer sent back a plow, claiming that it would not work at all. When Sears looked into the matter, the company found that the entire farm had been tilled before the machine was deemed a failure.

Illustrations were essential for feeding the customer's fantasy. At first woodcuts were used, then halftones of drawings and photographs. Richard Sears insisted on accurate renditions of the products, but never resisted a bit of whimsy. In one early book, the head of Teddy Roosevelt was placed on the drawing of a suit for stout men.

The book was itself a hot item. In 1897, some 318,000 were sent across the Midwest. They represented a substantial financial burden for the company. So a charge was levied for the purchase of the catalog. By making a customer pay for the privilege of receiving the catalog, the company attempted to weed out those who wanted the fantasy without making any purchases. The price varied from year to year and in the early years of the twentieth century reached the substantial sum of fifty cents. Yet Sears wanted to get the book into as many hands as possible and realized that the charge discouraged some potential customers. In 1904, both Sears, Roebuck and Montgomery Ward announced that, in the future, no charge would be made.

Richard Sears was not a person to let such a revolutionary change pass without exploiting it. He developed a scheme called "Iowaization" because it was applied on a state-by-state basis with Iowa first. The company wrote to all of its Iowa customers and asked them to distribute 24 catalogs to their friends and neighbors. After each "distributor" had given the books away, he wrote the company with the list of names of the recipients. The company kept a careful record of the orders submitted by those new customers within the next 30 days. The "distributor" would receive premiums increasing in value in line with the total volume of the orders submitted by people on his list. This technique turned "distributors" into salesmen because they had an obvious interest in getting their neighbors to make purchases. At the same time, as satisfied customers of Sears, Roebuck, they could provide living testimonials. Word-of-mouth advertising turned out to be the most effective gimmick ever used by the company because sales in Iowa soon topped those in any other state. Richard Sears set out to "Iowaize" the country.

Distribution of the catalog skyrocketed. By 1908, some 3.6 million were being sent at one time. Every customer who placed an order received a catalog if his name was not already on the list. Today, customers must order at least $25 in merchandise every three months to stay on the list. If they fail to keep up this constant pattern of purchases, no matter how high their orders in any one three-month period or how much they buy in Sears retail stores, they may stop receiving the Wish Book. The seductive power of the big book is so great that few customers, once hooked, allow their purchases to fall below the required amount.

Some people feel positively left out if they do not receive a catalog regularly. A couple of years ago, this letter arrived:

> Dear Sears:
>
> Our family has been faithful, loyal, credit-worthy, praise singing, banner waving, bill-paying patrons of Sears since 1968. But one thing we are not, and that is proud possessors of a Sears catalog.
>
> After repeated visits to the catalog sales counter, my faith has been shaken in your great institution. Is there really a Sears catalog or is it a myth . . . perhaps another Howard Hughes?
>
> If there is a great Sears, Roebuck and Co., in the sky beyond, we pray He will hear our humble plea: let us have just one catalog! In return, we promise to use it with reverence, to love and to cherish it. The book will occupy the most honored place in our home, on top of the television set, and we promise to order from it on a regular basis and we will encourage others to do the same.
>
> Revolving Charge No. 64817360-X2

"Well, that last part really touched our heart," says a Sears official, "and we sent a catalog."

Actually Sears wants to get as many catalogs into circulation as possible, provided that they pay their own way. Every catalog order is now fed into a computer, which analyzes the frequency and prices of purchases, the use of credit, and the geographical location of the purchaser (to allow for the best mailing patterns for catalogs). The operating cost of the catalog distribution centers is a factor in determining how many catalogs should be sent to each area to guarantee at least break-even sales levels for the company. In other words, the number of catalogs available in a given region depends on just how efficient Sears itself is there as well as the area's traditional buying habits.

Catalog distribution has settled at about 15 million in recent years, so the company is testing ways of finding new devotees for the big book. In a Texas test, Sears distributes the catalog automatically to those on its mailing list and offers to sell it to others at two dollars a copy. In each catalog that is sold a two dollar gift certificate is redeemable for purchases made from that catalog. Company research indicates that nationwide circulation might rise by 2.5 million copies if this test were extended. Because only half of Sears credit card holders receive the catalog, the company is also testing the effects of mailing it to those who have good records of active purchasing in retail stores and of prompt payment. This should help the catalog penetrate urban and suburban markets where credit is a good deal more popular than in rural America.

Richard Sears knew that his catalog, with its studied amateurism, was magic. And it was the only way of advertising that was completely under the company's control. Local merchants could and did block Sears, Roebuck's attempts to take ads in their community newspapers. *The Ladies Home Journal* refused to carry Sears's ads at all because publisher Cyrus Curtis objected to their homespun makeup and sometimes wild claims. To counteract the negative publicity given the mail-order business by the independent merchants it hurt the most, Sears, Roebuck and Company used the catalog as its own tribune to proclaim the enormous scope of its operations and the Iowa prices it could offer.

At the same time, the company began to clean up its advertising in the big book, a move that indicated the waning of Richard Sears's influence on it. Of course, it soon became too big a task for him to write the entire book single-handedly. The men who purchased merchandise for the company proved to be poor copywriters, so editors were hired. Still, Sears insisted that they adhere to his style. Finally, in 1908, when Sears left the company, the catalog editor prepared a booklet setting standards for copy in the big book.

The catalog began to take on a new style. Coats might still be offered as made from "Baltic Seal" or "Electric Seal," but the fine print also indicated that they were, in fact, made out of dyed rabbit. Flamboyant selling of patent medicines became more restrained and finally disappeared from the catalog altogether in 1913. This change had come about as the result of the opening of Sears's own testing laboratory in 1911. The company could not hire reputable people for the lab unless it followed their findings. Descriptions of merchandise had to correspond to what the lab had found, a constraint that Richard Sears would have once considered insufferable.

The Sears catalog had succeeded in gaining the consumer's confidence. The constant effort to "clean it up" helped keep that confidence as consumers demanded increasingly to be dealt with on the basis of absolute honesty. (Even Richard Sears is reported to have said: "Honesty is the best policy. I know, because I've tried it both ways.") As the American population grew and millions fled the farms for the cities, the catalog climbed in popularity. The biographer of the catalog wrote at the end of the 1930s: "Wherever the traveler goes in the United States, he will find the catalog . . . wherever it is found, a curious affection surrounds it, an expression that arises perhaps out of a subconscious longing for an America which is vanishing but which still continues to be exemplified by the catalog."

The company's correspondence over the years reveals the changing clientele. Most people would be embarrassed and far too sophisticated today to drop a note to Mr. Sears and Mr. Roebuck. And the company itself would just as soon not be inundated with piles of letters requiring individual responses. But the letters bring back the feeling of neighborliness and concern that Sears, Roebuck worked so hard to cultivate.

"Can you send me a 'love powder' from your drugstore?" wrote a woman decades after Sears had stopped selling medicines. "I can't keep my man home nights. I've tried everything from buying a television to hiding his pants. It's no use. Please help me. P.S. I do not want to buy in this town. . . ."

All manner of personal problems were referred to Sears for solution. "I have a new hired man," wrote a Missouri farmer. "This morning my wife found a bug in his bed and we would like to know what kind it is, so I am sending along same with this letter. Please answer soon."

Perhaps the classic letter and response resulted from an unfortunate event in Kentucky. A woman returned four bottles of medicine she had previously obtained from Sears. "My husband died after he had finished only the first two bottles of the lot," she said without a hint of complaint. The order clerk promptly sent the widow a condolence note and then added a copy of the Special Tombstone Catalog.

Customers believed that the company cared about them as individuals and indeed even thought about them that way. So it was not so great a surprise when a New Mexico woman wrote enclosing one dollar to pay for an item that she had ordered 20 years earlier. She had requested 10 yards of colored cotton material at ten cents a yard. Instead, she received white cloth. Finally, the proper material was sent, but she never returned the original shipment. "I have never been satisfied with myself," she confessed, "so I am sending $1 to pay the bill, and ask your forgiveness for the delay. I am glad that at last I can be free."

One thing about the catalog remained constant through the years, making the big book a permanent nostalgia trip. Although each page might be more tidy, it still remained crammed with temptations. A recent catalog of more than 1500 pages contained about 70,000 different items for sale.

Other things have changed. Blacks and members of other minority groups have appeared as models. Although Sears could rarely be accused of setting the styles, it has certainly kept up with them. Today's readers might wonder what catalog customers of the early twentieth century would think of the considerable expanses of feminine flesh exposed on its pages. Such advertising merely keeps the catalog even with such other prestigious media as *The New York Times* magazine section. Of course, it reflects the changes in standards of taste and advertising, but the ads of an earlier period seemed to readers then just as avant-garde as those today.

Sometimes readers see more than Sears puts on the printed page. Such was the case of the Scandal of Page 602 of the 1975 winter catalog. Calls started coming in to the Sears Tower about a case of indecent exposure involving a male model for men's boxer shorts. Orders flew through the building to find out what had happened. Then, somebody noticed that the same ad had appeared in an earlier catalog without any such "indecent exposure." A printing mistake had occurred in the final stage of the catalog printing process, leaving a titillatingly false impression. But the truth never caught up with the myth, carried on the national newswires to the effect that the indignant model allegedly "overexposed" would sue Sears.

If the illustrations in the catalog are, well, downright sexy, the language is usually more chaste. Over the years, the emphasis has been placed on saying things in the most simple language.

Making a Sears, Roebuck catalog once consisted of Richard Sears sitting down with a few sheets of paper and a pen. His notions of items to be sold, fair prices, and provocative descriptions would spill onto the paper, which would then go directly to the printer. Today, the production of the Sears catalog is one of the most complex operations in the world of publishing.

Sears merchandisers decide what the company should sell. They are constantly besieged by potential suppliers who want the company to carry their products. At the same time, Sears turns to its traditional suppliers for updated versions of the items that are sure to appear in every catalog. About 30 percent of the goods are ordered from firms Sears partly owns. New products are sent to the Sears laboratory for testing before any final decisions are made.

The selection of merchandise is an educated guess at best. It is also a big gamble, given the enormous quantities that must be ordered to serve a multibillion dollar national market. The company's buyers are given considerable latitude in forecasting what will sell. Sometimes they are wrong, painfully wrong. A few years ago, a senior buyer decided that gardening dresses would sweep the country that year and ordered 50,000 of them. Total sales amounted to exactly 100 gardening dresses. In an act of resignation and charity, sweetened by a tax write-off, Sears donated the rest to a Hungarian refugee organization.

Finally, the decisions are made, and the merchandising departments prepare Full Merchandising Information, known as F.M.I. cards, for each of the items that will go into the catalog. For the Spring 1977 catalog, these cards were ready in June 1976. Enough such cards to account for about 15 pages of the catalog go to a copywriter who studies them with a group copy chief, the manager of the merchandising department responsible for the goods, the buyers, and even the people who will prepare advertisements in the general media for the same goods.

The copywriter then prepares the rough layouts of the 15 pages for which he or she is responsible. Guidance comes from a strictly confidential, red loose-leaf advertising policy manual. Some 78 copywriters hone the product information and fiddle with layouts on the twenty-first floor of the Sears Tower. Meanwhile, in New York, another 16 copywriters are handling other sections of the book, covering items purchased through the office there. The copywriters are mostly young people who hope to advance in the company. They are closely watched by top management, for a lot rides on their ability to induce customers to order their products.

When the copywriter has finished the rough page layout, the group chief sends it to the layout department. An artist's comprehensive drawing is prepared. One copy goes back to the writer and the sales manager to insure that creativity has not damaged accuracy. Another copy goes to the typography division, where printing specialists determine just what kind of type will be used. The typographers tell the copywriter just how many lines and even how many letters will fit in the space alloted.

At the same time as the copywriter is struggling to fit his or her prose to the available space, the art department has sent layouts to some 35 photographic advertising studios, mostly in the Chicago area. Models are called in. And Sears manages to attract the best, always the wholesome image of their average American customers. Again, the selection of models is an exercise in catering to customers' fantasies about themselves. Some who debuted on the pages of the Sears catalog are Susan Hayward, Lauren Bacall, Ginger Rogers, and, believe it or not, Gloria Swanson. No wonder men used to write to Sears trying to order a wife. One Montana rancher asked for a housekeeper "or someone to cheer me up. I'm very lonely and the girls out here are too young and too few."

In the photo studios, the models pose in and with everything from bikinis to tractors received from suppliers. The art buyers can pretty well dictate what they want the studios to produce, using the layouts prepared by the copywriters and artists. A harried production control department tries to keep track of where each page is located. The people there know how each page is supposed to be progressing in order for the book to be produced on time. A special group in the editorial department prepares the index as the book begins to take shape.

Finally, the copy is ready to be set in type. Sears does not do its own typesetting or printing; it relies primarily on the huge R. H. Donnelley Corporation, which prints everything from telephone directories to the competing Montgomery Ward catalog. When the proofs come back from Donnelley and other printers, the artwork prepared by the photo studios is added. The copywriter makes sure that everything fits on the page, often a neat trick when the object is to crowd a lot of information into a small space and still keep it readable. The buyer also gets another look at the pages to make sure that the products he has selected are accurately and attractively described.

At last, the pages go to the editorial department, which looks after the major headings. Even more importantly, it checks to make sure that all advertising meets Federal Trade Commission requirements and the dictates of other regulatory bodies. From the editorial departments in Chicago and New York the copy and artwork go back to the printer. Quality control analysts go along to the printer as well. Only one more set of proofs comes back for a final check; then Donnelley's presses roll. The entire process, from the time the F.M.I. cards come to the copywriter until the proofs are returned to the printer, takes a little more than three months. For the Spring 1977 catalog, the book was placed in the printer's hands on October 10. He provided more than 15 million copies just two months later.

There has never been just one big book. Even in the earliest days, Richard Sears was turning out revised editions at least twice a year. Now there are no less than 35 different catalogs published each year, so that the production sequence is going on for many of them at the same time.

Two big books dominate, of course. The first is the spring/summer catalog. It reflects the season by including swimwear, tennis togs and a healthy display of garden equipment. By contrast, the fall/winter edition is heavy with warm coats, sleds, and long johns. Each catalog runs about 1500 pages and remains valid for a year.

Three additional "general" catalogs are published. Following the spring/summer big book comes a slimmer summer edition, running about 200 pages. In early fall, the famous Wish Book itself, the Christmas catalog, appears, and it is packed with thousands of gifts. Later, the mid-winter sale catalog weighs in, also at about 200 pages.

All of these are full-color, rather hefty books. The larger ones cost about $2.50 each to produce. The total circulation of general catalogs is about 65 million copies each year. Some 28 million people make catalog purchases these days—about 40 percent of all American households—but only about 55 percent of them achieve the pattern of buying necessary to assure that they will automatically receive these books. If these people just barely meet the minimum amount required to qualify, they must spend something like $1.5 billion. Total catalog sales in 1974 were $2.7 billion.

In addition to the five general catalogs, the company also publishes 14 tabloid catalogs throughout the year. They each run about 80 pages in length. Many of the items also appear in the big books but are placed temporarily on sale. You might think that Sears would try to move its weakest sellers by cutting prices and advertising them in the tabloid. But top company officials would remind you that the object is to boost sales, and if an item has not sold well in the big book, it is unlikely to generate a large sales volume if the price is cut. So some of the company's best sellers come in for price reduction in the tabloids. However, special mailings of "shopper"-type tabloids are used to help reduce overstocked items through price reductions.

All of the price decisions are made well in advance, so that sale items are chosen even before the big books appear. Sears still believes that lower prices bring in customers, so it gambles on prices that will have to remain valid for many months, simply because of the production time for the catalog. Some prices, like those on bedding, are never cut in the tabloids because the original profit margins are set at a relatively low level. Sometimes, of course, advance guesses on price turn out to be woefully bad. For example, Sears was unprepared for the energy crisis that devoured the profit margin on some items. Yet the company was bound to go on selling them at the catalog price, which is never raised during the period the catalog is valid. Because there are so many catalogs, a customer may order an item on which the price has been cut without even knowing it. The company will automatically charge the lower price, even if the customer's order includes the higher one.

All told, some 250 million tabloid catalogs are mailed out each year. Like the big books, each has its own expiration date, meaning that at any one moment several Sears catalogs may be valid. That is more than a little confusing for the recipients, so the company figures that the tabloids are merely of passing interest to customers, while the big books remain the staple of catalog sales. Tabloids are generally valid for 4 to 12 weeks.

But that is not all. In addition to the general catalogs and tabloids, Sears has long published special interest catalogs. Typically, they vary from 32 to 200 pages in length. The number of such books changes from year to year because Sears is constantly researching each market to determine if it is large enough to sustain all the cost and effort that must go into producing a catalog. For example, in 1976 Sears introduced a catalog of cameras and photographic equipment, including cameras from a wide variety of well-known manufacturers under their own trade names, something of a departure for the company, which prefers to use its own stable of brand names. The new catalog revealed the success of its new marketing strategy.

The 16 specialized catalogs currently in print reveal a lot about Sears's catalog customers. They must be pretty big people because there is a catalog for big and tall men and one for heavy women and those who want half sizes. While there is no catalog of high fashion, there is one for uniforms and one for western attire. Many must live in mobile homes or own campers because there is a special book for them. They are do-it-yourselfers because books are provided for home improvements, power and hand tools, and even home health care. They tinker with their Jeeps and foreign cars with the help of appropriate catalogs, and they cut their grass and till their gardens, guided by the suburban farm and ranch book. They are not just outdoors people because one whole tome is devoted to their floor coverings. Finally, they have time for some recreation, aided by books on boating and fishing and winter sports.

Of course, the company loves to reel off the statistics of such an enormous production of catalogs. It requires 175,000 tons of paper each year, which works out to one million pounds of paper daily, including Saturdays, Sundays, and holidays. Eight full-size N.C.A.A. swimming pools would just barely hold the 3 million gallons of ink spread across the thousands of pages. And, ah yes, here is the clincher: A pile of all the general catalogs alone, all 65 million of them, would rise 1,002 miles.

Actually, there are even more varieties of catalogs than all of these. Each general catalog and tabloid is specially made for the 14 markets served by Sears's 14 catalog distribution centers. Most of the pages are the same in all catalogs. However, the index sections differ because the shipping information depends directly on the distribution center. Some pages are also changed to reflect local legal requirements. For example, New York State requires that bikes have reflecting tires, but customers in California or Texas probably will not want to buy a bike made just to suit New York. So the pages describing the two-wheelers are changed. Finally, the catalog reflects some variations in taste and climate. Sears says that customers in the Southwest and West like brighter shades than those living in New England.

Obviously, the purpose of all this care in preparing the catalogs is to sell more goods. Even after the catalog was "cleaned up," Richard Sears believed that the company should combine this attention to presentation and distribution with a bit of honest "puffery." But, over the years, items have been allowed to sell themselves, with promotional language gradually being reduced.

The final abandonment of the founder's approach was the adoption of the grand-sounding Segmented People-oriented Copy in 1976. Known as SPeC at the Sears Tower, this approach required the end of any pretension that the catalog is a work of literature. Some of the people who prepare the catalogs suggested, with more than a bit of genuine concern, that SPeC really meant "Specialized Program to Eliminate Copywriters."

Clearly, the decision to eliminate "throwaway adjectives" in the catalog was a traumatic one for the company. After all, puffery, or what Sears admen call "narrative-style copy," had always worked. In addition, to drop the vestiges of informality that remained in the description of Sears's goods was to reject at last Richard Sears's belief that the catalog was an informal and folksy means of communication between the store and its customers.

But the increased sophistication of Sears's customers and the rise of consumerism had their effect. George Troll, catalog advertising and sales promotion manager, notes that even such a phrase as "big two-quart capacity" could raise eyebrows. "I'd like to see a 'small two-quart capacity,' " he quips.

Catalog sales officials were pushed to make the change by the results of a national public opinion survey. It showed that a decreasing number of people believe that advertising helps customers in making buying decisions, whereas almost two-thirds of us believe that advertising tries to convince consumers to buy things we do not need and cannot afford. Because selling by catalog is entirely dependent on the ability of the ad to convince customers to buy, Sears felt it had to come to terms, and quickly, with growing consumer skepticism.

George Troll takes apart one of Sears's former ads to show just what the problems were. The ad read:

> This newly designed table captures the elegance of the court of King Charles IX of France, where pocket billiards first flourished. Then, it was only a crude triangular table without cushions or rails. Today our table combines elegance with modern playing features.
>
> This massive 8-ft. table is accented by wrought-iron-like ring fittings on the sides and a regal brass-plated heraldic shield on each end. 3-inch thick honeycomb core bed. Cherry finish hardwood cabinet. 100% wool green billiard cloth. Black, leather-grained corner protectors. Four brass-plated score counters. End ball return. Two 57-inch cues; 2 ½-inch phenolic balls; triangle; chalk; bridge stick. . . .

What's wrong with this copy? Says Mr. Troll:

> The customer, asked to pay $575, is left with the following questions:
>
> 1. What are the cushions made of? How are they made? The

material and construction all affect a major consideration of the game—the need to make predictable bank shots—remember the price, $575.

2. Are there leg levelers that allow for uneven floors? This is a common problem in basement game rooms.

3. What are the cues made of? Are they made of warp-resistant materials like Canadian maple or fiber glass?

4. Prospective buyers might also want to know what "phenolic" is and why the balls are made of it.

Thus ended the long, happy reign of King Charles IX.

The shift to SPeC also was expected to help in the handling of phone orders for catalog items. Formerly, the copy might confuse the customer or the order-taker, with the result that the goods delivered were not what the customer had in mind. What is more, the old ads often failed to explain why one item was more expensive than a similar one.

Sears is not abandoning puffery completely. It is phasing in S.Pe.C. slowly when it comes to the tabloid "sale" catalogs. And it will not change its advertising in print media or on television and radio, on the grounds that people do not make direct purchases from such ads.

About one-fifth of all of the company's sales comes from catalogs, although less than one-half of 1 percent of total sales results from mail orders, where it all began. About three-fifths of all catalog sales are now made over the phone, mostly through catalog sales counters in the retail stores. These counters are the biggest single department in terms of sales in almost all of the retail stores.

Retail managers love to bury the catalog sales counter deep in the bowels of their stores. They reason that customers may stop to make some immediate purchases as they head for the catalog counter to order items not available locally. But the catalog-selling people want the counters out front. They argue that catalog sales are so successful and profitable that the company ought to boost them by letting casual shoppers know they can place orders while they are in the store. That is the way Richard Sears would have done it.

The catalog has proved to be perhaps the most effective way of getting customers into Sears retail stores. Many people see that Sears carries an item they want and rush off to the store to buy it. That is particularly true for children's clothing. Half of the store sales of such apparel is estimated to result from catalog advertising.

Sears levies additional freight charges for home delivery of goods ordered through the catalog. As a result, most people pick up their orders, even if they have placed them by phone. In addition, Sears frequently sends out post cards when a new catalog is available for distribution, instead of simply mailing it. That saves on postage and weeds out customers who are no longer interested in catalog buying. But, most important, it brings the customer into the retail store to pick up the book.

Actually, the catalog is an invaluable supplement to Sears's retail stores. Even the largest of them cannot carry the enormous variety of goods in the catalog. Major appliances sell better through the catalog than in the stores, even though almost all of them stock such items. It seems that customers prefer the detailed product descriptions of the catalog to the aggressive salesmanship in the stores.

Apparel has always been a major part of catalog sales, although clothing is, of course, available in all kinds of retail stores across the country. Rural people still seem to find the Sears selection superior. But apparel sales have not been very profitable for Sears because of high handling costs, the great number of returns once the customer has had a chance to look at the clothing, and the problem of getting rid of overstocked items. As a result of these problems, Sears decided to pull such high-risk merchandise out of its regional catalog distribution centers, and, in 1976, it opened a National Catalog Fashion Distribution Center. That allows it to centralize inventory control, develop new ways and equipment to handle apparel, and deal with returned items. One immediate impact was to send clothing on hangers so it is in better condition when it's unpacked; Sears hopes that fewer items will be returned as a result of their improved appearance on delivery.

Despite the increased concentration of the American population in urban and suburban areas, Sears has not abandoned the rural customer who may only rarely set foot in the retail store. About 43 percent of Sears catalog sales are made in rural or sparsely populated areas. Many are served by catalog offices or independent sales merchants. Located in 2,300 small communities across the country, these offices can generate sales as high as $1 million each in a year. Surprisingly, Sears is just beginning to tap the potential from their independent Catalog Sales Merchants. Most of them draw their entire business from Sears catalogs, receiving about a 9-percent commission on sales. The company has recently conducted successful tests in hiring part-time Catalog Sales Merchants who are located along Sears's truck routes. Insurance and real estate agents can easily supplement their incomes by handling Sears catalog orders. Although there were only 100 such part-time agents in 1976, the number might go as high as 1000 in 1980.

President Franklin Roosevelt once suggested that the best way to deal with anti-American propaganda from the Soviet Union would be to fly planes over Russia and drop Sears catalogs. In the late 1940s, when the Associated Press Moscow bureau chief returned home, he reported that "the Sears, Roebuck catalog and the phonograph record are the most powerful pieces of foreign propaganda in Russia. The catalog comes first." It was another way of saying that the catalog has become authentic Americana.

Richard Sears succeeded because he knew his customers. The catalog was in them, waiting to be pulled out and put in print. But it would never have kept selling over the decades if a man called Julius Rosenwald had not been around to turn the fantasy of the catalog into commercial reality.

CHAPTER 4

THE MAN WHO SAVED SEARS

> The aim of my life is to have an income of $15,000 a year—$5,000 to be used for my personal expenses, $5,000 to be laid aside and $5,000 to go to charity.
>
> —Julius Rosenwald, said in the mid 1890s

> Chicago, Dec. 29 [1921]—Julius Rosenwald, President of Sears, Roebuck & Co., the big Chicago mail order house, pledged approximately $20,000,000 of his personal fortune today to see the company through the period of business depression and readjustment.
>
> —*The New York Times,* page 1

Julius Rosenwald was one of the few people who achieve their aim in life. The son of a peddler, he had been required to work almost from childhood. He never went to college. His personal economic survival was at stake in two depressions and that of his company in a third. Yet his genius was not in the way he survived, but in the way he used his resources. He became one of the great pioneers in business management and in philanthropy. In a memorial address at Fisk University, which Rosenwald had aided, James Weldon Johnson said: "Julius Rosenwald used his brains in disposing of money. Had he used them only in acquiring it, we should not be gathered here today."

What was true of Fisk University was also true of Sears, Roebuck and Company, the source of Rosenwald's wealth. The company was a business that had not been created by a businessman. What Rosenwald could contribute to it, what Richard Sears must have seen in him, was his ability to give a constitution to the chaos, to turn Sears, Roebuck and Company into a viable business.

Although both Sears and Rosenwald came from humble backgrounds, they could not have been more different. The fusion of their talents and drives provided the firm foundation for the giant enterprise that grew out of the former freight agent's watch business.

Samuel Rosenwald, Julius's father, had arrived at Baltimore in 1854, an immigrant from Bünde, Westphalia, Germany. Like hundreds of thousands of others, he had fled Europe because of his hatred for compulsory military service. When he stepped off the *Wilhelmine* at Baltimore, he was 26 years old and had $20 in his pocket. His story is a familiar one. He first hit the Winchester trail in Virginia, working as a merchant on foot, a peddler. Then, he graduated to a horse and wagon. By 1856, he had gone to work for the Hammerslough brothers who ran a clothing business in Baltimore. Then came marriage to their sister, Augusta, and the assignment to manage their store in Illinois.

Julius Rosenwald was born in August 1862, in a house one block from Abraham Lincoln's in Springfield. "I remember as a boy watching the wagons of the early pioneers going through Springfield on their long journey west," he wrote many years later. One of his first commercial ventures was selling pamphlets describing the newly dedicated Lincoln Memorial in Springfield. On the day it was unveiled, he earned $2.25 and saw Ulysses S. Grant. Ever the son of a clothier, he recalled, "He was the first man I ever saw who wore kid gloves."

Julius was raised in the Jewish faith and was often subjected to the jibes of his young friends. After two years in the high school at Springfield, he was packed off to New York to learn the clothing business from his uncles, who had moved there from Baltimore. At the time he went east, a man by the name of A. Montgomery Ward was already developing the mail-order business in which Rosenwald would later prosper.

After working as a stockboy for his uncles, Julius was given a job as a salesman. Although he also worked for other clothiers in order to supplement his income, he had time to drop into the local vaudeville shows in the company of his friends Henry Goldman, who would later head Goldman, Sachs, the investment banking house, and Henry Morgenthau, who would make a fortune and serve his country as an ambassador.

Finally, Samuel set his son up in the clothing business in New York. But the depression of 1884–1885 almost bankrupted the enterprise before it got off the ground. Undeterred, Julius was always looking for new opportunities. One day, a supplier of summer clothing told him that his firm was unable to keep up with a flood of orders. Rosenwald hardly paid attention to the remark. But, later that night, he was awakened by the realization that here was the business for him. With his brother, who had also been sent to the East to learn the clothing business, and Julius Weil, a cousin who was then working for the Hammerslough brothers, he pulled up stakes and headed for Chicago to open his own wholesale clothing business. Like their competitors, Rosenwald & Weil ordered their garments from men who ran sweatshops, where immigrant labor worked long hours under often harsh conditions.

Rosenwald & Weil prospered, and eventually Samuel sold his business in Springfield and joined his son in Chicago. In 1890, Julius married Augusta Nusbaum, who lived near the family house on Wabash Avenue. Julius continued to build his business, emerging unscathed from the 1893 depression. He also began to live out his commitment to charity. Attending a meeting to support Jewish charities in Chicago, he blurted out a pledge of $2500, then a considerable sum of money for him. When his wife caught him sulking around the house, he confessed that he had given away such a large sum that the family would have to tighten their belts. For the rest of his life Rosenwald would maintain that this was the largest gift he had ever made because it represented such a big share of what he had. Although he was later fond of saying, "I have my generosity under complete control," he ultimately gave away about $63 million.

But the main focus of his life was to be Sears, Roebuck. By 1897, Rosenwald had become actively involved in the management of the company, concentrating first on expanding the clothing department. As he would later in other departments, Rosenwald found chaos. One story of the clothing merchant's early experiences concerned a complaint from a southern customer who reported that he had received a heavy suit when he had ordered a lightweight one. When the new corporate executive asked the man in charge of shipping why a different and clearly improper garment had been sent, he was told that there was no lighter suit in stock. "Why didn't you send a watch?" snapped Rosenwald. The need to reform the clothing department was obvious. The company was losing a lot of money as a result of suits being returned because they did not fit, were badly made, or were totally unlike the garment offered in the catalog.

Sears's advertising brought in floods of orders. Often they had to be piled in wash baskets, waiting to be processed. One customer ordered a baby carriage. Later, he wrote to ask that the order be changed to two plugs of chewing tobacco and a shotgun because the boy was now grown up. In its haste to fill orders, Sears, Roebuck often sent the wrong item. One story that made the rounds had a Sears, Roebuck truck driver and his colleague from Montgomery Ward arguing about which firm did the most business. Finally, the Sears man shouted, "Hell, we get more goods back than Montgomery Ward ships."

Rosenwald insisted that customers must be kept happy. When they complained about not receiving an item they had ordered, another was sent. Eventually, the extra item had to be recovered from the freight station where it had been left. The loading docks at Sears, Roebuck became so crowded that trucking firms threatened to stop handling the company's business.

What the company needed was a system for processing orders and the space in which the system could work. Sears was reluctant to see the company expand into larger headquarters, but Rosenwald insisted that they proceed with plans for the huge West Side plant, where the operations that had gradually spread all over downtown Chicago could be pulled together. The massive brick edifice, topped by the first Sears Tower, turned out to be the lever that turned Sears, Roebuck and Company into big business.

Not only did Rosenwald take charge of raising the money to build the plant, but he also supervised its construction. Here was a clothing merchant, with no experience in either construction or high finance, up to his neck in both. He was obviously confused as one contractor after another trooped through his office to bid on the job. Finally, Louis J. Horowitz of the Thompson-Starrett Company took a gamble on Rosenwald. He offered to put up the plant for a $250,000 fee, but would make a contract for just $1. If Rosenwald were unhappy with the completed building, he would have to pay only costs plus $1. The construction firm, eager to try its hand at a large industrial plant, backed up their man although they never expected Rosenwald to come through with the full payment. The job completed, Rosenwald wrote to Horowitz. The contractor opened the letter with obvious concern. Three checks fell from the envelope. The first two covered the $250,000, made up of the contracted fee (actually $40,-000, not $1) and the amount verbally agreed upon. The third check was for $50,000, because Sears, Roebuck was so pleased with the work. The solid, high-ceilinged building was meant to last, and now, almost seven decades later, it still houses the Sears laboratories.

The construction of the new plant also provided the key to the system for handling orders. O. C. Doering, the company's operations manager, was responsible for making sure that there were always enough bricks on hand for the work to continue uninterrupted. He had to make sure that suppliers knew in advance just how many bricks would be needed and when.

From the successful management of the brick supply, Doering evolved the "schedule system," which made it possible for Sears, Roebuck to process orders efficiently and reduce the number of returned items. The heart of the problem was that the orders called for items from several departments. Suits, watches, bicycles, and cream separators lacked the splendid uniformity of bricks. Yet the solution was simple: a timetable.

Orders flooded in at a rate of 100,000 a day. Each mail sack was weighed because the company had determined that there were usually 40 orders per pound. The letters were taken from their envelopes, with the help of the first automatic openers used in industry. Each order was numbered, and the time the goods were to be shipped was also stamped on it. All of the items in that order would be collected and placed in a bin, which would be held for no more than 15 minutes. Payments and orders were checked and labels prepared. Then the various parts of the order were sent to the various departments. The merchandise there was stored on numbered shelves, the numbers corresponding to those in the catalog. Boys and girls would pull the items ordered from the shelves and drop them on conveyers, which eventually brought them to shipping rooms. Heavier items went to the loading docks while precanceled stamps were slapped on the lighter items. Some goods were shipped directly by Sears, Roebuck and Company's own suppliers. They were required to adopt order-processing systems, too. The order was shipped at the end of the alloted 15-minute waiting period whether or not all of the items were ready. Late items were sent separately by express, prepaid. The cost of shipping plus a fifty-cent penalty was assessed against the department's profit showing. That caught the attention of department managers whose advancement depended on how much of a profit they could produce. The system worked so well that orders from a single department went out the same day and mixed orders were shipped the following day.

This "schedule system" may seem elementary in an age when orders are filled by computer, and following a timetable is an obvious requirement for handling orders. But much of what Sears, Roebuck did was innovative, and certainly within the company itself there had never been so much organization. Henry Ford picked up the "schedule system" and used it to create the assembly line in his factories. For Rosenwald, it was simply a requirement for growth. The company would strangle on its own success if it did not develop a system for taking care of orders in a way that reduced the volume of returns significantly.

Although Rosenwald often gets the credit for financing the expansion of Sears, Roebuck and for imposing order on its operations, the installation of the "schedule system" reveals that it was often others in the company who had the ideas and carried them out. Rosenwald had to approve their plans, but they were able to take the initiative in solving the problems that Richard Sears's advertising campaigns imposed upon them. Rosenwald's obvious skill as head of the company was in attracting and retaining inventive and dynamic people and then letting them get on with the job. While such a skill may seem today to be a basic requirement of corporate executives, Rosenwald acted at a time when only a few small enterprises would be transformed into huge corporations. Without his ability to solve the problems of such a transformation, it is likely that Sears, Roebuck and Company would not have been able to survive. It would have died of its own weight. To a great extent, Rosenwald was one of a small band of executives who wrote the book on successful management of large corporations. Years later, when Charles Kellstadt, one of Rosenwald's successors at Sears, was asked if Rosenwald was the Alfred P. Sloan (head of General Motors) of retailing, he replied: "I think I would say that he was more than that. Sloan took the residuals left to him by Durant and molded them into something. What Rosenwald did was pioneer. He did something that hadn't been done before."

Even some of the old-timers, who had first been hired by Richard Sears, were pleased that Rosenwald took an interest in all aspects of company operations, while the Founder kept on grinding out ad copy and dreaming up new ways to increase sales. Richard Sears was respected and even loved by some of his employees, but they all knew that the company needed the cool, management skill of "J. R.," as they called him. They could feel the steady growth of Sears, Roebuck as the thousands of orders passed through their hands. And they believed that Rosenwald was concerned about their ability to do a good job. For that reason, the employees of Sears, Roebuck gradually came to support Rosenwald in his disputes over management of the company with Sears. They felt that they and Rosenwald actually knew the company better than the Founder. It is to Sears's credit that when he saw that the company was slipping from his control because it was forced to face problems in which he had no interest, he gracefully left the field to Rosenwald. With his departure, the bold salesmanship of the previous century gave way to the progressive management of the twentieth century.

That Rosenwald was an excellent business executive was a great piece of good fortune for Sears, Roebuck. But it was not altogether exceptional; there were other good businessmen. What was rare was the combination of business skill and idealism that Julius Rosenwald brought to the company. He had long quarreled with Richard Sears over the need to be absolutely honest in the catalog and other advertising. Although Sears came to appreciate the importance of promising no more than could be delivered, he had a hard time suppressing the urge to take the farmer on a flight of fantasy, in which his dreams could be fulfilled at rock-bottom prices. As soon as Sears had retired from the presidency of the company in 1908, Rosenwald made his move. He called in the department managers and told them that henceforth the company would make only the most truthful statements about its goods. He believed that Sears, Roebuck had a moral obligation to its customers and its suppliers. He was concerned about the continual need of Sears, Roebuck to raise money to finance its operations and worried that banks would be increasingly reluctant to deal with a firm that was continually in hot water. Finally, Sears, Roebuck was as much a reflection of his own personality as his own small firm of Rosenwald and Company had been. If a customer was disappointed, Rosenwald took his protest personally. However large Sears, Roebuck and Company would grow, Rosenwald would always call it "the store," just as though it were his simple outlet for men's clothing.

Although he had grown to dislike Sears's selling methods, he never disliked his former colleague personally. When Sears retired, he had washed his hands entirely of the company and sold his stock to Goldman, Sachs for $10 million. The investment bankers offered some of his shares to Rosenwald, who tried to accumulate all of the company's stock he could. But Rosenwald refused on the grounds that he never wanted it said that he had profited at Sears's expense. By the time Rosenwald gave up the supervision of the company, the value of the stock he had refused had grown to more than $200 million.

Once the company began to operate in a more businesslike way, Rosenwald turned to his other interests: philanthropy and civic action. Most of the gifts that Rosenwald gave during his lifetime reflected his feeling that he was obligated to give. The federal income tax was just coming into use, so Rosenwald reaped little advantage from the deductions that might result from his philanthropy. But, because he gave out of a spirit of generosity, the organizations that benefited from his support soon found that Julius came along with the money. He was forming his own ideas about what should be done with gifts such as his in order to promote social welfare. He attracted advisors who actually became his teachers, making up for the college education he had never had. When he had learned their lessons and seasoned them with his own experience in the business world, he expected to have a major influence on how his money was spent.

This was a life apart from Sears, Roebuck. Of course, the company basked in the reflected glory of its president, but Rosenwald, as philanthropist, acted as though he were in a different world from the catalog, the mailroom, and "the store." His interests were as broad as the catalog—ranging from the city of Chicago, for which he had developed a deep affection, to Jewish philanthropies, from the cause of blacks to the cause of the Republican party.

In the early twentieth century, charity had become increasingly the domain of the millionaire businessman and less the responsibility of church and state. In a sense, "welfare" was as much a problem then as now, but the burden of paying for it was assumed by the wealthy. Some, it was said, did so because their consciences were troubled by the ways in which they had amassed their fortunes. It was said that the Carnegie libraries that dotted the nation were the interest on the debt incurred when Pinkerton guards gunned down striking workers at the Homestead Steel mill, owned by Andrew Carnegie.

Julius Rosenwald had little to make amends for. Yet the mere accumulation of wealth had its effect. "I really feel ashamed to have so much money," he said. In part, he reflected the inevitable pressure that was applied in the press and public opinion on those of great wealth. Perhaps more important was his background in the Jewish tradition of charity. In fact, his initial gifts, small in comparison with what he would later contribute, were to the traditional, local Jewish welfare organizations.

For all of his generosity, Rosenwald is often remembered with a trace of bitterness by those Jews who recall his opposition to Zionism, the movement for creation of a Jewish state in Palestine. He had come under the influence of Chicago Rabbi Emil G. Hirsch even before he had the funds to become a major backer of social causes, and Hirsch was a lifelong opponent of Zionism. In part, Hirsch's stand was based on his German background. Jews were not yet persecuted there as they were in other European countries. In addition, he believed, and Rosenwald probably agreed, that American Jews had no need to consider a retreat to Jerusalem. Although he was an idealist, Rosenwald was never convinced that the creation of a Jewish state could be a practical reality or that the solution to the problems of oppressed Jews did not lie elsewhere.

Yet Rosenwald was, in fact, a major benefactor of Jewish causes in Palestine. If he could be convinced of the value of a specific project, he would readily open his checkbook. Among his early contributions were gifts to support a publishing house in the then small city of Tel Aviv and the Jewish Institute of Technology at Haifa. In addition, he was attracted by Aaron Aaronsohn, a fervent advocate of the agricultural development of Palestine. Rosenwald was impressed by the young discoverer of wild wheat, who had been supported by Baron de Rothschild. The man was so persuasive and so well respected by American botanists that Rosenwald found himself as president of the Jewish Agricultural Experiment Station located at the foot of Mt. Carmel. Aaronsohn even succeeded in inducing Rosenwald and his wife to visit Palestine, although he never made a Zionist out of the philanthropist.

It was the persecution of Jews in Russia, beginning with the pogroms of 1905, that had first interested Rosenwald in the problems of Jews abroad. He was convinced that if they were allowed to resettle and to learn agriculture or a trade, they would find a place in Russian society. In the early 1920s, the time seemed ripe for action. The Russian people and the Soviet government appeared more favorably disposed then ever before to let Russian Jews live and work in peace, provided they were resettled. Rosenwald, together with such other American Jewish leaders as Felix Warburg, Herbert H. Lehman, and Louis Marshall, backed the Russian resettlement effort. This brought Rosenwald into direct conflict with the leading American Zionists. The Chicagoan's gift of $1 million for Russian resettlement was denounced as being opposed to the goals of Zionism. Actually, Rosenwald's feelings did not run that deeply, but he considered it would be more practical to resettle people in their own country than to move them thousands of miles. In the end, the two sides compromised, with some funds going to Russia and some to Palestine.

Rosenwald became involved in Jewish causes because of his heritage. He became concerned with the plight of colored people or Negroes (the word *black* then implied a discriminatory attitude) because of the influence of one man: Booker T. Washington. A friend had given him Washington's *Up from Slavery,* and Rosenwald came to believe that it was the single book that had influenced him the most. He found that Washington shared many of his own values. Rosenwald, who was always acutely aware of his educational shortcomings and, as a result, always refused the honorary university degrees that were offered him, admired Dr. Washington's learning. He agreed with the black man that if people started their lives with obstacles to overcome, they would probably be spurred to greater accomplishment. Rosenwald never thought of challenging Washington's basic assumption that the goal of blacks should not be social equality, but improvement of the individual and increased trade among blacks.

Washington turned the president of Sears, Roebuck and Company into "Cap'n Julius," the most beloved white man among southern blacks after Abraham Lincoln. Rosenwald's millions poured into the South, almost invariably in the cause of education. "Separate, but equal" was the doctrine laid down by the United States Supreme Court, but the actual practice fell far short of that rule. In fact, Julius Rosenwald, more than any other person, tried to insure that blacks did receive an equal education by contributing to the construction of some 5,357 public schools, shops, and teacher's dwellings. His contribution of more than $4 million was a spur to local and state governments to increase their own efforts. He became a legend to the black children educated in his schools.

But he was a living part of the Tuskegee Institute, the educational base of Booker T. Washington. In October 1911, he hired a private railroad car and, with a group of friends, journeyed to Tuskegee. He was deeply impressed by what he saw. "Your Principal, Mr. Washington, to my notion has done the greatest work of any man in America," he told an assembly of the school. That trip became a regular event in the spring for Rosenwald, who had become a trustee of the institute, and his friends.

Rosenwald never seemed to attach great importance to public fights against anti-Semitism or on behalf of the rights of black people. Once, when a chauffeur in Chicago objected to driving Washington, Rosenwald simply told him that he would have another driver take his place. The chauffeur asked him if he would be riding with the black man, and Rosenwald said he would. "Well," replied the driver, "if you can stand it to ride with him, I guess I can stand it to drive him." That was fine with Rosenwald, who concentrated more on helping the disadvantaged than on trying to change other people's minds. His own personal attitude was beyond question. Mrs. Washington wrote to Mrs. Rosenwald: "I want you also to know that we

love Mr. Rosenwald and you for what you are to us and not for what
you may or may not give. . . . Mr. Rosenwald makes you forget all
the hard things in life. His presence takes off the *chill.*"

There were many other philanthropies, many other millions given
away. Out of it all, Rosenwald developed a philosophy of giving that
he advocated to the other millionaires who set up the foundations,
built the hospitals, financed the universities. He strongly opposed
endowments that tied the recipient in perpetuity. He argued that the
donor was giving to an institution with which he was familiar, not
to the institution as it would develop decades later. And perhaps the
income from the endowment would be unnecessary because of
changed events, such as increased government involvement, long
after the donor's death. When he contributed to a cause, he lobbied,
often successfully, with other major contributors to cut the strings
on their gifts.

At one time, Rosenwald's fortune was valued at more than $200
million, much of it in Sears, Roebuck stock. When he died, his estate
was worth more than $17 million. Some he had given away to friends
and family. But $63 million had gone to the causes that he supported.
He had come remarkably close to meeting the goal he had set for
himself as a young man of giving one-third of what he made to
charity.

Rosenwald did more than give money; he gave himself. Often his
personal involvement in civic life, the war effort, and Republican
politics managed to embroil the good name of Sears, Roebuck and
Company.

His role in the war effort developed out of his belief that war was
inevitable and that the United States must be prepared. In the 1916
presidential campaign, Rosenwald supported Charles Evans Hughes,
the Republican, mainly because he wanted to get ready for war.
President Woodrow Wilson, sensing that public opinion was shifting
toward preparedness, appointed a Council of National Defense,
which included a seven-member Advisory Commission. Rosenwald
was one of the seven, along with such others as Samuel Gompers,
the head of the American Federation of Labor, and financier Bernard
Baruch.

At the first meeting of the council, Rosenwald took charge, immediately advocating that it support universal military training: the

draft. Within four months, he had convinced all but one member of the council, and the President and Congress went on to create the draft.

As part of his responsibilities on the council, Rosenwald, who had given up day-to-day supervision of Sears, Roebuck, took charge of getting private industry to produce the supplies needed for the war effort. Rosenwald used the Sears, Roebuck techniques of having the government, which had replaced "the store," deal directly with producers at a fixed price. These merchandising methods came under increasingly sharp attack from the middlemen who normally would have played a role in an open market purchasing system. They lobbied Congress for an end to Rosenwald's approach, although there was little question that it was saving the taxpayers' money.

Rosenwald, always a stickler, barred Sears, Roebuck from making any sales to the government under this system. He also refused to accept his salary from the company while he served in Washington. Occasionally, government officials brought great pressure to bear on Rosenwald to allow certain goods that Sears, Roebuck could supply at a good price to be sold, but he then insisted on elaborate precautions to insulate himself from the deal. He did agree to the use of Sears's laboratories for testing fabrics and other goods at no charge to the government.

Finally, Congress began to criticize the system that Rosenwald had created on the grounds that members of the council could insure that their own firms got juicy government contracts. Rosenwald was furious, and, in an interview with the *Chicago Tribune,* he lashed out. "This is very stupid. It is shortsighted. It is nonsensical and foolish," he said.

Congress does not like being called stupid, whatever the facts, and Rosenwald's disastrous interview assured the end of his system. It aroused the opposition of politicians who disliked being told what to do by rich men. Said Mississippi Senator James K. Vardaman, "His stupid utterances are but the emanations from a mind uninformed and a spirit inflated with the vanity of riches."

Rosenwald was disheartened by his experience, although no one had ever alleged that he had operated his supply system for his own advantage or that of Sears, Roebuck. His was the case of the blunt businessman, somewhat lost in the world of politics, which he clearly did not understand. In the end, the functions of his office were transferred to the quartermaster general and were handled by General Robert E. Wood, who had once been the chief quartermaster of the Panama Canal under General Goethals.

Rosenwald was not totally discouraged by his brush with public life, however, and became a key backer of Calvin Coolidge and then of Herbert Hoover, a man he considered the best qualified to be president in the history of the Republic. As a "fat cat," Rosenwald occasionally found himself invited to the White House and once was considered for the post of secretary of commerce.

But his political activities on the state level brought him some grief. In 1926, Frank L. Smith, chairman of the Illinois Commerce Commission and the person chiefly responsible for regulating public utilities in the state, won the Republican nomination for the United States Senate, defeating incumbent Senator William B. McKinley. After the primary campaign, it was revealed that Smith had received $125,000 in cash contributions from Samuel Insull, a utility magnate. He had dipped into the till of the Commonwealth Edison Company to make the payment at a time when Smith was still head of the I.C.C.

Rosenwald's instinct for political reform was aroused. He did not want Smith in the Senate. First, he backed an independent candidate, but when he decided that his man would have no chance, he asked for a meeting with Smith. At Chicago's Congress Hotel, he offered the Republican candidate a cool $500,000 in Sears, Roebuck stock if he would pull out of the race. Rosenwald told Smith that he stood no chance of being seated in the Senate in any case. Rosenwald had blundered again, totally ignoring the inconsistency between his passion for reform and his attempt to buy a candidate. Smith refused his offer and was elected. But, just as Rosenwald predicted, when Smith went to Washington, the Senate refused to seat him by a vote of 61 to 23. Smith tried again in 1928, but was defeated in the G.O.P. primary. Rosenwald emerged unscathed from his involvement in the campaign. There was virtually no criticism of his cavalier ability to dispense Sears, Roebuck stocks. In the end, the local press praised him for an impulsive act on behalf of the public.

Philanthropy and business were two different worlds so far as Rosenwald was concerned. The trouble was that the rest of the world did not see this separation so clearly. If Julius Rosenwald was such an idealist and supporter of the downtrodden, many people could not understand why he did not practice what he preached.

As president of the company, Rosenwald felt that he should pursue those policies allowed by law that would promote its growth and development. If he got Sears, Roebuck and Company involved in social betterment programs, business might suffer. In short, good deeds did not always make for good business.

In 1913, the Illinois State Senate created a special committee "to investigate the subject of white slave traffic in Illinois." It had been alleged that local employers paid such low wages that young women took to the world's oldest profession as a way of surviving economically. Sears, Roebuck and Company became a target of the committee's investigation because it was a major employer and because Rosenwald was such a well-known benefactor of the poor. The company then paid an average wage to women of $9.12 a week, although girls under 16, who presumably lived at home, were paid as little as $5.00 weekly. Those who did not live at home received at least $8.00. Under cross-examination, the committee tried to get Rosenwald to admit that, if he paid wages that were too low, he had a moral obligation to raise them in order to prevent his employees from turning to prostitution.

"I say the question of wages isn't a moral question," he told the investigators. "It ought to be treated on an entirely different basis. I wouldn't combine the question of prostitution with wages. I say in my opinion there is no connection between the two."

Rosenwald could see no reason why his philanthropy or the size of Sears, Roebuck imposed any special obligation on him to pay higher wages than his competitors, even if the company could afford it. But he came under continual pressure from Jane Addams, whose Hull House he supported, and from other social reformers. Although he never gave ground and opposed the effort, eventually successful, to establish a federal minimum wage, he was probably pushed toward the creation of Sears's profit-sharing plan, one of the first in the nation, as a result of the hearings into wages and prostitution. The plan, described later, would serve as the company's pension program until 1977.

Although he had wandered off into philanthropy and civic action,

Rosenwald kept "the store" always as his highest priority. It continued to prosper as the American people prospered. But when the national economy faltered, Sears would be in trouble.

When Rosenwald had returned to the active management of the company in 1920, he found that millions of dollars worth of orders were being returned unfilled because demand so far outstripped supply. The shortfall was not simply a question of bad advance planning; postwar purchasing absorbed more than could be produced. Immediately, Rosenwald set about building up inventories in an effort to keep sales growing. As the company swung into mid 1920, its volume of business was six times as great as in 1908, when Richard Sears had left its active management.

Then, the depression struck. Customers found prices too high and stopped their purchases. Wholesale price-cutting could not seem to bring them back. Unemployment moved upward; it would reach six million by July 1921. Sears, Roebuck, with masses of items in inventory that had been ordered at high cost, was unable to move them. The company's stock, which had once hit 243 in 1920 could muster a high of only 98 the following year on its way down to a low of 54. In October 1920, the company needed cash and sold $50 million in notes at 7 percent interest. They were to be paid back in three years rather than the ten urged by the bankers. Rosenwald argued that the company would be able to make repayment within three years or never.

In February 1921, Sears, Roebuck and Company was forced to pass its quarterly dividend. Instead of simply making no payment, the company issued scrip, paying 6 percent interest and due in August 1922. But Rosenwald worried that small investors, who counted on their dividend checks, would be forced to sell their scrip to traders at a big discount. He said that he would buy the scrip of all stockholders who held less than 50 shares of company stock in order to protect them. He paid the full face value.

The president also cracked down hard on the executives who had grown soft on the golf links during his absence. Some were unceremoniously fired. Executive salaries were reduced, and he abolished his own entirely. Total operating savings amounted to $20 million.

But all of this was not enough. Rumors circulated through the financial community that Sears, Roebuck and Company would soon go the way of other mercantile corporations—either into bankruptcy or through a reorganization that would place it under the control of the banks. By the end of 1921, the company showed an operating loss of $16,435,468, a setback unprecedented in its history. It looked like a classic case of "the bigger they are, the harder they fall."

If Sears was to be saved, Rosenwald would have to do it. Or, rather, his money would. A plan was prepared by Albert H. Loeb, the number-two man in the company. He had joined Sears, Roebuck while serving as the attorney handling the details of the arrangement that had brought Rosenwald and Nusbaum in as part owners.

Loeb proposed that Rosenwald donate to the company treasury some 50,000 shares, which would allow Sears, Roebuck and Company to reduce its capital stock by $5 million, with only Rosenwald suffering a loss. Loeb also suggested that Rosenwald take over the real estate assets of the company, which were valued at $16 million. He would pay $4 million in Liberty bonds to the treasury and would give the company his note for the remainder. The note would be secured by the real estate itself and not by Rosenwald's own funds. Yet the note would be acceptable to banks as security for loans, whereas the real estate itself would not have been.

At first, Rosenwald was reluctant to agree. Loeb urged him on, telling him that other executives were willing to turn back their stock but only he had enough to make a difference. Another official told him that Sears's problems were only temporary. Its traditional customers were not deserting the company; they had simply reduced the volume of their purchases.

But Rosenwald would not budge. His own attorney advised against making such a gift to the company. Finally, an outside lawyer was called in. He told Sears's president that he was under no obligation to lift a finger to help the company. But, he argued, the gift could be turned into a sound investment. He could take an option to buy his stock back at $100 a share at any time within three years. Although he was now more attracted by Loeb's proposal, he was hesitant to give himself this option, protesting that he would appear to be taking advantage of the situation. Finally, he was persuaded. Rosenwald was also said to have been investing in those companies that were Sears, Roebuck's suppliers, so that if the company went down, he would lose on those investments. Whatever the reason, Rosenwald made his move only when he was convinced that it made good business sense.

Even if Rosenwald's gift was not the generous act it might have seemed, it was still unprecedented in American business. Because of his unique move, Rosenwald was showered with praise from John D. Rockefeller and from the smallest stockholders. The financial press was ecstatic, hailing him as a "commercial genius." His gamble would work out only if the projections were right about the company's long-term growth potential, however. And it would be Rosenwald's job to see that Sears, Roebuck regained the road to prosperity.

Sears, Roebuck and Company was able to pay off the bank loans falling due. It was able to borrow more, when needed. And the company, which had been headed toward another disastrous deficit of more than $16 million, actually showed a surplus of almost $2 million.

In the end, recovery came and with it the resumption of Sears's growth. Rosenwald exercised his option to buy back his 50,000 shares. After his death, his estate was repaid the $4 million on which he had been receiving 7 percent interest. The heroic gesture had paid off. But never before and never again in the annals of American business would a stockholder of a huge corporation step in with his personal finances to save the company. At Sears, Roebuck and Company, "J. R." had become a saint.

But even saints are mortal, and Rosenwald had to begin thinking of who would take over the succession that had passed from Richard Sears to Julius Rosenwald. In 1924, the Leopold-Loeb murder case broke. One of the defendants was Richard Loeb, the son of Rosenwald's right-hand man. Albert Loeb, already ill, never recovered from the shock. He died in October of that year.

Rosenwald was already deep into a talent search for his own successor. He had asked his son Lessing, who had worked his way up in the ranks until he was manager of Sears's Philadelphia operations, to draw up a list of the most able railroad executives for his consideration. Rosenwald believed that railroad men would have the necessary sense of organization and procedure required to keep Sears growing. In short, he wanted, if possible, to find somebody who could reproduce his own special contribution to the company.

Executives within the company were miffed that they were obviously being passed over. But Rosenwald made it clear that he left no room for sentiment in his decision. "I have no time for 'seconds,' " he said.

Finally, Rosenwald hired Charles M. Kittle, senior vice-president of the Illinois Central. Kittle was young enough to look forward to a long reign at Sears. To fill Loeb's slot, he brought in General Robert E. Wood, whose work at the Quartermaster Department during the war had impressed him. Wood had left the Army and had joined Montgomery Ward. But his desire to promote and expand that firm had clashed with management's more conservative approach. One day he heard on the company grapevine that he was to be fired. He quickly summoned a messenger, and while the boy waited, he wrote out his resignation. The boy was instructed to get it onto the desk of President Theodore Merseles immediately. Then, Wood went to Sears. Rosenwald hired him quickly because he sensed in the general the kind of drive that he had once seen in Richard Sears.

Rosenwald himself remained as chairman of the company until he died in early 1932. He kept to himself the power of determining who would be in charge of Sears's operations, always under his general supervision. And there was yet one dramatic gesture left.

In October 1929 came the great crash. Within a week, Rosenwald had moved to guarantee the stock trading accounts of all Sears employees. He pledged to help those accounts, not only in Sears stock, but in all of the holdings of his employees. He took over the management of some 300 accounts personally, borrowing $7 million from the Chase National Bank to have the working capital necessary. Almost two-thirds of the accounts were able to stay afloat without his financial help. In all cases, he succeeded in saving his employees who had bought on margin from being ruined financially. Why did Rosenwald do it? In part, because he liked to help people and believed that if they could survive the initial setback, they would again prosper. But, perhaps more important, he thrived on "the action." He would sit in his office making a hundred decisions a day, just as in the early days of the company. Again the praise poured in. His friend Henrietta Szold wrote him, "Such acts demonstrate that moral heights can be reached in our condemned commercial era as in the eras glorified by historians."

In the life of Sears, Roebuck and Company, Julius Rosenwald had occupied a pivotal position. He had devised no innovation in merchandising. He had not been the author of the reforms that allowed the company to handle an avalanche of orders. He had not been a financial wizard. He had not placed his company on a higher standard than his competitors. He had not been an advertising genius.

But he believed in his business—the mail-order business—and was determined to adapt it to changing conditions and make it work. He was able to bring out the best in his subordinates and to make sure that new ideas were put into effect. He could rely on the most talented people to raise money for his company and to make sure money was wisely spent. He understood his business and the nature of competition completely. He kept the gains made by Richard Sears's supersalesmanship by developing satisfied customers.

He was the model of the modern corporate manager. But he was more than that. He was honest, and he demanded honesty. He believed that fair management of a private company could bring benefit to society as a whole. He realized that business was not everything in life and devoted himself to an extraordinary philanthropy with as much zeal as he ran Sears.

Above all, Julius Rosenwald saw himself as a trustee. He had an obligation to less fortunate people. And he had an obligation to Sears, Roebuck and Company. So he saved it.

CHAPTER 5

THE MAIL-ORDER WAR

In 1869, E. C. Allen of Augusta, Maine, had an idea. Americans had been buying products by mail from the time of George Washington, but no company was wholly dedicated to sales by mail, and most of those which dabbled in mail orders usually carried only a single line of products. So Allen hit on a plan to sell nationally a selection of specialty items ranging from recipes for washing powder to engravings and to do it only by mail. He founded the *People's Literary Companion,* whose object, despite its title, was commercial, not educational.

The idea worked, and in the next decade, Augusta, Maine, became the direct-mail capital of the United States. In its second year, Allen's paper, priced at fifty cents a year, sold 500,000 copies. There was big money in the mails.

If Allen's paper and the competing *Fireside Visitor* could make big money in Augusta, the big city boys knew they could do even better. One former traveling salesman who had once run a general store did not waste any time. In 1872, Aaron Montgomery Ward opened the first large concern selling a range of goods by mail. His initial capital was $2,400, and his first catalog was a single sheet of paper, 8 by 12 inches. By the time that Richard Sears had begun selling watches, Montgomery Ward and Company was publishing catalogs of hundreds of pages, containing thousands and soon tens of thousands of items.

Ward's biggest coup was in getting his firm named the official supply house for the Grange, the rural organization known as the

Patrons of Husbandry, who were then adding members at a furious pace as the populist mood swept the prairies. Ward also introduced the notion of a guarantee allowing people to return an item after examining it. This was a powerful inducement for distant customers. The third element vital to Ward's success was the homey style in which he wrote his catalog.

Just as Ward had imitated the Augusta merchants, so, too, others imitated him. Richard Sears was the next, but many others launched their own companies, some of which still survive. Spiegel, May, Stern Company, and National Bellas Hess were soon on the scene. Even the big department stores like R. H. Macy and John Wanamaker gave mail order a try. In fact, hundreds of companies had entered the field by the time that Richard Sears settled down to try to build his company into a mail-order power.

The lure of mail order to young entrepreneurs was obvious. You did not need to lay out money for an inventory. In fact, it would be years before some mail-order houses built up large stocks of goods instead of making their purchases only after orders had been received. The post office, the railroads, and private freight haulers were eager for the business; so the mail-order houses had surprisingly little trouble in getting their products to a waiting market in rural America. Starting a mail-order outfit in the late nineteenth century was cream skimming. It was hard to miss finding a market when there were millions of Americans too far from the big cities to have any real choice about what they purchased and openly unhappy about their domination by the local general store operator.

The business E. C. Allen started has never stopped growing. Selling by direct mail has become a fine art, a profession in itself. Not only can you choose from the wealth of items offered by Sears, Ward, or others, but you also are regularly assailed by firms that want to sell you everything from automobile spare parts to a gadget that promises "Ugly Blackheads Out in Seconds."

The mail-order business is a war. It is a war for the hearts and minds and, most importantly, the wallets of Americans. There are perennial skirmishes among the outfits that sell gimmicks to reduce your waistline or to help you "Grow World's First Blue Roses" or to serve as the "Exploding Toilet Seat." But the real battles are fought among the giants like Sears and Ward. The battlefield is the nation, but the general staffs of the giants are in Chicago. Ward and Sears and the others went there because it was the real capital of the United States, at least of that country of farmers and ranchers who felt themselves excluded from the commercial life of the bustling East.

The first stage in the mail-order war was not among the budding mail-order houses but between them and local merchants. The store-keepers just plain hated the mail-order people. Racism was a tool right at hand; if the mail-order merchants could not be seen, there was no problem with spreading the story that Richard Sears or A. C. Roebuck or Montgomery Ward were blacks. In later years, that Rosenwald was a Jew much interested in black causes was also used as a weapon against Sears, Roebuck and Company. The logic, of course, was that these fellows could not afford to show their faces as retailers, so they took refuge in the mail-order business.

But the local shopkeepers did not stop with racism. In small towns, merchants brought pressure to bear on the local citizenry to destroy the hated catalog. Shopkeepers would give prizes to the person bringing in the most catalogs or simply bought them outright at ten cents a copy. Kids were given free admission to a picture show if they could produce a catalog. When all available copies were accumulated, a public book burning might be held. The good old American version of this good old "know-nothing" custom was not designed to stifle the free expression of ideas, just free competition.

The local newspapers, dependent on the advertising of the town merchants, joined in attacking the mail-order houses. They were often the butt of journalistic jokes. Hence, the origin of "Monkey" Ward. Another local wit wrote that a fellow had just bought a watch from "Rears and Soreback." He got it for half price, but it ran twice as fast as any watch you could buy from the local jeweler. One Arkansas newspaper actually caused a complete about-face in company policy. Sears, Roebuck and Company had been planning to close its grocery department, but word leaked out in advance of the actual move. The newspaper tied the decision to the passage of the new pure food and drug laws. In order not to give any support to the story, which could have hurt sales of all items, the company determined to keep the unprofitable grocery department in operation for several more years.

The mail-order executives were understandably exasperated. Finally, Montgomery Ward decided that the best defense was good offense. In 1902, his catalog reprinted an article entitled "The Tyranny of Villages," which read, in part: "We believe the farmers of today are tyrannized over by the country merchants to a far worse extent than they realize. . . . Mail-order business has solved the problem for the farmer and released him from serfdom."

Richard Sears agreed, but his pen dripped with sarcasm and charm rather than venom. The same year, the Sears, Roebuck and Company catalog carried his editorial entitled "Our Compliments to the Retail Merchant." He said: "As a rule, the merchant from whom you buy adds as little profit to the cost of goods as he can possibly afford to add; for example: if a certain article in our catalog is quoted at $1.00 and your hardware merchant asks you $1.50 for the same article, we wish to say in behalf of your hardware dealer that this difference of 50 cents does not represent an excessive profit he is charging you. . . ." because he could not buy in as large lots as the giant Sears, Roebuck. The point was neatly made and, incidentally, with a finesse that showed why Sears was passing Ward as the leading mail-order house.

The opposition of local merchants and the social and economic pressure they could exert led Sears, Roebuck to introduce the plain, unmarked wrapper. The company claimed that if Sears shipped its goods without placing its name on the package, merchants themselves could buy from Sears, Roebuck.

While they all worked at defeating the guerilla warriors of the towns, the mail-order companies paid even more attention to the war among themselves. Their ever-mounting profits showed that they were beating off the attacks from the shopkeepers and the provincial press. Sears was more concerned with Ward's balance sheet. By 1900, Sears, Roebuck had edged ahead as the leader in the mail-order business, and it has never since been in second place.

Other stores would periodically enter the field to attempt a run at Sears, Roebuck and Ward. R. H. Macy went so far as to lift some of Richard Sears's own prose in an attempt to get cosy with its prospective customers. But there was more to mail order than the catalog copy, and, by 1911, Macy had dropped out of the mail-order race, just before the business would enter its golden era.

The golden era for the mail-order business corresponded with the economic resurgence of the farmer at the time of World War I. It brought new demand for American agricultural production, both at home and abroad, and with it came higher prices. Between 1914 and 1918, farm prices more than doubled. Today, when farmers speak of a desire to receive parity, they refer to a farm income equal to what they got during those halcyon days.

Why Sears, Roebuck could come from behind and seize leadership of the field can be explained by a single factor: Richard Sears's superior ability as a salesman. As one of his colleagues said at the time, "He could probably sell a breath of air." Ward, then as in later years, was more conservative. All-out domination of mail order by Sears, Roebuck leadership was due to the Rosenwald management team. Until 1919, Sears, Roebuck was consistently saddled with a smaller inventory than Montgomery Ward. When it had to disappoint so many customers because it was out of stock, Sears temporarily conceded the inventory advantage to Ward. But it had already strengthened its hold on the lead. Keeping the inventory as small as possible without letting its reduced size hinder the business was the essence of success. While mail-order houses could buy in big lots, they also were relieved of maintaining much of the inventory that retail stores could not avoid, simply because they did not have to stock stores with merchandise. They could wait to gauge demand before placing big orders with suppliers. Even though the 1921 debacle had pushed Sears, Roebuck and Company into the red for the first time, it is remarkable how well Rosenwald managed to keep costs under control. The net sales per employee remained relatively stable throughout the period after 1908, when Rosenwald took complete charge of the company.

The events of 1921 threatened to take away the lead that Sears, Roebuck had been building over Ward. The older company rebounded better from the depression. Although it was remarkably secretive about its progress, Ward undoubtedly showed a higher rate of return on investment than did Sears. A few years later, *The Wall Street Journal* would report on the reason for Ward's strong showing: "As vice-president of Montgomery Ward & Co., it was generally understood that General Wood contributed largely to the comeback of that company. . . ." When Wood went to Sears, Roebuck, the permanence of its lead was assured.

The biggest ally of the mail-order merchants was the United States

Post Office. Rural people insisted on being able to read newspapers and magazines published in the big cities and, perhaps more important, to be able to keep tabs on their government. The politicians responded and the post office grew. By 1901, there were 76,945 post offices, more than at any other time.

But even more important than the expansion of post offices were the classification of the catalogs as second-class "educational" material and the introduction of rural free delivery (R.F.D.) and parcel post. The low postage rates for catalogs had come into effect even before Richard Sears had begun his business. He immediately recognized that the post office was actually subsidizing his advertising effort.

R.F.D. was a major breakthrough. In order to mail his order or correspond with the mail-order house, the rural customer had usually been required to journey to town. If he had wanted his mail delivered, he would have had to pay somebody locally, in addition to the postage charges.

In 1891, Postmaster-General John Wanamaker, the Philadelphia department store magnate, first proposed a system of rural free delivery. The post office would hire carriers to take the mail from town to letter boxes at the roadside throughout rural areas. There would be no charge to the country dweller. It took several years for Congress to save up the sum of $30,000 needed to launch the system. Starved for newspapers, entertainment, and even companionship, rural America took to R.F.D. with enthusiasm.

Most important, at least commercially, R.F.D. gave the farmer what all Americans have always liked in their shopping: convenience and choice. Of course, the farmer would still make trips to town and frequent the general store. But he could compare the store's prices with the catalog's. And perhaps even more vital was his ability to place an order without leaving home.

So well pleased were they with R.F.D. that farmers' organizations of all kinds peppered Congress with demands that the parcel-post system be extended throughout the country. It was one thing to be able to correspond easily with the mail-order house; but the real revolution would come when it was no longer necessary to journey to the freight depot in town to pick up the goods that had been ordered. That was precisely why every volley of demands from farmers was met with an answering volley of opposition from chambers of commerce, retail merchants' associations, and hosts of businessmen.

Hearings dragged on before Congress from 1910 to 1912. Battalions of witnesses on both sides appeared. But both Sears, Roebuck and Company and Ward held back. Rosenwald was unsure that parcel post would benefit the company. He feared that increased use of the mails would lead to more small purchases when the company had been asking customers to place large orders or to group them so far as possible. The handling costs to Sears, Roebuck could skyrocket with parcel post. Nor could parcel post make it cheaper to mail the catalog because it was already classified third class, even less expensive than the fourth-class parcel post. One Ward executive told Congress, apparently sincerely, that he did not know whether his company would support parcel post. He did not expect that the share of goods shipped by mail would increase.

Parcel post went into effect on January 1, 1913, and was an immediate success, especially for the mail-order houses. Gradually the service was improved to include ever larger and heavier packages.

The Post Office Department had, in effect, endorsed the mail-order business. Of course, R.F.D. and parcel post were a response to a broad popular demand. In opposing them and in attacking the mail-order houses, the local merchants were doomed to lose because the people, especially those in rural America, were changing their buying habits and perspectives. History would show that the small store could never stop the mail-order house, but it could survive along with it. Somewhere down the road were the larger department stores and discount houses that would do more to eliminate the local store than would the mail-order houses.

If the mailman brought the "Chicago houses," as Sears, Roebuck and Company and its competitors came to be known, a bonanza, he also brought some of them a new nightmare of organization. Rosenwald had brought order to the company only to have parcel post impose new chaos. The shipping department had to be rearranged to handle a flood of orders, and within a matter of months after the introduction of parcel post, Sears, Roebuck and Company was its biggest single user. Both the Chicago Post Office and Sears scrambled to keep up with the mail, which soon hit 20,000 pieces a day. In the end, it was worth the effort. Reshuffling the shipping department kept costs from rising. In short, parcel post forced the company to streamline its shipping operations, which would have been necessary, in any case, to deal with steadily increasing demand.

The revolution in the mails also induced the company to enlarge its product line. Mail delivery prompted people to "shop" for smaller and lighter items that caught their eye. The strength of Sears, Roebuck had always been in the heavy, hard goods, which could not be shipped by mail. Now, it introduced a larger soft-goods line. There was no science to this shift in merchandising. It was all trial and error.

One soft-goods sales effort that was an unmitigated flop was an effort to break into the world of high fashion. In 1916, the company introduced the "Lady Duff-Gordon" line of women's clothing. *Printer's Ink* wrote, "Romance and a sense of surpassing smartness are thus brought into the remotest homes that the Sears, Roebuck catalog reaches." Somehow it did not work out that way: Lady Duff-Gordon was not a hit on the farm. Each of her gowns was given a romantic name. One was "I'll Come Back to You," which is precisely what the dress did to Sears. Good-by, Lady Duff-Gordon.

The general merchandise manager of Sears, Roebuck and Company fancied himself something of a style-setter and was not about to be deterred by the failure of the lady's line. After a foray into fine linens proved profitable, he rushed into high-priced shoes. But there would be no wing-tips in the manure piles, so that experiment was a complete failure. Finally, he put $500,000 into a factory to manufacture men's high-priced clothing. Management had had enough. The whole plant was written off as a loss before a single suit could be sold.

While it was trying to find soft-goods lines that would sell, Sears, Roebuck and Company also went into the ultimate of hard goods, selling houses by mail. Starting with sales of building materials, the company edged closer to selling the whole package. The first complete "Modern Home" was sold in 1909. Although Rosenwald was somewhat reluctant to get into mortgage loans, the company finally took the plunge. The company not only sold building materials under mortgage arrangements, but also actually put up cash for homebuyers.

The selling of the most elephantine of mail-order products—a complete home—was a success. Some of the houses were handsomely designed; one was spotlighted in an article in *The New York Times* as late as 1976. They helped fill the demand for new homes in suburbia, where many of Sears, Roebuck's traditional customers were moving, but in the late 1920s demand for new housing began to slack off and the final coup de grace was delivered by the Great Depression. Profitable until 1930, "Modern Homes" plunged into the red thereafter. Some mortgage loans turned sour, and Sears, Roebuck, the farmer's friend, was put in the unenviable position of having to foreclose. But for a while, Sears, Roebuck, as well as Ward, had actually pulled off a major marketing success with the ultimate product.

Mail-order sales grew steadily through the 1920s, and competition between Sears, Roebuck and Ward remained keen. In 1929, Sears said it would prepay all postage charges, and Ward retaliated by offering to cover freight as well. So would Sears, according to its next catalog. Actually, the depression intervened, and the company limited itself to giving customers a credit for the cost of postage, covering only the smaller shipments, which could be mailed. By 1933, both of the mail-order giants had backed away from this expensive way of attracting customers. In today's Sears, Roebuck catalog, where the company implies that handling and shipping costs have always been in addition to the cost of the item, "since our founding in 1886," the brief flirtation with free shipping is forgotten.

The depression not only forced Sears to charge for shipping, but it also cut deeply into mail-order sales. The company countered by cutting prices. The catalog began to sound again as though Richard Sears was writing his hard-selling prose about lower prices. Then, prices began to rise again as the federal government restored individual sectors of the economy. In fact, the price changes in the Sears, Roebuck catalog were a reasonably accurate barometer of the economic recovery.

The rise of retail stores which, during the depression, topped catalog selling, meant that traditional mail-order operations would be increasingly interwoven with sales in the stores. Again, Sears and Ward vied with each other to come up with the latest wrinkle in catalog selling.

Prices in Sears, Roebuck's retail stores were a few percentage points higher than in the catalog to take into account the increased cost of selling. But customers would often complain about the difference in price. Clerks were first told to suggest that customers examine the item in the store and then return home to place their order. Yet Sears had just spent a lot of money trying to get the customer to the store. The obvious answer was to install a catalog sales counter in the store itself.

Curiously enough the introduction of the catalog sales counter aroused the same kind of animosity as had existed between the mail-order houses and the general storekeepers. Clerks were already too busy, the counter took up valuable selling space, and catalog prices were often lower. But management was firm. It gave the retailers a share of the profits from counter operations and then simply ordered store managers to make way for the catalog. The vestige of the original conflict between retail and the catalog is the location today of most catalog sales counters at the rear of the stores. Presumably customers, wending their way toward the catalog, will be tempted along the way. And the best selling space is not sacrificed. Gradually, retailers recognized that the catalog sales personnel relieve the customer of the responsibility of filling out forms and computing costs, so that the catalog actually draws people into the stores.

The overlap of catalog and retail sales is greater than ever and not merely because of the use of retail outlets to make what once would have been mail-order sales. In the 1950s and 1960s, Sears conducted tests to determine the impact of the catalog retail sales. In some markets, catalogs were widely distributed while they were held back in others. The result was an increase in sales in those areas where there were more catalogs. About 45 percent of the added sales was in retail. Sears has measured the impact for each of the groups of goods it sells and has found that the greatest stimulus for retail purchasing by the catalog is in children's clothes.

Sears management was reluctant to accept the survey findings because, at the time, only two general and three supplemental catalogs were being distributed. Now, with the monthly tabloids being mailed to catalog customers, Sears admits that the catalog generates big retail sales. Yet catalog and retail are still competitors. Some storekeepers do not like having any of the catalog advertising costs charged to their accounts. One investment advisory house has discovered that the method for calculating bonuses for sales has also helped keep this rivalry alive.

Although the rivalry between retail and catalog is waning, some store managers are still adamant. One grumbles about the 11 percent charge he must pay on each catalog item his store handles. "Don't overestimate the catalog," he warns a visitor. Because people are often dissatisfied with the color or size of an item when they receive it, some 16.5 percent of catalog sales end up as returns. Then, the retail store has to sell these items because it is usually barred from sending them back to the catalog distribution centers.

Ward got the jump on Sears, Roebuck in instituting the service that would keep the mail-order business flourishing: taking orders by phone. In 1934, it began offering phone-order service in five cities where it had mail-order plants. A customer in such cities could be promised delivery at his or her door within two days. Sears was not to be left behind and tested the technique in Chicago. It was a natural move for Ward, which had no retail stores in large cities. As a result, it advertised its invasion of urban areas with full-page announcements. Sears had to be more careful because it did not want the mail-order system, which it called Telethrift, to keep customers away from its department stores.

Sears extended the service into scores of cities during the 1940s. Deliverymen would collect payments, even on installment plan purchases, and could pick up merchandise that the customer wished to return. The result was that catalog customers increased the frequency of their purchasing. Sales grew in later years to the point where orders by phone now represent about 60 percent of all catalog orders. In a subtle transformation, the mail-order business had become the phone-order business.

Eventually, Sears began encouraging customers to come to a nearby retail store to pick up their purchases. Of course, that brought even more catalog customers into the stores, and it saved them the added delivery charges from the store to their home.

The complete hybrid of the maturing mail-order business and the retail stores was the catalog sales office. In towns too small to justify even the smallest Sears store, offices were opened exclusively for catalog sales.

Take Exeter, New Hampshire. Everyone knows the Sears store, just up the street from that old-fashioned New England town hall. You might mistake it for a small department store. When you enter, it looks like an appliance outlet and, in fact, Sears is the biggest seller in town of the merchandise on display: water heaters, refrigerators, freezers, kitchen cabinets, television sets, and even a small tractor. But this is not really a retail store. It is a catalog sales office. Just like the iceberg, what you see is only about one-tenth of what there is.

The merchandise display is a sort of three-dimensional catalog. You get a chance to look at that stove, for which you are about to part with as much as $534.95, before you place your order. A lot of people feel more reassured when they can actually see what they are ordering rather than just the photo in the catalog. About one-fifth of the office's sales, which total over $1 million a year, come from sales of items on the floor.

Then there is the counter. People are streaming in all day to pick up their orders. But if you are unsure about size or about how to make an order or if you are just out shopping, you will place an order for a catalog item at the counter. Another 30 percent of the store's business is done that way.

But half of the business in Sears's Exeter store is done in a small office tucked away behind the catalog desk. Here five women are hard at work taking orders over the phone. They sit at wooden desks, designed especially for Sears to hold all of the catalogs from which orders may be placed, some on a slanting shelf just in front of the operator and others in a warren of cubbyholes under the rack and along the side of the desk. Under a glass plate on the top of each desk are shipping charts, so that the operators have an idea of where an item ordered is located, how long it will take for an order to arrive, and how much it will cost. To many customers, these disembodied voices are Sears, Roebuck and Company.

If you step out of the telephone office, you are in the largest room in the Exeter store, the one where incoming orders are kept. It is a miniature warehouse. In effect, this is the store's inventory, but, unlike most inventories, it will all be sold because it represents just what customers ordered. Of course, there is no need to display these goods, so the cool and efficient atmosphere of the warehouse displaces the more lavish surroundings of a retail store. Obviously, this is a pretty cost-effective way to sell.

Most catalog sales offices are smaller, with a lower volume of business. And what you find in one of these offices, you will also find in every Sears retail store.

By 1974, Sears was ringing up $2.8 billion in catalog sales while Ward trailed badly in second place with only $870 million. How had Sears been able to build such an impressive lead?

The answer lies in the kind of management that Sears had and their ability to gauge what the market wanted. The Sears labs were concerned not merely with testing the quality and characteristics of items the company sells; leave that to the Federal Trade Commission and Consumers Union. The lab was and is concerned with finding out what people want and how Sears can provide it. The characteristics of any product are important not in the abstract, but in relation to what consumers are looking for.

Above all, Sears management knew how to sell—or, more exactly, how much and when to cut prices without reducing profits. The mail-order market, actually called catalog sales now, was so alive and well in the mid 1960s that *Barron's*, the financial weekly, took a close look at this venerable and thriving industry. And what it found was that Sears was in the process of blitzing the competition. The then president of Ward grumbled, "I regret to report that in the catalog portion of our business we did not keep pace with competition." Other Sears competitors were complaining that the giant was trying to wipe them out. The Sears president was indignant. "We made an intensive effort, but retailing is a business that requires an intensive effort every day. When all the chips are down, we'll make more money than ever before, so I don't see how anybody can say we went out to buy business." Meanwhile Ward had fought back and had achieved a big jump in sales, although at great cost.

The battles chronicled by *Barron's* in the 1960s represented an extension of the competition to suburbia. Increased catalog production and the mailing of hundreds of millions of flyers cost big money. New York-based J. C. Penney tried to break the grip of the Chicago Four—Sears, Ward, Spiegel, and Aldens—by purchasing the General Merchandise Company in 1962. It promptly ran up big losses. Even Ward took it on the chin to the tune of a $25 million loss in a single year.

Amazingly enough, Sears did not really know how it performed its profit-making tricks. It was not until the late 1960s that it began a systematic survey of the market to find out why the catalog continued to thrive.

The poll showed that the catalog's main appeal was the enormous assortment of articles and the complete descriptions of their characteristics, usually far better than what could be extracted from relatively untrained sales people in the retail stores. In addition, customers were impressed by Sears's barrage of tabloid catalogs and flyers. Finally, the ease of ordering by phone was becoming increasingly attractive to people.

People do not want to use the catalog in order to avoid going to the store; most of them actually go to the retail outlet to pick up their order to avoid paying extra for home delivery. What is unique about the catalog is the presentation of more information than the customer could probably obtain if he or she actually examined the product. It is like buying a car on the basis of how it looks. That will not tell you much about its gas economy or how often you will have it in the shop. In short, today's more discerning customer finds that the catalog allows for more careful shopping. Sears's move to more detailed catalog descriptions was not, as it seemed, a reluctant bow to consumerism. It was what the customers wanted.

So the catalog is the complete department store. Originally it was the store-in-the-book for the farmer just up from poverty. Even today, most catalog customers think most other catalog customers are just poor hayseeds. Each thinks of himself as an exception because most are suburban families with school-age children, Dad with an above-average education, and the family income in the $15,000 to $20,000 range.

But one thing about the stereotype is still true. A great many of Sears's catalog customers still live in rural or nonmetropolitan areas. And that market is still growing, in part perhaps because of the return-to-the-country movement that has rapidly boosted the population of such disparate states as New Hampshire and Colorado.

Sears has spent more than a quarter of a billion dollars expanding its catalog sales in the period between 1970 and 1977. That is the biggest growth in catalog sales investment in 25 years. Two new catalog distribution centers were built, and five others were expanded. Other older facilities were modernized. And, perhaps most important, Sears again took the plunge into the fashion game by opening a distribution center devoted exclusively to this "high-risk" area.

The enormous appeal of the catalog is demonstrated by the purchases made from it by millions of people who do not even receive it. "This implies to us that Sears has considerable inherent strength and untapped potential in its catalog operations," says one investment house, pretty heady stuff in the conservative world of finance. On an average, Sears gets $90 in sales every year from each of the catalog customers, including those who do not even get the big book. And sales have been growing in recent years at about 10 percent annually.

Ward and Penney are still trying to come up with catalog lists that can duplicate, even on a smaller scale, Sears's success. The cost of catalog advertising at Sears is about 5 percent of total sales (as compared with 2.8 percent for Sears's retail). It has been estimated that Ward must pay at a 7 to 8 percent rate, and Penney's catalog advertising cost is higher than 15 percent.

Many people see Sears as synonymous with the mail-order business. And, like General Motors in the automobile industry, it is, in fact, larger than all of its major competitors combined. After Ward, with 31 percent of Sears's catalog sales, trail Penney with 21 percent, Spiegel with 14 percent, and Aldens with 8 percent. Of the total market for the major stores, Sears has managed to maintain a remarkably steady 57 percent share. But it cannot rest on its laurels. Penney is beginning to move up and seems determined to challenge Sears's dominant position. So are smaller specialty houses.

In the next few years, the tight little world of the catalog companies promises to see the vigorous pursuit of its seemingly age-old war. In Chicago, Ward has been merged into a conglomerate called Marcor and then bought up by the Mobile Oil Corporation. At Sears, there are subtle signs that Ward is no longer regarded as the prime competition. Until late in 1976, Ward's (actually Marcor's) price was posted on Sears's daily stock quotation board for the purpose of comparison. But as Ward was "conglomeratized," it became less worthy of notice to the folks at Sears, so its stock price was banished (to be replaced by that of K mart, the retailer that worries Sears the most, but that story will come in a later chapter).

The growth of Penney does not seem to be coming at the expense of Sears. Instead, Spiegel has actually seen sales slip, and Aldens perks along without much actual growth. Spiegel started out as a retail operation, gave that up during the depression to stick with mail order, then bounced in and out of the retail business while building a reputation as a mail-order house. The name that it got was not always what it wanted. A United States senator was convicted of taking a bribe from Spiegel to vote in favor of postal legislation designed to help its sales. Spiegel also strongly favors credit sales. Some people complain that they cannot buy from Spiegel unless they have its card. It is now owned by Beneficial Finance; so that may be the reason why.

Aldens started out as a hats-by-mail business under the name of Chicago Mail Order Millinery Company. In 1946 it opened its first retail store and took the name of Aldens, after its men's-wear line. It is owned by Gamble-Skogmo, the Minnesota conglomerate.

In New York, in a splendor notably less than that of Sears, sits J. C. Penney, the new challenger. It began in 1902 as a retail operation. Mr. Penney located his stores in rural county seats, and the customers flocked to him. He was able to exploit the bulk purchasing skills used by Sears or Ward while selling over the counter. Actually, it was Penney far more than the mail-order houses that hurt the small local merchant.

Later, Penney also decided to take on Sears in the catalog-sales field. The key was obviously Sears's success with catalog selling in its stores. Penney, which began adding stores at a rapid pace in the 1970s, found the catalog market an obvious attraction. While it could not yet challenge Sears head on, it soon passed Spiegel and Aldens. In 1970, its sales were 42 percent of Ward's; just four years later, sales were 66 per cent of Ward's and still growing.

More frequently, these days, Sears finds itself in head-to-head competition with Penney. But a visit first to a Sears catalog counter and then one to a neighboring J. C. Penney shows why there is still a lot of confidence in Chicago. Penney's manager is a retailer, mail order having been a fairly recent addition to his company's operations. So he feels he has little stake in how well catalog does; that it does not draw many customers to his store is not of great concern. The catalog counter is almost deserted. The catalog itself looks, at first glance, like a carbon copy of Sears's big book. But the similarity is superficial. Shipping information is far more complicated, and Penney relies heavily on the mails. Penney has only 3 catalog distribution centers, as compared with 14 for Sears. The selection of goods omits many of the bigger items sold by Sears. And, most surprisingly, the guarantee seems to stop short of the all-out promise of satisfaction from Sears. But they are paying close attention to Penney in the Sears Tower, where its stock quotations have achieved the honor of being posted daily, perhaps as a warning, certainly as a challenge.

So here is competition on a grand scale. But it is still the old-fashioned kind of sell–cut prices–cut costs competition that is supposedly the essence of the free enterprise system. And, as it has for every year in the twentieth century, Sears, Roebuck and Company wins just about every battle in this mail-order war.

CHAPTER 6

BIOGRAPHY OF AN ORDER

The enormous mound of brick on the northern edge of Philadelphia looks like one of those forbidding factories where thousands toil to produce a million widgets every day. The only relief is the architect's half-hearted stab at a gothic style on the window frames of the top floor. Even in a day when huge factories are commonplace, the building is impressive. Hard by stands its own power plant, sufficient to light and heat a fair number of American towns. Almost as a pledge of fealty, the city of Philadelphia has added a fire station, whose sole task appears to be the protection of the brick giant.

Nothing is produced here; except for profits. This is a Catalog Merchandise Distribution Center of Sears, Roebuck and Company, one of 14 the company has scattered across the United States. It is the third oldest of these plants, yet all are much the same. They are the link with Sears's past, with the origins of the greatest direct-mail house in the United States (and, hence, in the world).

If any single building is characteristic of Sears, Roebuck, it is this plant. No customer can enter its doors, yet hundreds of thousands are served here every day. New equipment and new business techniques have invaded the premises, but the basic rules of operation are precisely those that were first used in 1908. To enter this sanctuary is to get close not only to Sears, Roebuck today but also to how it must have been in the early years. Here everything is done the Sears way, with no compromises. You do not get into the place without being cleared for an identification badge, and everybody, including the general manager, wears one at all times.

Sears's main task is getting the goods from the manufacturer to the customer, and the Catalog Merchandise Center serves as a way station. Yet here the abstractions of the Wish Book are translated into reality, and thousands labor to see just how fast they can make wishes come true.

Mary Hamilton could care less (her name, like all others in this story, is fictitious). All our heroine cares about today is the weather. In a word, it is awful. Snow is falling again, and the temperature is around zero. On top of that Monday morning depression engulfs her. So, it is a perfect time, perfect to go shopping.

The weekend was a good one to stay indoors, and yesterday afternoon the family had browsed through the Sears catalog. The kids had wanted just about everything they saw, but Mary and her husband Joe had said no to all of their demands. This was no time to be making unnecessary purchases. Just stick to what we need. Mary had gone along, sticking bits of paper into the pages displaying items the family required. Now, on Monday morning, she flipped to those pages and reviewed their choices. Joe, Jr.'s parka would not make it through this winter, so she had picked a new "survival" model from the catalog. He wanted a green one. She will also get a new set of sheets and a pillow case for her daughter Ellen, in a comic book print. I hope Ellen remains faithful to Snoopy, at least until the sheets wear out, she muses. Dad, who is trying some reupholstery work in his shop, has picked out a staple gun and a box of staples. Mary hopes that, by getting her order in today, he will have the stapler in time to use it next weekend. Mary wants to pick up a small braid rug to use in the guest room. That is all for now.

Now to call Sears. Mary always places her orders through their local store, located in Hicksville, Long Island. As she dials, she recalls that her mother always asks for the same salesperson and will not place her order with anybody else. Sometimes, she says she will wait until "her friend Betty" calls her back. Mary does not care that much, although she feels that Sears must know who she is by now. Sometimes they call to inquire if she would like to place an order. She probably does not know that that means she is a good Sears customer, one who probably will not mind the call from an operator with time on her hands.

The phone rings on operator Helen Mikovski's desk. She has been working for Sears for eight years, all of that time at an order-taker's desk. She likes the work, especially dealing with people. And she knows the catalog intimately and watches it closely as it changes over the years. As she picks up the phone, Helen pulls a blank order form to the center of the desk. Mary thumbs from one book mark to the next, reading off the catalog number, color, size, name of the item, price, and shipping weight. The number itself is a key, and Helen will check it to make sure it is right. It indicates not only the article, but also the catalog in which it is listed, the catalog plant where it is kept, and even the color of the item. All of this information goes into a box on the order form. Helen knows from the item numbers that Mary is ordering from the 1976 fall big book. But haven't we been offering that survival coat in another catalog as well? she wonders. She flips out her Midwinter Sale catalog and quickly leafs through it to the proper page. The coat is now $22.99, not $27.99 as in the big book. A quick look at the codes tells her that none of the items Mary has ordered are shipped direct from the supplier or from the special fashion distribution center near Chicago or from some distant catalog center. Mary can pick up her order by Thursday.

As she hangs up, Mary smiles to herself. Sears, Roebuck could easily have charged her the extra $5 for the survival coat, and she would never have known the difference. In fact, if other items are being sold at reduced prices in tabloid catalogs, the bill will automatically be reduced. That makes for happy customers. What about when the cost increases during the life of a catalog? In such cases, Sears will not raise its price. In 1973, for example, when the oil embargo hit with amazing suddenness, the company found that it was advertising antifreeze at bargain prices. In fact, Sears lost money on every gallon sold. Top management huddled in Chicago. Should we simply let Sears run out of the stuff? They stuck with their announced price and kept on buying high-priced antifreeze to resell at a lower price. Their only concession to commercial reality was to limit the number of containers that any one customer could buy. Sears would meet the legitimate demand of its customers, but it did not want to become a cut-rate supplier to the market as a whole.

Before Mary's order will leave the catalog office she has called, it will go through the first of many sortings. Does it call for items coming from several departments or locations or is it for a single item? These orders are separated. Several times each day, an operator will take all the orders received by Helen and a dozen other operators in Hicksville and retype them, punching a paper tape in the process. Then, the tape is fed into a teletype, which will transmit them to Chicago, where it is retransmitted by computers, talking with each other in the middle of the night, to the Philadelphia catalog center.

The Chicago computer will do a number of other tasks. Mary has charged her order to her Sears credit card, and this information is pumped out to the credit central on Long Island, where another computer keeps Mary's account up to date. Yet another computer will keep tabs on the supply of coats, sheets, staplers, and rugs, and when supplies at the Philadelphia plant get below a predetermined level, will print out an order for more. However, a merchandising executive will have to clear the order before it is actually sent.

The huge I.B.M. 370 in Philadelphia is also sorting information that will be used later. How much purchasing is coming from each area? Perhaps a recent burst of orders from Hicksville means that Sears should think about expanding its operations in that area. Has a customer ordered an appliance that can be covered by a Sears Maintenance Agreement? The original guarantee may last for a year, so the computer must remember who should be sold a maintenance contract and send a reminder to the local sales outlet just before the guarantee expires. Finally, the computer keeps track of the value of purchases that Mary makes during the year to determine if she is still eligible to receive the catalog. If so, it will, at the appropriate time, print a label so that the next catalog can be mailed, or a card so that she can be invited to the Hicksville store to pick it up.

Not all orders are as easy to process as Mary's. About 8 percent of those received in Philadelphia come directly by mail. (Nationally, the Sears average is 5 percent.) These orders are opened in a specially secured room, where any checks, cash, and money orders are removed. The orders are then passed to an office where clerks huddle over computer screens and the rushing sound of the computer's cooling fans dominates. Here, the orders are punched into the computer manually. Some orders come from abroad or from discontinued catalogs. A special group works on translating such orders into the computer's language.

Now the 370 begins issuing orders. It has been told when the truck will leave for the store nearest Mary's home, so it can calculate a schedule for processing her order. She has ordered items from four of the eight floors of the catalog center. The computer spits out order tickets for each of the items. On each ticket, just as it was decades ago, a time is imprinted. This is the key to Sears's venerable schedule system. Mary's ticket reads Tuesday, 9:45. That means that for 15 minutes, beginning at that time, the packing room will be waiting for Mary's shipment. All four tickets must be back in the packing room at that time, each attached to the item Mary ordered.

Promptly at eight o'clock emissaries from each floor come to the ground floor to pick up their order tickets. They hurry back to their home bases because in order to meet the 9:45 target, the items will have to be sent down between 9:10 and 9:30, a precisely scheduled 20-minute period. At times, activity of the stock floors can be feverish. At Christmas, the Philadelphia center can be filling as many as 340,000 orders a day. Even on a slow day, some 100,000 orders leave the plant.

Each floor in the catalog center is a military model of neatness and order. The old wooden floors have been varnished to a mirror shine, and the brick walls look freshly painted. At one end of the floor, the soft piped-in music is accompanied by a low rumble you might mistake for a far away railroad train. Closer inspection reveals a number of cages, each almost as tall as a man, pulled along tracks embedded in the floor. These cages bring in the goods newly arrived from Sears's suppliers. Each catalog plant is located near suppliers of most of the items that it stocks. Of course, some are trucked in from manufacturers that have only one base of operations, but the idea now, as when the catalog system was created, is to keep supply lines as short as possible. Sears is a good customer; so suppliers must agree to keep their goods flowing steadily into the innumerable cages.

At the loading dock on the ground floor, trucks are arriving continuously through the day. Goods are unloaded into carts, in what looks like a switching yard. On the front of each cart are a series of holes into which flexible rubber rods are inserted. The carts actually are moved by a kind of cog-railway system that runs through the track. It carries them from the loading area to huge elevators. The rods "tell" the railroad the floor and the aisle where they are to go. After an elevator is loaded, it shoots up to the merchandise floors at the speed of one level per second. When the doors again open, the cages automatically roll out and proceed to their destination. There, they are unloaded, and goods are placed in temporary storage. Later, goods will be transferred to the merchandise bins at the other end of the floor.

Mary's order will be filled by "pickers" on each floor. They shuttle from one bin to another, pulling items for the 9:45 delivery. Once, pickers used roller skates and even bicycles to hurry from one bin to another. Sears people tell the story of the day the company president was visiting a catalog plant and rounded a corner in time to crash into an oncoming bike. That was the end of wheeled transportation for the pickers.

Each picker has received a batch of order slips. In the case of Mary Hamilton's order, four different pickers have each received a slip for part of what she wants, but all slips indicate that the order is scheduled for 9:45 in the packing room. The pickers move through the aisles quickly, plucking items off the shelves according to item number. They do not even have to pay attention to color, as that is included in the order number, and each size has its own bin. The goods are dropped into the special wheeled carts used by pickers. The orders are dropped into one side of the cart and are emptied later all neatly stacked, from the other side. On top is what amounts to a small desk. The picker must note the number of items requested and occasionally indicate that Sears is out of stock. Until recently, the pickers checked a box marked "Memo" on the order ticket when an item priced at $9.90 or higher was out of stock. That meant that the customer should be informed that the order would be filled later. On lower-priced items, the picker would check "Omit" indicating that the customer would have to reorder if he or she wanted to obtain the item when it came back in stock. But Sears found that once customers had ordered by catalog, they were generally willing to wait, if necessary. So Sears is increasingly using the "Memo" box and will hold orders for as much as 180 days, if the customer agrees.

The picker attaches the order slip to each item. When the cart is unloaded, the orders are stacked and ready to be dropped to the wrapping room at the appointed hour. For those items that are out of stock a message is sent. On each of the storage floors, there are five metal cylinders, perhaps 10 feet in diameter. Each tube has three "blades" or spiral slides which wrap themselves around a central core. The items due in the wrapping room at 9:45 are dropped into an opening on the side of the cylinder during the scheduled 20-minute period and are carried by gravity on one of the blades to the ground floor. The blades are like giant children's slides, and it looks tempting to wait for a lull in the merchandise delivery and hop on for a ride. Some stock people at Sears have tried it, much to their regret. The drop is pretty sharp, and the blades have been honed and polished through decades of use. Those who have taken the plunge probably recall it as the fastest slide of their lives.

When the cascade of items arrives at the ground floor, it flows onto a network of moving belts, each about 3 feet wide. These belts pass in front of sorters, who are able to determine from codes that the computer has printed on the slips where the items should be sent for wrapping or packing. In only two cases does the catalog plant actually put all of the items for a single customer into a single container. One of these is what they call "D2C," direct to customer, and includes any order (except for large items stored in warehouses) that will be shipped, usually by mail or United Parcel Service (U.P.S.) to the customer's home. The other time a customer's order will be packed is when he or she has ordered through a catalog sales merchant, a person who runs a catalog office but who is not a Sears employee. This saves the merchant from having to make up the orders on his own premises.

The packers who handle these orders stand in a kind of cockpit. In front and above them is a hopper into which are fed the items that they must assemble in the next 15 minutes. The packer drops these goods onto a desk and then sorts them by order. She must handle 15 orders of no more than four items each, every 15 minutes. As the orders are completed, she dumps them onto another belt, which passes below the hopper. It is monotonous work, requiring real concentration, and the tedium is relieved only by the piped-in music.

Those items that will be mailed are carried to another room where they are weighed and postage is placed on the package. In some places, Sears has begun using machines that can automatically calculate whether it is less expensive to ship by mail or U.P.S. The company is still a big mailer. At Christmas, four trailer trucks and a dozen postal vans pick up orders every day. If the customer has not paid enough in advance for postage, Sears sends its bill. These postal billet-doux are sent only once, because the company has found that its customers are remarkably honest and pay what they owe after that one reminder. For those who have overpaid, Sears issues checks on the spot.

About 80 percent of the goods leaving the catalog center are not individually packed for each customer. Instead, the items pass along an amazing and somewhat terrifying series of belts, at a rate of as many as 30,000 in a single hour. Repeatedly, along their way, they are pushed off by sorters onto other belts until they are finally slid into bins for each store or catalog sales office. The computer has calculated when the pickers must pull merchandise and when it must arrive in the packing rooms; this strict schedule ensures that the items will go into a store bin in time to make the truck that will carry them to the store.

Mary's items, which are not to be mailed, are to make a noon "cut-off" in the sorting room. They all are carried to the bin for her store and are mixed with scores of other items for other people's orders. As the bins fill, a slide on one side is flipped up and the goods are put in what are called consolidated cartons. Sears buys these expensive boxes, which it tries to use on as many as four round trips, from companies that have rejected them because of misprints of their commercial messages. So it is not surprising to see boxes for everything from toilet paper to potato chips being used to carry customers' purchases.

A rolling belt carries the boxes to an area where they are loaded on giant caged or flat carts. These carts, about eight times as large as those that trundle in new goods, also run on tracks and move to a collection point where shipments for the noon "cut-off" are assembled. Again, the Sears people can route the carts to the appropriate loading dock by setting devices that determine the tracks they will follow.

In the loading room, scores of trailer trucks and large vans are drawn up at a seemingly endless number of docks. Goods too large to store even in the mammoth catalog center arrive from a separate warehouse elsewhere in Philadelphia. At Bay 159, there is a sign with four store locations listed. On the right are Hicksville and Farmingdale; on the left, White Plains and Ramsey. That means the Long

Island stores are handled by the morning truck; the second two, in the afternoon. Consolidated cartons for the Hicksville store are loaded in the "nose" of the trailer because the truck will stop at that store last. Then goods for the Farmingdale store are put on the truck.

The trucks make a run every day. Often they will leave their trailer at the last store they visit each day, as in Hicksville, and pick up the trailer left the day before. It contains returns. The Sears vehicle may also stop at suppliers on the way back to pick up more merchandise.

When the shipment arrives, containing Mary's purchases, the cartons are opened and once again go through a sorting process. Her order is assembled by clerks in Hicksville on Wednesday morning and placed in bags. Off they go to storage racks, where they will be held until she calls for them. Often the store will call Mary to tell her that her order has arrived or to let her know that an article is out of stock. If it is an "Omit" item, she will be asked if she wants to reorder.

The order that Mary placed on Monday was nothing out of the ordinary, and it has been filled in a typical way. Julius Rosenwald's "schedule system" has worked in 1977 just as it was planned to work in 1909. By locating catalog distribution centers in strategic spots around the country, Sears is able to fill most orders in three or four days. Some catalog centers are far more automated than the venerable establishment in Philadelphia. Pickers have been replaced, and the sorting onto the appropriate belts is done automatically. In the giant carpet storage center, great rolls are lifted automatically from high racks, laid out, and cut to the customer's measure by a machine, all under the direction of a computer.

Of course, had Mary ordered a tractor or a fancy dress, the mechanism for meeting her order would have been more complicated. Because of its size and limited demand, the tractor might have been located at another catalog merchandise distribution center, and it might have been shipped from there directly to the Hicksville store by a private trucking company. Or it might have been shipped directly from the supplier. If she had chosen a frock from the National Fashion Distribution Center, near Chicago, her order would have taken a day longer because trucks shuttling between Chicago and Philadelphia would have brought it on Tuesday night.

One product Sears neither makes nor sells is vital to the catalog operation: the computer. The system devised under Rosenwald's supervision is essentially labor-intensive, and it was developed at a time when labor was plentiful and cheap. But the growth of the American population has made it impossible to continue without the help of the computer. Sears would simply have strangled in its own success. The cost of labor would have forced the company to limit its own growth because costs would, at some point, have outstripped profits. Now the computer transmits and processes the order, prints the merchandise slips, routes goods through the catalog center, prepares and prints the bill of lading, and helps the catalog outlet keep track of the orders it has received. Yet all this electronic wizardry has not put Sears people out of work. Able to handle an ever-increasing volume, Sears needs more people to handle the merchandise, operate the stores, mail the packages, and, of course, run the computer. Because the catalog operation is a classic example of mechanization replacing rote functions, it is a textbook study of the beneficial effects of automation.

Mary has come in to the Hicksville store to pick up her order. When the package is opened at home, everybody grabs his or her purchase as though it were a Christmas present out of Santa's bag. All except Mary. Now that she has seen the rug in the room where she wanted to place it, she does not much like the color. Although the color is close to what was pictured in the catalog, it is just a shade off. That is always a possible problem with catalog orders because even the multicolor pictures in the catalog cannot do justice to some colors. On her next run into the store, she takes the rug along. Some places might not take it back because there is nothing wrong with the rug. But the return is made quickly and easily at Sears, and she is immediately given a credit on her charge account. "Satisfaction guaranteed."

But Jack Wilson, one of the Hamilton's neighbors, is not satisfied. He has recently bought a snow-blower from Sears, and it just is not working to his satisfaction. He can never get the choke to work as it is supposed to, so he has to pull the starter cord more than he would like. Back goes the snow-blower to Sears for adjustments under the warranty. But Jack also wonders if it is worthwhile complaining. Probably, it will not make any difference.

Back at the Philadelphia plant, they want his complaint. They worry that people will think that it is not worth the effort to complain. "It's just like your vote," says an official there. "It may not seem to count much, but it does."

Sears wants to avoid having to repair too many snow-blowers. That just costs them money. But if customers begin complaining, that is a warning for Sears. Many items are test marketed in a few retail stores before they go into the catalog or all other retail stores just to see what customer reaction will be. If Jack's complaint comes in and is backed up by a few others from other stores, the complaint office will swing into action. Its inspectors, who are sent into "key stores," may be asked to check to see if there is something wrong there. The supplier will be notified or, if the level of complaints is too high, may be told to stop shipping and correct the defect. Sears even issues recalls for items it has sold that, as a result of complaints or its own research, may develop problems later. Once again, the computer makes it possible to find out which customers have bought the item in trouble.

Complaints are so important to the catalog operation that sometimes Sears actually invites them. In one tabloid catalog, Sears published three complaint letters it had received, together with its answers and asked for more. One man griped that he could never find a telephone number to place an order. A fellow in California said he had moved and was not getting his catalog any more. Most interesting was a letter from a Michigan woman who recorded all the times she had returned items and noted that her Sears kitchen floor had cracked and her two toilets still leaked and she could not get repair parts for them. It takes a certain amount of confidence about your business to print 15 million copies of that kind of complaint, for which, incidentally, Sears made no excuses. The net result of this one exercise in soliciting complaints was a raft of letters that kept the complaint department busy for weeks.

Philadelphia also handles complaints about retail operations in its area. The operating rule is "don't bounce the customer." That means that complaints are not referred up and down chains of command before they are handled. If complaints come in concerning a single retail outlet, for example, a Philadelphia representative will call the store manager directly. Sears is proud of this system, which relieves the complaint department of passing its inquiries through central catalog or retail headquarters. In fact, they will tell you there that some folks from the federal government were in recently to learn how to keep the taxpayers as happy as Sears keeps its customers.

Of course, keeping customers happy so they stay customers is a prime goal for Sears. But, in dollars and cents terms, Sears wants to bring down the returns, which run at a rate of 16.5 percent. The more goods it can get right the first time, without having to service them under a warranty or take them back because they are the wrong color or size, the higher are Sears's profits.

When perhaps half of the households in America are buying through the catalog, repeat purchases are essential. Sears cannot go somewhere else to find customers. Making the guarantee of satisfaction with their product is not the gesture of the Good Samaritan. Sears would rather take a loss on one sale than turn the customer off on the company for good. The company knows it will make a lot more sales in coming years if the customer feels that it handles returns and complaints willingly and eagerly.

For Dick Lamb, the general manager of the Philadelphia plant, the catalog business is high commercial adventure. Computer specialists, merchandisers, and systems people troop through his office every day. It is the office built by Lessing Rosenwald. Lessing eventually rose to the chairmanship of Sears, not only because he was his father's son, but also because this plant was successful.

Today, Lamb, an old-style free-enterpriser who would have made old J. R. proud, thrives on the challenge of keeping his aging monolith of a plant responsive to his customers needs and to the competition. Through the orders processed there, he can keep his fingers on the economic pulse of the Northeast. He knows if there is unemployment and where old markets are fading and new ones growing. As he walks through the plant, perhaps as Rosenwald did decades ago, he feels a geniune affection for the old building and the people in it. They will stop to talk a minute, but they soon dart off, never forgetting the demands of the "schedule system." It is both their master and their servant. If they keep feeding the hungry blades and empty bins, customers will come back. The pickers, the packers, the sorters, the shippers, the clerks, all can work together efficiently because of the system. Of course, there is always some grumbling. Workers do not always like the tedium. Lamb and his men do not always appreciate government regulation. Yet, for all, there is pride in a smooth-running operation.

The clanking cages on their phantom railroad, the giant chutes and blades, the whirring belts and the people, the 4,500 who make the Philadelphia plant hum, all contribute to what corporate biographers like to call the romance of industry. There is romance here, growing out of a sense of fellowship in making the schedule system work.

Oh, by the way, Mary Hamilton got her mail today and is already planning another trip to the Hicksville store. She received a card telling her that she can now pick up the new spring catalog.

CHAPTER 7

THE GENERAL

Robert E. Wood was

a. a genius
b. a fool
c. a liberal
d. a conservative
e. a dangerous right-winger
f. the man whom the army carried out of his office during World War II.

The third great man in the history of Sears, Roebuck and Company was all of the above, except one. He was not the man whom Franklin Roosevelt had bodily ousted from his office during the War. That man was Sewell Avery, the president of Montgomery Ward, but the story has become part of the mythology of Robert Wood.

Like Richard Sears, he was something of a swashbuckler, and like Julius Rosenwald, he was one of the best business leaders of his time. That is enough to start a mythology, and Robert Wood himself was probably the most determined promoter of his own myths.

Like Richard Sears, Wood was a child of the Midwest. Born in 1879 in Kansas City, Missouri, he was the son of the owner of a prosperous ice business. And like Sears, he knew economic hardship because the 1893 depression just about destroyed the father's business and ended the boy's hopes of going to Yale. Instead, as ambitious but poor boys did, he took the examination for West Point and went off to get a free college education. When he graduated in 1900, he was shipped off to the Philippines to perform the customary tour of duty: chasing insurrectionists. But he was already growing tired of the army, which offered him little hope for advancement or major responsibility. He returned to West Point for a while to teach French, which only made matters worse. Then he learned that work was beginning on the Panama Canal and easily wangled a transfer since few officers wanted an assignment in the land of yellow fever.

But Wood saw opportunity and packed off his wife, Mary Butler Hardwick, a nurse he had met at West Point, and his two daughters. They were to become well settled in the Canal Zone, and two more children were born there. (A fifth child was born after the family's return to the United States.)

"Anyone who stayed was promoted," he later said, "I was promoted every month for three months in the canal organization and, more important to me, reached a position near the top of the organization at the beginning of the work." He eventually became chief quartermaster, handling all supply for the canal project, and was named director of the Panama railroad and steamship operations.

His most important task was to keep the supply of cement flowing. In the hot and humid Canal Zone, cement did not last very long in the sack. Wood had to keep his stock small, while always having enough on hand to meet immediate needs. "The day we run out of cement," General George Washington Goethals warned him, "you're fired." Wood kept his job by casting aside the government rule that contracts would only be awarded to those who had made closed bids. He simply could not find a single supplier that would meet his schedule. So he called three suppliers to his office and worked out guaranteed purchases from each, provided they kept the cement coming on schedule.

By 1915, he was again growing tired of his job and retired from the army as a major, with a generous pension as a token of appreciation for his efforts in Panama. He joined the Du Pont company. "It was a good job," he later remembered, "and they raised my pay nearly every week. But I had looked around the company. I saw there was no room at the top. The Du Pont family was too able." So he quit and got a job with the General Asphalt Company, where he thought there was more opportunity.

When war came, Wood volunteered for military service, although he did it more out of a sense of duty than real desire. He handled supply and transportation problems, was promoted to colonel, and was put in charge of all port and shipping operations for the American military in Europe. In 1918, Goethals called him back to Washington, made him a general at the age of 39, and named him acting quartermaster-general. That put him in charge of a multi-million dollar purchasing and distribution system. "The commissaries were actually a chain of small department stores. My first ideas on the nature and problems of mass purchasing came from that experience," he recalled.

One of his civilian assistants happened to be Julius Thorne, president of Montgomery Ward. When the war ended, Thorne asked him to come back to Chicago as vice-president. Wood, who would forever after be known as "the General," left the army that he had never liked with the firm intention to make his way in the business world.

Montgomery Ward soon ran into difficulties because the post-war recession caught with it too large an inventory. Wood found the solution: Open retail stores to get rid of the surplus. Within a year, the backlog was gone, and Wood was sure he had made a valuable discovery. Unfortunately, Thorne was also gone, worn down by the economic crisis of 1921. In his place was Theodore Merseles, an Easterner (by definition somebody Wood did not much like) and a conservative, who did not like his brash vice-president. He closed the retail stores. Ward had "regarded the retail outlets as the funnels through which to drop the lemons from the mail-order inventory," Wood said bitterly. "I'm afraid I developed a profound contempt for them." The feeling was mutual, and Wood went to Sears, Roebuck and Company as vice-president.

Wood wasted no time in pushing the retail idea at Sears. J. R., who had seen the company become the largest mail-order house, was unenthusiastic, but he stuck to his principle of allowing his brightest people to test their ideas. Wood's biggest convert was President Kittle, who knew nothing about the business but who had the rare ability to make hard executive decisions. What is more, Kittle's contract provided that his pay would be a function of gross sales; so he was eager for a scheme that would push them up, even though he did not know what the ultimate impact on the company might be.

Within weeks of their taking office, Kittle and Wood agreed to open their first store in the mail-order plant at Homan and Arthington streets in Chicago.

Wood never made any claims to being an intellectual, and part of his myth is that his favorite book was the *Statistical Abstract of the United States*. This annual tome summarizes the findings of the census. "I always had been interested in population movements," he said. "It was a hobby with me—and I thought I saw the movement of the farmers to the cities and the extension of good roads." If the farmers could drive to town, they would have less need of the catalog. The same, of course, was true of city folks. Wood thought that you could figure out from the *Statistical Abstract* the direction the shifting population was taking and then build stores to serve them when they got there. In addition, he felt, Sears should build along the highways, down which thousands and then millions of cars would travel. That is what he set out to do.

In 1925, the first eight stores were opened. Only the one in Evansville, Indiana, was operated in a city where there was no mail-order plant because Kittle and Rosenwald wanted to be cautious about their company's venture. In that first year, retail represented 4.5 percent of the company's total sales, but the next year, in which only one more store was added, it reached 8.5 percent of sales.

Meanwhile, Ward was catching on. A mail-order agency in Plymouth, Indiana, started selling saws over the counter and kept asking the mail-order plant for more. When Merseles heard about the retail operation, which undermined the claim that mail-order was cheaper because it eliminated overhead, he was furious. But the profit figures were finally persuasive, as was Sears's performance, and finally Merseles gave in. But, by waiting two years, Montgomery Ward had lost the initiative and its chance to catch up with Sears, Roebuck and Company. Yet, from 1927 on, the competition between Ward and Sears was unrelenting. They raced each other to open more stores, to enter the choice markets first, and even to get into the smaller towns.

In January 1928, Kittle suddenly died. His record, built largely through Wood's efforts, was impressive. But his death, which undermined Rosenwald's hope that the third company president should have a long reign, as did the first two, set off a brief struggle for

power. Senior old-timers, who had been angered by being passed
over four years earlier, now expected to move to the top. Two vice-
presidents, Max Adler and Otto Doering, the man who had developed the schedule system, each believed they had a right to the top
job. It was rumored that they had agreed to stay on with Sears if
either was selected. Lessing Rosenwald, Julius's son, had another
story. He said that both Adler and Doering had already told Kittle
that they wanted to resign. Given their frustration at having been
passed over previously and the likelihood of a long Kittle tenure, the
story is probably true. When Kittle died, Julius sent Lessing to find
out if Doering wanted to be considered for the presidency. Interpret-
ing the feeler as an offer, Doering said he would stay if selected.

Meanwhile Lessing himself was angling for the job. He felt that
he had put in his time and had worked through every department
of the company. While passing on Doering's reaction, he also told
his father that he would resign if he were not chosen for the job. Here
was a ticklish problem for J. R., one that he let his wife handle. She
reminded Lessing that, if he took the job, he would always be in his
father's shadow in Chicago. He had gone to Philadelphia to avoid
just that situation and had deep roots there. Lessing surrendered and
told his father that he no longer wanted to be considered.

The choice was down to Doering and Wood. J. R. wanted to pick
a young man who had a chance at a long tenure as chief of Sears.
On that score, he would have to choose Wood. In addition, Doering
had already acquired a fortune, while Wood was still clearly a man
on the make. The success of retail operations, still in the future, made
little apparent difference to Rosenwald. Wood got the job, and Doering quit.

Wood had always wanted to work for a company where he could
aspire to the top post. The General and Sears were made for each
other. J. R. was still chairman, but his health was failing. When he
died in 1931, Lessing would, at last, succeed him. But Lessing would
never leave Philadelphia, and he would be continually occupied with
his father's estate. Thus, from the moment he became president in
1928 until his retirement in 1954, General Wood would be the undis-
puted boss of Sears.

Sears's entry into the retail business is remembered as Wood's
greatest accomplishment. Within just six years, the retail business

topped mail-order as a source of corporate income. Wood became a rich man, his $30,000-a-year salary at Ward having turned into $300,000 at Sears. But, despite his foresight and boldness in the retail business, Wood's contribution was far broader. Almost every major aspect of Sears, Roebuck and Company today, with the exception of the catalog, was developed by the General and his aides. He established new relationships with suppliers, expanded credit operations, turned to foreign markets, and created the Allstate Insurance Company. He reshuffled the organizational deck that J. R. had left him and reshaped the company. It is really no wonder how often top management refers to the General today because many of his ideas have demonstrated such a vitality that later executives have been hard put to improve on them.

Actually, Wood took charge of Sears at a time hardly conducive to achieving an impressive performance. Part of his early success must be attributed to the optimism, if not the euphoria, that accompanied the ever-rising stock market. But when the crash came in 1929, it hit hard at the kind of people who were Sears's most reliable customers. Wood had to bring the company through the most difficult economic period it would face.

The retail operations turned out to be the key to survival. In 1921, the company had been a mail-order business still closely tied to agriculture. Because it was still so specialized in mail order, it was vulnerable. The downturn in farm prices was felt almost immediately at the Chicago headquarters. Retail meant diversification. By building strong mail-order and retail operations, Sears was selling to all elements of American society. Of course, the depression hit everybody, but still people had to buy the basic necessities of life. Ward had looked at the growing prosperity of the 1920s and had grandly announced that it would no longer cater to the bumpkins, in effect soft-pedaling the rural mail-order business. "We take orders from everybody," said a Ward man. "We no longer depend on hicks and yokels. We sell more than overalls and manure-proof shoes." The depression revealed the inherent weakness in attempting to abandon the prime market, however colorless it might seem, and Sears kept on selling its plain and reliable goods. Everybody needed what Sears was selling, and Sears was now selling to everybody.

Retail also made it possible to cut prices quickly as demand slackened. The company was locked into its catalog prices by its long-term arrangements to purchase goods. But in the retail field it could adjust its inventory and its profit margin much more frequently.

Sales fell in each of the four years after the crash, and Wood moved to counter the effect of decline by reducing operating costs. As a result, the company showed a net loss only in 1932 and Wood never let that happen again. Still, it was a trauma for Sears to lose money because it simply was not used to the idea.

Not everybody greeted Sears's entry into the retail business with unbounded joy. Just as the chief competition to Sears as a mail-order house had come not only from its competitors but also from local stores, so, too, it and other chains were subject to a renewed attack by those same interests when they began retailing. This time the independent businessmen were better organized and financed, and they tapped a reservoir of public suspicion about the retail chains.

Suddenly, Sears found itself in the much-maligned company of the A&P, F. W. Grand, W. T. Grant, J. J. Newberry, Walgreen Drug, and Western Auto Supply. Such chain stores were actually nothing new in the United States, but by 1929, they represented one-fifth of the total volume of retail sales.

The attack against them took the form of proposals in virtually every state legislature for discriminatory taxes against the chains. The depression would not help matters because local retailers would be particularly hard hit and would strike back at the chains, which seemed better able to survive. The small businessmen believed that if the chains could be kept out of their markets, they would hold on to their customers. Their rationale was that theirs was the old-fashioned American way of doing business, a system that relied upon a middleman in the chain of distribution between the producers and the consumer. The cause was buttressed by Supreme Court decisions that said such discriminatory taxes were lawful, even if the tax rate increased in line with the number of stores a chain had. The battle was ultimately joined in the United States Congress when Representative Wright Patman attempted to have a federal antichain statute passed. If it had been enacted, it would have reduced Sears's pretax profit by 45 percent. Perhaps the key factor in the defeat of the Patman bill was an extensive study by the Federal Trade Commission, which showed that consumers benefited from the operation of the chains.

The obvious appeal of the chain stores was their ability to sell at lower prices because they could make large-scale purchases and had their own distribution systems. Their opponents attacked their lower prices through "fair trade" and similar laws, designed to force them to keep their prices at the same level as the small retailers. In some states, stores were banned from using "loss leaders," items sold at or below cost as an inducement to get customers into the store. To a certain extent, Sears and others could avoid some of the penalties inherent in such legislation by marketing products under their own name.

Sears fought back on other fronts. While it did little direct lobbying of either state legislatures or the Congress, it was a powerful member of trade associations. In this way, Sears could avoid calling attention to itself, both among its consumers, many of whom liked Sears and opposed chains, and among legislators.

In this time of trial, the General fell back on the techniques of Richard Sears. The company sought to reaffirm its close ties with the American farmer. The catalog again took on a folksy tone, stressing that Sears was really interested in the welfare of its customers and well acquainted with their problems. Wood openly supported New Deal social legislation, which he thought would be good for business, and wrote in the catalog that Sears recognized that it had to accept new responsibilities as a good citizen.

But Sears found that appealing to public opinion through the catalog, however wide its distribution, was not enough. The Federal Trade Commission took after the Goodyear Tire & Rubber Company on the grounds that it was giving too large a discount to Sears, which resold its tires under its own name. Goodyear argued that it did not have to handle the distribution or advertising of the tires Sears sold. But the FTC found that Sears had increased its tire business faster than any other retailer and concluded that its success was the result of Goodyear's discount. Soon, federal legislation against such alleged discriminatory pricing and in favor of fair trade made it clear that Sears would have to shift its suppliers. It could no longer rely on firms like Goodyear, which were selling tires with the Goodyear name at higher prices to other retailers. In fact, Wood had already begun to shift Sears into arrangements with suppliers more closely associated with the company. New federal laws meant that Sears found itself forced to step up the pace of developing new sources of supply, including those in which it was a part owner.

But the lesson of the attack on the chains was clear: Sears should increasingly become a "local" store. The catalog argued that Sears could sell at lower prices than local stores, but kept up its neighborly chatter. Retail store managers plunged into community life with an enthusiasm made necessary by public opinion. Only the coming of a new war would take people's minds off the struggle between the chains and the local stores.

Even Wood's confidence in his own ability and in the staying power of Sears, Roebuck and Company was undermined by competition and the depression. Mergers were frequent as corporations fought to survive. With so much duplication by Sears and Ward, it was inevitable that they would discuss the possibility. Rosenwald was in favor of it and worked up figures to show that merger would benefit the stockholders of both companies. But the talks broke down over the obvious question: Who would run the new company? Wood's liberalism and Merseles's conservatism clashed once again. An attempt at a merger with J. C. Penney was also doomed, in part because it was becoming evident that Sears could prosper without merger.

As retail developed, Sears paid a good deal of attention to carving out a special role for itself as opposed to the traditional department stores. If you are a man, how often have you sat uncomfortably in the middle of a department store's dress department, waiting for a woman? The General noticed such unhappy fellows. "The department stores were essentially for women. Eighty percent of their business was in women's wear, apparel, hosiery and all other apparel," he observed. "A man in a department store was lost. He was jostled around by the females and he had nowhere to go."

The obvious solution was to put monkey wrenches in the same store with fancy frocks. "We made it a store for the family; in other words, for the men, too. We added hardware, tires, service parts and other items of particular interest to men."

Perhaps the most typical family purchase was the "big-ticket" item such as a washing machine or refrigerator. People preferred to examine them rather than choose on the basis of a picture in a catalog, although they might ultimately order from the book. By the beginning of World War II, the retail stores had come to be dominated by such hard-line items, while the catalog was concentrating increasingly on soft-line goods.

The war brought new problems. New national priorities made it difficult to obtain the metal needed to manufacture appliances and the tools that had become a staple of the retail stores. In 1942 and 1943 sales would again fall, but profits held firm. Again, it was possible to retrench and cut some costs. And this time, the farmers came to Sears's rescue. The war meant higher prices for their produce and more money in their pockets. They wanted to buy the soft goods that remained in the catalog. Between 1940 and 1943, mail-order sales of soft goods doubled while retail sales of big-ticket items fell by 36 percent.

The Sears fall catalog issued in July 1942 told the story. It was 196 pages shorter than the catalog a year earlier.

Missing were those items that were Sears's best sellers: virtually all electrical appliances, tractors, gas ranges, cookwear. *Fortune* magazine wrote: ". . . by observing how government regulations have affected Sears, one can gain a good insight into their effect on the civilian economy as a whole. In a sense, Sears has already become an auxiliary of government: it is a rationer of goods. . . ."

Ward was better off because of its concentration on soft-line items. In two of the war years, its profits rose at a faster rate than did Sears's. Shortages continued to make things worse as the war continued. The catalog kept getting smaller and smaller, and Sears was forced to return a quarter of a billion dollars to its customers as late as 1946 because it simply could not fill their orders. Yet Sears did find one good customer during the war: the government itself. It was one of the few firms that was large enough and with sufficient sources of supply to meet the burgeoning demands of the war. In an odd way, Wood again became part of the Quartermaster Corps, selling certain items that had disappeared from the catalog to priority customers who in turn fed the war effort. Tank builders used Sears tool kits, army commandos slept in Sears sleeping bags, and munitions workers wore Sears coveralls, specially designed without pockets or metal snaps. Confident of the company's ability to find what was needed, Wood returned to the days of Richard Sears and had the company sell items it did not have in stock. Then, it would scavenge among its suppliers. Of course, there were profits to be made, but they were uncertain and, as everybody at Sears was well aware, temporary.

It was a tough time for Sears, just as for almost everybody else. Wood could not have helped being somewhat bitter because he had never wanted the United States to become involved in the war in the first place.

The General had started off as a supporter of Franklin Roosevelt and the New Deal. In fact, in later years, he would take pride in pointing out that he had twice voted for Roosevelt. But, as Hitler began to turn his plans for European conquest into reality, Wood split with his president.

Wood was ever the Midwesterner. He thought of himself as a model American, one who took to heart George Washington's admonition that the United States should avoid entangling alliances, especially with Europe. Wood knew Europe, or at least thought he did. What he saw was a continent in inexorable decline, and he worried that the United States would be dragged down with it if it became involved in Europe's affairs. To him isolationism was the essence of political liberalism. A liberal, according to Wood, was a person who looked to the future, and the future was at home. If you worried about Europe and insisted in remaining involved in events there, you were a conservative, a person excessively concerned with the past that must be put behind us.

The General was passionate in his isolationism. He viewed America idealistically as "the New Jerusalem," an experiment in Western civilization. Millions had fled Europe in pursuit of this dream, which he wanted to keep untarnished.

He believed that if the United States stayed out of the war, Germany would certainly conquer the entire European continent. Then, in order to preserve its empire, Britain would come to an agreement with Hitler. Its economy would be saved. At the same time, the United States would be safe, protected by a 3,000-mile moat over which Hitler could not cross. Wood admitted that such a world would be far different. The United States would have to gear its production to the same system that Hitler was using, while figuring out a way to preserve individual freedom. The economic relationship between America and Europe would be based on a return to the barter system.

Perhaps these changes were not to be desired, Wood reasoned, but they were preferable to the alternative. If the United States went to war, it would obviously be involved in a prolonged conflict. Britain would not sue for peace and instead would exhaust itself economically in the battle against Hitler. In the end, it would be forced to give up its empire. For its part, the United States would have to reorient its economy drastically and set aside economic expansion in favor of the war effort.

Roosevelt had become the enemy. Wood believed that most Americans did not want to go to war but that the president was doing all in his power to make participation unavoidable. The General was outspoken in his opposition. Usually, he got a fair hearing because his arguments were essentially economic and his patriotism beyond question. But he sensed that his warnings were falling on deaf ears, at least so far as the White House was concerned. In 1938, he had been sounded out as a possible candidate for president. Now, as the decade came to an end, he may have regretted that he had no political organization at his disposal to counter what he saw as Roosevelt's war policy.

Then, in early 1941, he heard about the efforts of one Robert Stuart, a student at Yale Law School, at the very university he had so wanted to attend. Stuart was trying to start an organization called America First. The General summoned the student to Chicago and listened to his plans. He liked what he heard and agreed to back the organization. Even more important, he would become its chairman, instantly giving the campaign a prestige and notoriety that it could not otherwise have achieved.

After Wood took charge of America First, other prominent leaders joined. One was Lessing Rosenwald, who had recently given the chairmanship of the company over to the General. Even in the 1930s, it had been clear that Rosenwald had allowed Wood to run the show, and J. R.'s son had clearly come under his influence. Lessing Rosenwald's decision to join America First drove a bitter wedge between him and the American Jewish community, which, in reaction to Hitler's open anti-Semitism, had swung behind Roosevelt's policies.

Then, the movement got out of hand. While failing to pick up the mass support of average Americans that Wood thought was inevitable, given American opposition to involvement, America First chapters nevertheless continued to sprout up all over the country. Wood and Stuart were somewhat bewildered by the influx of new members, who seemed to care little about their leadership and who often forgot to forward their dues to national headquarters. The newcomers were Nazi sympathizers, crypto-Communists, anti-Semites, and other people whose motives for wanting America out of the War were far removed from Wood's idealistic isolationism. *Harper's* magazine would later write that Wood's vision, held by Jefferson, William Jennings Bryan, the La Follettes, and other prairie populists, had "been kidnapped by a variety of reactionaries." Most of them were nobodies.

One of them was somebody. Charles Lindbergh, whose solo flight over the Atlantic more than a decade earlier had been sufficient to keep him America's darling, joined America First. He had been a frequent visitor to Nazi Germany and one of the most ardent believers of its claims to superiority and eventual success. Lindbergh was a big drawing card for America First and could have been just what the movement needed to build a respectable membership. But "Lucky Lindy" would not submit his speeches for advance clearance and said pretty much what he wanted. One of the things he wanted to say was that American Jews were responsible for the war.

His remarks threw America First into confusion. The national board met to decide if Lindbergh should be repudiated but failed to agree on any action. Lessing Rosenwald finally had had enough and quit. The membership recruitment drive ground to a halt. Lindbergh kept right on spouting his line, although he was sharply criticized in the press, and Wood continued to hang onto the movement for all the same reasons he had always professed. He said nothing about Lindbergh.

Wood still believed that a majority of the American people and, more important, a majority of the Congress agreed with him. In late 1941, he wrote President Roosevelt, urging him to ask Congress for a declaration of war against Germany. Roosevelt's reply was a masterpiece of patriotism and evasion, lending obvious support to Wood's belief that Congress would refuse to declare war. The president and the General both knew that a declaration of war was only a matter of time, but Wood gambled that if Congress went on record in opposition, it would be slow to change its course, and Roosevelt might be checked. Roosevelt knew that as well.

After Pearl Harbor, Wood quickly folded America First and pledged his complete support to the war effort. He knew he had lost his battle and watched as much he had predicted, as a consequence of the war, actually took place. But years later, he still believed that the United States would have been better off staying out of the war no matter who had won. "They answered me then by warning that if we let Hitler win, we would have to become an armed camp and spend as much as $50 billion on armaments. Well, what are we doing today?" he asked.

The General always blamed the war on Roosevelt and his military chief of staff. "President Roosevelt and General Marshall knew the Japs were coming," he said in a later analysis. "We had broken the Japanese code. They let 'em come, to get an incident which would unite the American people behind a war they wanted. They have the blood of Pearl Harbor on their hands."

Not only did American entry into the war rankle, but also the charges that he was motivated by more than isolationism in his opposition to involvement. He would always call the charge "the smear," arguing that he had not espoused the views of those who flocked to the movement. Who was responsible for this smear? The General would always say "they" were responsible, without being more specific. But his close friends said they understood him to mean "Easterners, minorities with strong ties overseas, international bankers, and foreigners." That hardly sounded like a description of Irish or Chinese. No, the description was pretty close to the code words used to describe Jews.

Perhaps the General was merely foolish in not realizing that his idealistic cause was being sullied by the rabble that joined the movement. He was something of a neophyte to politics, and it is possible that he had hoped his own personal integrity would far outweigh the motives of those who joined his organization. Yet when he was confronted with Lindbergh's statement, he failed to repudiate it, despite the glare of publicity about his lack of response. At that point, observers could only believe that the idealist was at the very least willing to do what was expedient. Wood did not seem ready to question the motives of his followers if he could achieve the desired end.

Ask an old-timer at Sears, somebody who knew the General, how they can explain his economic liberalism and political conservatism. One will tell you, almost matter-of-factly: "He was a bigot. He was anti-Semitic and anti-Negro." This executive says he thinks that the General's thinking was the product of his early training in the army officer corps. Such attitudes were common when Wood graduated from West Point. In fact, this executive implies that a man with such views could be selected to head Sears by Julius Rosenwald, a man who certainly had no patience with anti-Semitic or antiblack sentiments, because J. R. understood that such beliefs were nothing unusual in Robert Wood's milieu. Besides, even Rosenwald seemed to be able to separate his private concerns from the realities of the world of commerce in which Sears functioned.

Despite his outspokenness, Wood's America First adventure did not seem to have harmed the fortunes of Sears, Roebuck and Company. Obviously, some of the company's customers agreed with him. Others never associated the General with Sears stores. Of course, he led America First in an era when there were no television anchormen to brand Sears with Wood's political stigma. Still other customers were prepared to allow him to say or do what he wanted, so long as Sears kept on doing business as usual.

Whatever his attitude about the war, Wood cooperated fully with the war effort. Over at Montgomery Ward, Sewall Avery was more of a problem. He fought the efforts of the War Labor Board to have him accept what amounted to a closed shop under which all Ward's employees in the Chicago plant would have had to be unionized. The federal order came as a result of a bargaining election, under the supervision of the National Labor Relations Board, that indicated a majority of Ward's workers wanted such an arrangement. When the contract came up for renewal, Avery refused to sign, arguing that turnover caused by the war had left a majority of workers who now felt differently about the union. The War Labor Board insisted that Avery sign a closed-shop contract until a new election could be held. Avery refused. Although whether or not Ward was unionized might have little effect on the war effort, President Roosevelt felt he could not allow a major corporation to ignore the orders of an emergency agency. Finally, the Justice Department moved to seize the Montgomery Ward plant in Chicago. Still, Avery refused to be budged. In April 1944, he was actually carried from his office by two uniformed military policemen while doggedly sitting in his office chair, looking for all the world like a corporate Buddha.

Because of Wood's well-known opposition to the war, many people thought it was Sears's chief and not Ward's president who had been carried from his office. But Wood knew better than to let himself get into such an overt and widely publicized conflict with the government. Sears had artfully avoided unionization, so the specific issue never arose. Even more significantly, Wood was not the kind of man to let himself become such a blatant symbol of business conservatism.

Nothing could better demonstrate the differences between Wood and Avery than what they did with their companies in the postwar era. Avery took the conservative course, based on the experience following the First World War. Although orders were pouring in to both companies, Avery reasoned that, as soon as pent-up demand had been satisfied, the inevitable depression would follow. So he allowed Ward's cash reserves to build up, waiting to spend them on expansion when prices fell during the depression. This was the conservative, prudent, and wholly orthodox way to do business.

Wood, on the other hand, had remained the amateur demographer. He calculated that postwar demand was far greater than most people had predicted because of population growth and the rush to the suburbs. The war had accelerated the pace of technological development, and innovation would mean more jobs. In 1946, he decided to keep plowing profits back into expansion rather than build a nest egg. In the next six years, Sears would spend $300 million to open 92 new stores and enlarge and shift to the suburbs some 212 more. It was a big gamble, for, if the depression had come, Sears would have been in deep trouble. But the General was right. Sears's outlay for new construction was itself a big stimulus to the economy. The gamble paid off, and by 1951 Sears was selling $2.8 billion worth of goods, more than twice as much as Montgomery Ward. Sears was now the sixth largest American corporation in dollar volume of sales. The postwar expansion, Wood's last great contribution to the company of Richard Sears and Julius Rosenwald, made Sears what it remains today—one of the giants of the American economy. There would probably never again be such an opportunity for expansion; those who followed Wood would work hard to maintain the standing that Wood had achieved.

Sears, Roebuck and Company—the company *Time* magazine called "The General's General Store"—was a monument to him. In the business text books, it would always be a classic case. It was a tribute to Wood's judgment that he sought not so much to fight government regulation as to live with it, that he was always willing to shun orthodoxy in favor of the bold move; and, like Sears and Rosenwald, he regarded the company as an extension of himself.

Yet, even as Sears was expanding, Wood again showed that other side of himself, the Midwestern man with a weakness for right-wing causes. In 1944, a marine officer who had served as a state court judge, ran for the Republican Senate nomination in Wisconsin and failed. But that was just a calculated trial run for the race he would make in 1946 against "Young Bob" La Follette. This time, Joseph R. McCarthy would not fail, in large measure because of the support of Robert Wood. McCarthy had journeyed to Chicago to ask for support at the *Tribune,* a paper whose editorial views mirrored the General's. Robert McCormick, then the *Tribune*'s publisher, had continued his family's tradition of vituperative isolationism and virtually complete mistrust of Europeans. McCarthy came away not only with the newspaper's endorsement, but also with the financial backing of an organization called American Action, the postwar reincarnation of the America First movement. As before, Wood wrote many of the checks.

Why did Wood once again so readily sign up? For one thing, he and McCarthy shared the same political enemies, the nameless "they" who used "the smear." They both hated General Marshall, Wood for Pearl Harbor and McCarthy because of the impending "loss" of China. McCarthy did not think much of Europeans either and undoubtedly drew the support of Wisconsin's German-American community. Wood still longed for his ideal America, isolated and free to pursue its own development, and he sensed that "Tail Gunner" Joe could attract wide popular support for the policies necessary to achieve that goal. Undeniably, McCarthy was appealing to many of the unsavory elements who had joined America First. As before, Wood seemed little concerned about who became his associates.

Speaking of McCarthy, Wood would say: "He was being smeared for doing an unpleasant and necessary thing. It took a lot of courage to go after those people the way McCarthy did. I thought I ought to help him." Wood probably could not have told you who "those people" were, any more than McCarthy did, but his support was generous. In 1952, he organized a group of Midwestern businessmen to purchase national television time for McCarthy to present his case to the American people on the eve of the presidential election. On October 27, McCarthy delivered his talk, an obvious attempt to swing public opinion against the Democrats and to pressure Eisenhower to take up his anti-Communist cause. But he was badly prepared and had failed to marshall his "evidence," so the talk rambled. In fact, even his supporters were forced to admit that the senator, who had talked 40 minutes beyond the allotted time, had embarrassed the cause. Wood gradually withdrew from the McCarthy movement as it died.

Strangely, Wood did not share McCarthy's view of the Soviet menace. "What do we really know about their air force?" he asked. Even after their first A-bomb test, Wood said, "I don't believe they are making the bomb." Because he was so confident that the Soviets would not march on Europe, he urged a reduction in military spending, with the money saved going to roads and schools. Here again was the great isolationist, firm in his belief that the United States was safe behind its 3,000 mile moat. And in domestic policy, he showed himself to be on the side of the liberals in supporting social welfare programs. It was not that Wood was a do-gooder at heart. Instead, he saw better roads and better educated people as vital to the expansion of business.

Despite America First's overtones of anti-Semitism and antiblack sentiment, Wood had always argued that he had been "smeared," that his own motives were pure. Perhaps history could give him the benefit of the doubt, although the Lindbergh incident made even that difficult. But, if he had been fooled once, he could not use the same excuse for his involvement with McCarthyism. He was certainly intelligent enough to recognize that McCarthy's charges were reckless, unfounded, and damaging to the body politic; yet, at the very least, he again appeared to believe that the ends justified the means. He gave no sign of discomfort about being associated with the far right wing, and his prestige and money gave substantial succor to their cause.

Still, Wood's involvement in the America First movement and his

support of Senator McCarthy were far less significant than his contribution to the expansion of Sears. However controversial his political
judgments might have been, his stewardship of Sears left little room
for quibbling.

CHAPTER 8

THE QUARTERMASTER AND THE TERRITORIAL IMPERATIVE

In steamy Panama and later at the War Department in Washington, Robert Wood had shown himself to be a superb quartermaster. He could get the goods and deliver them where they were needed, when they were needed. Much the same thing was required in the catalog business.

But the retail business would be a lot different. Of course, the catalog experience helped, and Wood could fall back on his talents as a quartermaster. But he would also have to reshape the company. Getting and distributing the goods are only a part of retailing. Before he was finished, Wood would mount one of the most unusual research operations, transform buying practices, make Sears into a major manufacturer, develop a remarkably decentralized selling system, begin large-scale credit sales, and establish a big service organization.

Perhaps the retail development that bears the clearest imprint of the General's will was real estate. All phases of the retail business are linked. But it all begins with real estate—where to build the stores and what kind of stores to build. It was a big leap from the General's musings about the *Statistical Abstract* to opening hundreds of stores around the country. To translate Wood's vision into commercial reality, a real estate department was created. It quickly became one of the most important in the company, and, even today, after the period of the company's greatest expansion has passed, it exercises enormous power.

In St. David's, Pennsylvania, in the real estate section of Sears's

Eastern territorial headquarters, there is a plan for a new retail store, in fact for several of them. That may not seem unusual, until you take a close look at the plans spread out on drafting boards before a platoon of architects and designers; for the plan is detailed to the point of indicating where every refrigerator and dress rack will stand on the floor. Not only that, but the design for the store building itself is based on how the goods will be laid out on the floor. In effect, the building will be designed from the inside out.

The architects are normally friendly fellows, but they glance at you nervously when you walk into their room. What they are doing is classified top secret. Perhaps they are working out a new way to display a product, based on the experience of scores of store managers who have tried a number of different approaches. Or they may be working on plans for a store that has not yet been announced. They do not want to telegraph the news to their competition. If the land has not yet been acquired, they certainly do not want to announce Sears's plans prematurely because that would only serve to drive real estate prices up.

Like so much else at Sears, what is now done with a great deal of science was originally done purely by intuition. At first, the company built only the largest of its stores and rented space for the others. Even those it built were unimaginative and uniform, not very well suited to helping boost sales. For all his foresight, General Wood did not at first recognize that the store itself is a major help in increasing customer interest in Sears products. The architects of the time were not any real help because they knew little of the retail business.

In 1932, when it became obvious that retail would be the mainstay of the company, Sears created a Store Planning and Display Department. It gathered information from merchandising departments, from those handling freight and storage, and from employees who had to work in the new buildings. The most important questions were answered first: How much space should be given to each department? What items should be displayed, and where should they be located in the store?

In 1934, Sears opened the first store that had been planned by this new department, and it was an instant sensation. The headline in *Architect and Engineer,* reviewing the new store, said it all: "No Windows." For the first time a major commercial building had been designed to eliminate windows (other than display windows, of course). The store was located in the Englewood section of Chicago, and the local building code insisted that there be windows in case of fire. So the experiment was not complete; some windows had to be placed near stairwells. But Sears had made its point: The window had no place in a retail store.

The innovation of the store without windows also led to the first major commercial test of air conditioning. *Architectural Forum* wrote, "the building retained its heat at night, even in the coldest weather, for a much longer than normal time." Obviously, it would do the reverse in warm weather and represented an energy saver, however inadvertent.

The next year, Sears opened a store in Glendale, California, which had involved the store-planning people from the outset. They had decided where on the property the store was to be located, a matter of some importance since this was a store that allowed for a substantial parking area. The building was created entirely from the inside out. The major innovation? It was only two stories high, sharply reducing the problem of moving customers up and down over several floors and allowing merchandise in one department to tempt customers visiting other parts of the store.

From here on, Sears would plan every new store in exquisite detail. Nothing would be left to chance, in hopes that Sears would never find itself saddled with a loser.

The Sears real estate department now wields the power of life and death for the company's stores. Representatives in each of the five territorial headquarters continually monitor sales and population trends. Always on the move, these people visit cities and towns to determine if the present Sears stores remain competitive with other establishments. They check on local government development plans. They decide if a new store is to be built or if a new location should be found for an existing store. Perhaps their most crucial decision is how big a store should be and how much parking area it will need.

Just how carefully Sears examines this question of size is shown by a comparison of a Sears store in a medium-size New England town and a competing outlet of J. C. Penney. The Penney store is located in a space originally occupied by an outlet of W. T. Grant and covers 100,000 square feet. But Penney researchers have determined just how much merchandise the market can absorb, and it is actually insufficient to use all the space. The result is a cavernous and sprawling display floor, which seems thin on merchandise. By contrast, the Sears store has actually walled off some of its space and rented it to another retailer. It uses only 40,000 square feet, and its merchandise is far more tightly packed. To the untrained observer, this seems to be conceding a competitive advantage to Penneys, but Sears knows that customers respond better to its layout. Later, if Penney succeeds in bringing more customers into the shopping mall, Sears will be able to call on its 20,000 square feet in reserve.

Real estate experts also select the site of the new store. This is where greatest secrecy must be maintained because word that Sears is coming to town immediately boosts the cost of land. The company likes to own the land on which it builds to insure its complete independence. Even in large shopping malls, you are likely to find the Sears building at one end, a good indication that it has purchased its own site, immediately adjacent to the mall.

The company denies one widely circulated story about its site selection techniques. Competitors have claimed that Sears real estate experts ferret out the best two or three sites in a town and then buy them all. The store is then built on the best of these, the company keeping the rest in reserve, simply to prevent the competition from moving in there. That competitors have been able to find good locations in towns with already existing Sears stores tends to refute this story, however.

But Sears has been guilty of trying to determine just who its neighbors would be in a shopping mall. In 1975, the Federal Trade Commission found that Sears had engaged in a wide range of practices designed to discourage direct competition. Under so-called restrictive covenants, it could block the entry of other department stores into a shopping center, determine how much floor space a specific tenant received, and prevent discount selling by requiring that tenants not sell outside of a specific price range. Sears might also decide if a competitor would be located too close to its own store and, on that basis, refuse it a place in the shopping center.

Sears was bitter about the complaint. In a formal statement, it said: "This action is the latest in a series of orders directed against selected retailers who have been following industry-wide practices in the setting up of shopping center leases and other agreements. Within the past five years, the Federal Trade Commission has changed its position with regard to such practices that have been common for more than 25 years." In particular, Sears was angry at having been singled out because it believed that other stores had followed the same practices. It also argued that, in 1962, the chairman of the FTC had said that such covenants were probably not covered by antitrust rules.

Although Sears denied that provisions of covenants referring to a "popular price" dress shop or a "high fashion" dress shop amounted to price fixing in a shopping center, it agreed to an FTC consent order under which it would "cease and desist" from using covenants with such specifics. The FTC did not say why it had picked Sears. As the largest retailer and one that prides itself on its corporate virtue, the company was a logical target. If the FTC wanted to warn all other retailers against using such covenants, going after Sears was probably the best way.

By the time a decision is near on a site, the planners at St. David's territorial real estate office or in one of the other territorial headquarters are busy determining just what will go where in the store. Often, because putting a shopping center in the midst of a parking lot frees them from design constraints, they can use a design that has worked well elsewhere. For example, the big Sears stores in St. David's itself and in Hicksville, New York, and Burlington, Massachusetts, are virtually identical.

Once the size and shape of a new store is set, Sears may call in a local architect. The interior of the store must fit the Sears pattern, but the exterior is supposed to harmonize with local styles and, when possible, to use local building materials. That is why you will find a colonial-style building in Charleston, South Carolina, and one that looks like a government building in Springfield, Illinois, the state capital.

Store openings are almost a routine event at Sears. In 1975–1976, 35 new outlets were inaugurated, although 12 of these replaced older installations that were then closed. That brought Sears to 858 stores and about 2900 catalog sales offices. In order to keep up this pace, Sears spends about $275 million each year in capital improvements, although some of that money goes for distribution centers and warehouses. As routine as it may be, each store opening is a major milestone for the company. If corporate survival means there must be corporate growth, opening new stores has been one of the best barometers of the company's vitality.

Of course, the decision to open stores is not made on a piecemeal basis. There is a grand strategy. The most well-known and dramatic of these was to start building new stores at a furious pace right after World War II. While General Wood was gambling on steady postwar economic growth, Ward did not build a single new store between the end of the war and 1958. That effectively ended the race between the two old competitors. It would take bold managers at J. C. Penney and K mart to realize that they could open new stores and compete with Sears on what it had considered its own turf. But that discovery would not come until the 1960s, when Sears was already far ahead of the pack.

The decision to expand was accompanied by a major reversal of one of the General's favorite formulas. He had argued, wisely at the time, that most department stores catered mainly to women, so Sears should try to get men into the stores. That explained Sears's emphasis on tools and tires and on big-ticket items like appliances. But after the war, the company changed course. As it replaced outmoded downtown appliance stores, it decided that a majority of the new suburban outlets would be full-line stores. That meant getting far deeper into handling soft goods than ever before. This change of course caused serious problems for a company used to handling an inventory of appliances, which are hardly subject to style changes. As one Sears executive said at the time: "It's not a problem with refrigerators, say, where you just turn on a spigot in the factory if you run short. But in soft goods you can't do that; it's difficult to find sources for new materials that suddenly become fashionable, difficult to keep up quality and to get delivery in time at a certain place."

For all its foresight, Sears was slow to join in the movement to shopping centers. Its suburban stores, which it began establishing long before its competitors, were usually located apart from other retailers. Usually they stood alone, surrounded by parking lots. In the 1950s, developers began building shopping malls and centers, which Sears did not immediately accept. Yet these malls represented the same kind of commercial innovation as General Wood's own

plans for surrounding low-slung stores, which permitted many ad-
joining departments, with thousands of parking spaces. Because
stores were grouped together at the malls, customers might spend
hours on end browsing in one store after another. So people were
more inclined to shop there than at a single isolated store, much less
downtown. And all stores seemed to benefit from increased sales.

In 1960, Sears launched a major effort to catch up. It created the
Homart Development Company, a wholly owned subsidiary with the
job of developing shopping centers. Homart develops and operates
shopping centers either on its own or in joint ventures. It can also
take on related developments, including even residential, recrea-
tional, and office buildings. Sears does not necessarily become the
permanent owner of the shopping centers, because Homart sometimes sells out its share of joint ventures in order to begin new
projects. In early 1976, Homart was operating a dozen centers and
was a partner in four others. It was adding new ones at the rate of
three to five a year and was producing a tidy profit of $10 million
for Sears stockholders. The value of the property it held either alone
or with others came to one-half billion dollars. Not everything was
rosy at Homart, though. Like the parent company, it too had been
hit by the FTC for the use of restrictive covenants in the shopping
centers it had developed. It is still too soon to measure the impact
of the FTC decision, which could result in more head-to-head competition between Sears and its competitors.

It is obvious to almost any Sears customer that its retail stores vary
considerably in size. In fact, there is a strict caste system among
stores, although the company does not like to talk about it much. It
took General Wood only two years in the retail business to decide
that classifications were necessary. Stores that carried the full range
of the company's products were known as "A" stores. Today, they
each have more than 100 departments. In 1927, "B" and "C" stores
were opened. B stores may be only a bit smaller than A's, or they
may be only half as large. Typically, they may have 60 different Sears
lines. The C stores, also called "hard-lines" stores, are examples of
the stereotypical image of Sears as a purveyor of appliances, automotive supplies, and sporting goods.

From the outset, the B stores were something of a problem. Customers knew they could go to the biggest Sears stores and find just

about anything the company carried. Similarly, they had well-defined expectations for the smallest stores. In many a small town, the C store would acquire the reputation as the place to go if you were looking for a major appliance and not too much else. Just what you could expect to find in a B store was more a matter of chance. As a result, many customers in the 1930s took the easy course and simply went elsewhere. The key was in finding the proper-sized market for the B stores, some of which carried almost the full Sears line, whereas others were little more than C's with a few more square feet of sales space. That proved to be more of a chore than simply looking at the population figures for each town where a store was planned. But, over the years, Sears began to find a role for the B. For example, in 1975, although the uninitiated could not perceive the difference in the markets, it could gauge that the Ridgedale Mall in Minnetonka, Minnesota, rated an A store and the Sooner Fashion Mall in Norman, Oklahoma, would get only a B.

In the mid 1970s, Sears again began tinkering with the B store, this time in recognition of the growing population movement beyond the suburbs to small-town America. Both K mart and Montgomery Ward had been testing ministores, and Sears recognized that by putting such outlets into small towns, the company might find new markets, despite its near saturation coverage. Top management in Chicago tried to keep the "experiment" a secret but found it a little hard to deny the existence of what had come to be known as "Z" stores. That the first of these stores was opened in Maui, Hawaii, in 1972 is one indication of the lengths to which Sears went to start its new grouping without tipping off the competition. Then, too, if the plan flopped, not too many people would ever know about it.

The Z did not fail, although it represented a major change in Sears's way of doing business. The store looks like a slightly larger version of a C, but with an important difference. In addition to hardware, building supplies, automobile accessories, tires, curtains, and drapes—all of which might be found in a C—Sears Z stores stock women's and children's clothes. In fact, apparel may be the biggest single group of product lines carried. Many fewer salespeople are on the floor. Instead, customers push shopping carts and then pay for their purchases at check-out counters. Sears has traditionally spurned check-outs and carts. "Too much like a discounter," sneered one official. Now, they are being tested. These stores are so unlike the full-line department stores on the shopping malls that Sears has located them in smaller shopping centers side by side with supermarkets.

In these new stores, Sears is concentrating on those items that sell best. So you will not find high fashion for women or anything more than work clothes for men. Furniture, always a problem for Sears, is limited to those pieces that are known to be popular. There are not even very many toys.

About the only other kind of store in the Sears caste system is the "D," usually the smallest and located in a simple storefront. These stores carry only appliances. Like any of the smaller Sears retail outlets, the catalog sales desk is supposed to pick up the slack. Obviously, there really is not much difference between many C and D stores and catalog sales offices. Even Sears people get confused by the company's classifications. "I guess the retail stores are more often in cities and the catalog offices in the country," one store manager explains.

All this tinkering with the size and location of Sears stores goes well beyond the General's original directives to put the outlets in the path of a shifting American population. While that challenge remains, the company must now rethink its sales strategy, beginning with real estate, in the light of head-to-head competition from K mart and J. C. Penney.

CHAPTER 9

TAKING AMERICA'S PULSE —AND ITS BLOOD PRESSURE

At first, it was Richard Sears's intuition that gauged what the company's customers would want to buy. The burgeoning growth of the market and of Sears, Roebuck's sales compensated for the losses resulting from his occasional errors of judgment. Perhaps Sears's most important discovery was that the company was such a large purchaser of other people's products that it could demand that the goods be made to its specifications, actually those of its customers. General Wood was to push this attempt to please the Sears customer to the extreme, by supporting the development of a unique corporate laboratory.

Today, that lab and the company's merchandisers, the people who decide what Sears ought to sell, depend on the most scientific and detailed information about the company's customers that can be obtained. "In contrast to many of its competitors, Sears is acutely aware of the importance of consumer research," writes a leading investment house in its study of Sears. Yet the establishment of a consumer research department, equipped to go out and take the pulse of the American public, is a relatively recent innovation at Sears. Through most of its history, the company used its own sales —real world successes and failures—as the way to determine what the people wanted. Now, before the merchandisers act, they can draw on a dazzling array of studies conducted by the consumer research people. What is more, instead of going through the hierarchy, merchandisers can order their own research by going directly to specialists in their area on the consumer research staff.

Sears likes to know how well it is doing in comparison with the competition. But for each product line the competition may be a different retailer, so the company must run a variety of surveys. Just to find out how it is doing on hard-line goods, Sears has Trendex, a survey outfit, call some 70,000 people as often as four times a year. Another outside company handles a soft-goods survey. As a check, Sears itself conducts surveys, including one on home fashions that reaches 10,000 families. Samples this size are a good deal larger than those used by Gallup or Harris to tell us who the next president of the United States will be.

These surveys help Sears determine where it stands in the market, whether its goods are properly priced, and what customers want. Because the results are sometimes surprising, surveying is a much better way to operate than intuition. For example, one study showed that Sears auto batteries were priced above the industry average, but they were still the biggest sellers. It also revealed that people appear not to mind spending more if they are obtaining a quality battery. Another study showed that Sears boys' jeans, also priced above the market, were the nation's biggest sellers, while J. C. Penney's, sold below average prices, came in third. Of course, Sears is not always a winner. A study showed that for some men's apparel, shoppers would rather buy at local specialty stores than at Sears, even if it has lower prices.

With so many people coming into its stores, Sears wants to know what gets them there and why they buy or refuse to buy once there. By measuring what is called "drawing power," studies show what share of all purchasers of a given item check with Sears before buying. "Selling power" is quite another thing. That is the indicator of the share of actual purchases of that item made at Sears. If, for example, drawing power is low and selling power high for a given item, Sears steps up its advertising. However, if a lot of people come into the store to look but few actually make purchases, something may be wrong with anything from store display to the quality of the product itself.

Many of Sears's products are identified by the company's own brand names. Naturally, it has a healthy curiosity about just how aware its customers are of these names. One great source of pride to the company was the 1973 finding, in a brand-awareness survey conducted by its research department, that Toughskins, the name used for children's jeans, had become better known by mothers, than the century-old Levi's. Similar studies also allow Sears to determine whether people are going to pay an added price for special features. As a result, Sears has found that people are reluctant to spend as little as an added $5 for a gadget on a stove but will pay more for a television set if more features require a higher price.

Finally, the company wants to know what its customers think about it. In 1976, a study found that Sears was the most popular retailer among the income groups with the largest market share— those with incomes, after taxes, above $15,000 a year. Customers say they keep coming back to Sears because of its integrity, appliance service, the relationship between catalog and retail operations, and its broad credit system. In short, Sears must be doing something right.

Perhaps, more than anything else, Sears's lab is the answer.

Dinner is cooking in the kitchen, and everything smells delicious. Nearby, four sewing machines are started by an unseen hand, whir for a few seconds, then stop. In another room, a machine simulates the action of a person plopping himself down in a chaise over and over again. In still another room, a couple of people hover over a gold-plated peanut, trying to determine the poison level in the goober.

Sound like a house of horrors? It is not meant to be. All of these strange events and a good many more are taking place in the Sears laboratory, located in the great brick building on Chicago's West Side that was once the company's headquarters. A laboratory like this is unusual for a retailer to maintain, but its existence goes a long way toward explaining Sears merchandising success. It is not simply a safety lab, although it does monitor the performance of Sears products to see how well they meet government requirements. Its main purpose is to help Sears sell more.

The lab began in 1911 in response to the enactment of the Pure Food and Drug Act. Although all Sears products covered by the act conformed to its requirements, the company wanted to bring the entire catalog into line with the spirit of the new law. Obviously, this was a reflection of Rosenwald's desire to cut out the puffery in the catalog, the legacy of Richard Sears, and make the descriptions correspond to reality. The lab soon came to be known as "the watch-dog of the catalog." Perhaps the most immediate effect of the lab was the early elimination of patent drugs from the list of products the company sold. Other changes were less apparent but no less impor-tant as standards were imposed and the company's wares began to display a certain uniformity of quality.

The lab also allowed Sears to compare what it sold with the competition. Once, J. R. complained that the company was being beaten in the market place by a competitor's boy's wear. The lab insisted he was wrong and demonstrated, to his grudging satisfac-tion, that Sears was using better quality linings and that its sizing was consistent and honest, which was more than the other company could claim.

But Rosenwald did not really support the lab, saying he was "not interested in intangibles." While others in the company began to see that it helped them in selling the company's lines, J. R. could see little connection between its work and merchandising. Something of a struggle ensued within the company over the proper role for the lab. Some believed that it should remain an independent office, whereas others argued that it should simply serve as a training department for catalog merchandise managers, to acquaint them with the char-acteristics of the goods they were selling. The lab as training office seemed to be the accepted view until the 1921 recession almost put it out of business entirely. In the 1919 catalog, the company had devoted two full pages to describing the role the lab played in deter-mining the quality of its goods. While the refrain was repeated in the next two catalogs, the lab was actually being readied for a cutback. Max Adler, the general merchandise manager brought in as the company retrenched, actually told his buyers to stay away from the lab. The lab staff was cut by two-thirds and soon had little to do. Adler was more interested in boosting sales than in maintaining quality standards. The furniture department was one that he always kept under his control, and it never improved the quality of the merchandise. Later, Lessing Rosenwald would say, "The stuff was so awful that we used to wonder where Uncle Max managed to find it; nothing could have been quite that bad accidentally."

Three factors saved the lab and caused its steady expansion after 1928: General Wood, the Federal Trade Commission, and a change in the focus of its operations. As he took the company into the retail business, Wood recognized the value of having a place to determine the quality of the goods. His major interest was to keep costs down in order to keep prices down, and some of the lab's findings were particularly valuable in this effort. For example, it had generally been assumed that higher-priced goods were also of higher quality. But testing showed that, on occasion, quality and price were not directly related and that Sears could realize valuable savings by choosing lower-priced goods that were actually better than what the competition was selling at higher prices.

The Federal Trade Commission had been established in 1914, soon after the opening of the lab. Its task was to determine what constituted unfair trade practices, and the company wanted especially to avoid running afoul of the FTC because its mail-order business was so heavily dependent on another government agency, the United States Post Office. In the 35 years after the establishment of the FTC, the regulatory agency required Sears to change its advertising claims some 20 times. In almost all cases, the company had still been making exaggerated claims, à la Richard Sears. For example, it falsely said that its radios were "all wave" and its tombstones "last forever." But, it probably was spared a good many other problems with the FTC because the lab was constantly evaluating the characteristics of many of the best-selling goods.

Because Sears sold goods made by others under its own brand names, it became increasingly important to be sure that manufacturers' claims were accurate. The buyers themselves could not make such judgments, but the lab's examinations helped determine whether size 12 was always size 12 or if a washing machine could do everything Sears and the manufacturer claimed.

Wood did not consider this service as an "intangible," and his support for the growth of the lab was in sharp contrast with Rosenwald's somewhat surprising attitude. In 1929, he put an old army friend in charge of the operation, and in 15 years the payroll for the lab was ten times larger than it had been. Gradually, the functions of the lab were defined. Of course, it would conduct spot-check testing of manufacturers' or merchandisers' claims before items were advertised. In addition, this process allowed Sears to be sure that suppliers kept to specifications outlined in their contracts. To this task was added testing before an item was selected for inclusion in the Sears lines. The lab would evaluate possible new products in comparison with what was already available in the market. Another responsibility was to determine all the facts about items sold by Sears. This research covered what the item was made of and how it was made, how it stood up under use, and, when there had been a rash of complaints, where the problem lay. In short, the Sears lab is not a consumer testing operation based on some altruistic sentiment. It helps the company know what it is selling and makes sure that the claims made for each item are accurate, essentially a protective measure that spares Sears the ire of its customers and punitive action by regulatory agencies.

One of the most important functions of the lab and certainly the most fascinating is its program of merchandise development. Let us say that Sears wants to win a larger share of the market in automotive batteries. From its experience in the retail business, it has a good idea of what people want. It could simply let manufacturers know that it is interested in being supplied with a better battery and might even specify how it would like the battery to perform. But, for Sears, that would be leaving too much to chance. Instead, its own lab will try to build just the battery that the store wants to sell. In that way, it will know exactly the performance characteristics of the battery as well as how much it costs to produce, based on its precise knowledge of its make-up. Sears can make trade-offs between cost and performance in advance rather than wait to deal with the world of the possible as outside manufacturers see it. Then, when Sears has come up with the battery it wants to sell, it can ask manufacturers if they want to supply that specific battery within a cost range that Sears has already determined. That is exactly what Sears did in the 1930s when it decided that it wanted to capture a leading position in the battery market.

Actually, the process is a good deal more complicated than it sounds. People are submitting ideas to Sears all the time in hopes that they will strike it rich if the giant merchandiser adopts their idea. "We never get a good idea from an amateur," says a company official in charge of labs, but Sears looks for suggestions from "professionals who know the market." Of course, someday an "amateur" may come up with a money-making idea; so the lab is asked to look at every proposal that comes in.

Sears worries a lot about getting into patent disputes with people who submit ideas. What if the lab has been working on a similar item and finds a workable product similar to the one suggested? So before it will even look at a suggestion, it requires inventors to sign a submission agreement. Because ideas are sent in voluntarily, Sears can set stringent conditions. It tells those submitting suggestions that it will not necessarily keep the idea secret and that it may divulge it to suppliers that could actually manufacture the product. As a result, Sears tactfully suggests that would-be inventors should first talk with a patent attorney.

Even if employees come up with ideas, they and the company can run into the same kind of situation, as a major case, decided in 1977, revealed. In 1964, Peter Roberts, a clerk in the Sears store in Gardner, Massachusetts, suggested a push button on the side of socket wrenches, which would enable the sockets to be changed with the use of one hand. The company was glad to buy his invention, which gave it a clear competitive advantage. It told Roberts that it would use his invention on about 50,000 socket wrenches a year, and, in 1965, he signed a royalty agreement with Sears providing him with two cents per wrench up to a maximum of $10,000. Five years later, Roberts brought suit against his former employer. In a trial in United States District Court in Tennessee, it was disclosed that Sears had sold 23 million wrenches incorporating his push-button device. Finally, in 1977, a jury awarded him $1 million in damages to be paid by Sears, Roebuck and Company.

Because it has a far greater familiarity with the market and with suppliers and in order to avoid the unpleasantness of cases like the one brought by Peter Roberts, Sears handles most of its merchandise development as a purely "inside" operation. Like the push-button on the socket wrench, most ideas are not totally new inventions, but improvements of existing products.

Sears has developed a method of evaluating products, based on consumer and lab research, which enables it to define the various characteristics associated with each item and the value consumers place on each of them. "New ideas have to fit into a trade-off scheme," says a company official. "There are few totally new ideas like the Polaroid Land Camera."

What is meant by a trade-off scheme? Sears determines what might be called the total product cost to the consumer. In coming up with this item profile, factors that improve the product in the eyes of consumers are weighed against those that "penalize" the product. A kind of balance is established, which, in its simplest form, might look like this:

Total Product Cost

Penalize   Factor   Improve

Selling Price --------->

<---------Service Cost

Translated, this trade-off would mean the following: As the selling price of a product is "improved" from the customer's viewpoint—by decreasing it, of course—the service cost of the product increases. In other words, an inexpensive product is likely to require more servicing than an expensive one. To be sure, this trade-off does not indicate what customer preferences would be. For example, some would rather purchase a $15 blender every two years and may spend $45 over a six-year period. Others will be willing to spend $40 for a blender that will last for the full six years. Buying the more expensive model may be cheaper in the long run, but the customer may not have $40 available when it is time to purchase a blender. So the company will stock both kinds of blenders.

These trade-offs are the result of considerable research. Sears has found that for each product, there is a different set of factors. In evaluating floor wax, it learned that when the product produces a higher gloss, the finish is harder and more wear-resistant. On the negative side, a high gloss wax reduces safety and is more difficult both to buff and to remove. The lab must find out which of these factors is the most important to consumers. If consumers want high gloss, that means they are willing to accept the other disadvantages.

Sometimes the results are surprising. For example, people want great efficiency from hair dryers. They want machines that will thoroughly dry their hair fairly rapidly. The lab has found that, beyond a certain point, an increase in efficiency has a negative impact on all other major factors: The dryer is less comfortable, bigger, harder to store, hotter, noisier, and more expensive. Yet, efficiency is what people want. Much the same is true of vacuum cleaners. Above all, people want them to pick up dirt well. Yet, if they perform that function satisfactorily, they are noiser, less attractive in appearance, heavier, bigger, more difficult to move, and more expensive. Incidentally, however, Sears thinks a generally negative feeling about an efficient vacuum cleaner is inevitable. It is not that people hate vacuum cleaners; they just hate housecleaning.

Trade-off testing can actually lead to new product designs, not just a change in marketing of existing products. For example, people who bought window air conditioners did not much like them, research showed, because they cut off the view. So Sears came out with a slimmer model.

In one case, at least, trade-off research came up with the demand for a product that looked as if it had only positive characteristics. People hated lugging heavy ladders around, and they did not much like having rungs break under their weight. Sears came up with an aluminum ladder that was actually stronger than those that had been marketed before, while weighing less. The stronger design used less aluminum; so Sears was actually able to reduce the price. And such new design can mean profit dollars for a company the size of Sears.

Once the company was able to develop a new dishwasher door that reduced the cost of each machine by $3. The added profit that resulted from the saving on each washer was equivalent to the profit from $40 million in increased sales.

This procedure yields far different results than the findings in *Consumer Reports,* the magazine of the Consumers Union, which has its own lab. Sears studies the magazine's ratings of products it sells with great care and even publishes its own internal counter-magazine in which it analyzes the analysis. Even when *Consumer Reports* takes Sears to task and gives one of its products a low rating, the lab counters with explanation and analysis, not vituperation. Sears people believe that the Consumers Union raters are unaware of what people want in a product, and they doubt that the consumer organization even knows, in all cases, what people should want. Of course, safety is desirable, even if a product is somewhat less efficient as a result. But some products are given low ratings because they are noisy, whereas Sears finds that people do not mind the noise if they are satisfied in other ways. To a great degree, the Sears and Consumers Union labs are in the same business, and both are relatively rare in their coverage of such a broad range of products. But Sears thinks it has the advantage because it can devote greater resources to its testing. In contrast to Consumers Union, which may test only one model of a specific item, Sears buys many in order to come up with a composite picture. And, clearly, the lab is backed up with the kind of market research that Consumers Union cannot do. Yet there must be a kind of respect, perhaps somewhat grudging, between the two operations. In any case, Sears says that it is not concerned when one of its products gets a bad rating in *Consumer Reports* because such ratings do not seem to affect sales.

If the company fails to gain a big enough market share in a product line, the lab tries to find out what is going wrong. At one time, Sears noticed that the demand for aquariums was enormous and still growing, but somehow the company could not break into the market to the extent it wanted. Then, the research people suggested that the company should put all the aquarium parts together—tank, lights, pump, and feeder—and sell the package as an appliance. The company knew a great deal about selling appliances, and it soon was a lot happier about its share of the aquarium business.

Of course, not all of Sears's merchandise marketing research turns out well. One inventor came to the company with the idea for a sphygmometrograph, a blood pressure machine, that could be used by people in their own homes. When he came up with the machine, Sears redesigned it to make it commercially available. It was so proud of the $200 product that the machine was featured in the 1971 annual report. Only later did the company find that not many people had confidence in the idea of such a machine and would refuse to plunk down such a large sum for one. However, Sears figures that someday the market will be right, and they may try again.

The lab also helps Sears in the war against "returns." The company is always trying to reduce the number of items that customers bring back, once they have seen them in their own homes. The biggest problems are size and color. As a result, the catalog contains a "fitting room" feature designed to encourage people to measure sizes accurately before ordering. Then it is the lab's job to make sure that sizes are consistent. Color is a more difficult problem. The lab may never beat the color difficulties arising from catalog sales because of the limits on color reproduction in print. But customers are also quite familiar with products that seem to be one color in the store and another at home. That can be the sure cause of a return when the customer is attempting a delicate color coordination. The lab has developed color and material standards for suppliers to eliminate color variation because of differing lighting conditions, which, the company hopes, should reduce returns.

Julius Rosenwald might not be happy to see what has become of the brick colossus he had built to house the company's headquarters because now more than 125,000 square feet of it are given over to the labs. Everything from candy to chain saws is tested there. Buyers are constantly sending in new goods, which Sears is considering ordering, to be taken apart and studied. When Jimmy Carter became president, one buyer came upon gold-plated peanuts—the real thing —to be used as charms. But first the lab had to determine what would happen to the peanut inside. What would happen if somebody broke the charm open and tried to eat the peanut?

Not all research is done in Chicago. Tires are put on machines at the lab to test them for wear, but they are also put on cars in Nevada and given road trials. Then, the tires are removed from the cars and sent back to Chicago for X-ray examination. Real farmers test new farm equipment. Product-use instructions are sent over to the Sears Tower to see if people there can figure them out. The unspoken hypothesis apparently is that if company officials can understand them, anybody can.

Although the lab's purpose is to back up merchandising and not to duplicate Consumers Union or government regulators, it does look at product safety. In one corner of the lab, a Franklin stove may be fired up to see what kind of damage its heat does to nearby walls. And the lab does studies for the company's Consumer Product Safety Committee, which includes representatives of several headquarters departments, such as public relations and the legal staff. For example, let us say some reports have come in from the field about plugs on Christmas tree lights. The lab studies them to see if there is any hazard and sends its recommendation to the committee, which can decide on a product recall or stop all sales of the plugs in the stores or simply mandate that no more be shipped.

The lab and Sears's overall research establishment have become vital to the company's selling operation. Little is left to guesswork now because executives have learned that "Uncle Max's" technique of simply getting goods at the lowest price does not correspond to the demands of today's consumers. For once, at least, old J. R. was wrong.

CHAPTER 10

GETTING THE GOODS

"The core of Sears is the Chicago merchandising brain trust," a regional chief of the company once opined. "If you had to name the one most critical operating group in Sears, it would be this department, which first creates the product, assigns it a specific place in the catalog and a specific counter in the stores, and also provides the stores with a 'syndicated service' of display materials, advertising designs and selections for special promotions." Given the importance of this operation, it is not surprising that the chief of merchandising is always one of the inner core of officers who run the company. And it is the merchandising department that is the chief "client" of Sears's research operations.

In fact, the merchandising department is actually a group of smaller departments, one for each of more than 50 different product lines. Each is under the control of a supervisor, who is given considerable freedom of action by the company and who wields Sears's enormous purchasing power in his or her area. Many companies have people known as "buyers," who search the wholesale market for the latest styles or new products or staple goods at the best prices. But merchandisers at Sears are quite a bit more than the traditional buyers.

Enlightened by company research, they know what customers want. So they do not wait for manufacturers to appear at the door with a product line. Instead, the merchandisers prepare the specifications and styles for the goods they think Sears should sell. Then, together with people from Sears's own lab, they call in suppliers to

find out if they can meet consumer demand. The merchandisers are
not only concerned with the finished product, but also want to know
how an item will be produced; and, if Sears people can come up with
a better and less expensive method of production, they expect the
manufacturer to fall into line. Besides bird-dogging the suppliers, the
merchandisers must keep their fingers on what is happening in catalog development, retail display, and advertising relating to their
product line. In short, they are responsible for handing over a product and its selling package. They are left pretty much on their own
during this process. In the end, top brass will rate them on the basis
of the profit they bring in from the sale of the items under their
control.

One of the most critical decisions the merchandisers must make
is how many of each item the company will sell. With a company
as huge as Sears, an overstock can be a financial disaster, and a
shortfall can leave tens of thousands of customers unhappy. The
catalog is one of the best tools the merchandiser has to check on the
projections produced by the research staff. Just as soon as a new
catalog is delivered, the merchandise people can begin monitoring
sales of lines under their supervision. The catalog itself has been
studied down to the last detail, so adjustments can be made for the
size of a catalog display, location of an item on the page, and even
color in determining how well an item is selling when it first comes
on the market. Of course, the merchandiser will have had to go out
on a limb to place an initial order, but from then on, catalog sales
may indicate what will be needed. The merchandiser can make a
forecast for both catalog and retail sales and then place the orders
that will begin the long-term production process. His initial order
will have been designed to get enough goods on the shelf to begin the
season, but the follow-ups will determine if stock can or should be
maintained at that level. This is a tricky business because it may be
almost impossible for the merchandiser to shut off or even slow down
supply once an order has been placed. Sears tries to make purchase
commitments well into the future. Such agreements are meant to
insure that suppliers will have enough productive capacity to meet
Sears's needs, but they do not oblige Sears to take a certain amount
of a given item. Still, Sears is locked in, and the merchandiser has
to worry about being overstocked. On the other hand, if demand

zooms, the merchandisers have the right to ask for increased supply. Sears looks for suppliers who are able to meet bigger orders on short notice.

In fact, Sears's relationship with its suppliers is of major concern to the merchandisers. They must struggle with a problem that has plagued the company since the beginning: consistently providing a quality product. Richard Sears had made inflated claims for products the company did not even have in stock and then would rush out to try to locate a source of supply when orders started pouring in. Just about the only thing that saved him and his fledgling company from irate customers who had received an item far different from what they had expected was Sears's guarantee. But, after Richard Sears had left the scene, the company began lining up reliable suppliers who would be able to meet a constant demand while maintaining a consistent quality.

As Sears grew, it became a major consumer of the production of many companies. Some found themselves being gradually integrated into the Sears system because such a large share of their output went to the company. By the time it published its 1940 annual report, Sears was open in revealing just how much it dominated some suppliers. "The company . . . has sometimes told manufacturers not only what to make and how to make it but where it should be made."

If it could dominate its suppliers to this extent, could not the company also force them to set prices at whatever level it wanted? In 1938, *Fortune* magazine wrote that "the antimonopolists contend that by bringing this massive buying power to bear against small manufacturers and threatening to whisk it away once they have been ensnared, Sears can force them to submit to prices on which a living profit is often impossible." By implication, this meant that Sears could force into bankruptcy a company that had gone into debt in order to supply it with goods, and at the same time end up with a large supply of low-cost items. The stories continue to circulate about this brutal technique; so where there is smoke, there may very well have been fire. Even now company officials reluctantly admit that things of that sort might have taken place years ago. If a supplier today suddenly finds itself cut off from a Sears contract on which it had been counting, it may resuscitate the old charge, but there is no current evidence that Sears still uses this technique.

Sears's reason for insisting on being able to tell its suppliers where to locate was its desire to cut down transportation costs and delays. Often, it wanted them near raw materials and away from the higher labor costs of the cities. There is little doubt that, as result of this policy, Sears was one of the promoters of the move of industry away from traditional centers in the Northeast to the South and West. Another reason for Sears to urge companies to decentralize their operations in order to parallel its own structure was its belief that small units of production are often more efficient than large ones.

Relations between Sears and its suppliers are generally considered to be good these days, but the company still imposes tough standards on them. With those companies with which it expects to do business over an extended period, Sears concludes "basic buying" contracts. These usually run for three years and contain a renewal clause. Under such an agreement, Sears promises to buy a fixed share of its total requirements for a given category of merchandise. Although sales are guaranteed under this accord, profits are not because the supplier must keep its prices competitive with comparable goods sold in the open market. In that way, Sears can be assured of goods that it can sell at or below the price charged by its competitors. But Sears and the supplier do set a profit objective based on the return-on-inventory that is typical of the industry as a whole. In order to reach this target, the supplier keeps Sears informed of its actual costs of filling orders, and if, as a result of rising costs, profits fall below the agreed level, the supplier may increase its prices to Sears. In that way, the supplier is not locked into a price agreement that could drive it into deep debt or bankruptcy. But in order to be able to boost its prices to Sears, the company must be able to demonstrate that its increased costs are caused by conditions common to many others in the industry and not merely because of its own bad management. Usually, this arrangement has worked out pretty well, with suppliers earning a good profit. If profits exceed those set in the agreement, the surplus is shared by the supplier and Sears itself.

The basic buying contract is an open admission that many companies have tied their fate to doing business with Sears. But this giant customer cannot afford to become dependent on suppliers that get "soft" because of their guaranteed market; so Sears insists on the right to audit the books of those companies that sign such agreements. That is just about the only way it can determine why costs rise. Despite Sears's desire to conclude as many basic buying agreements as possible, many suppliers balk at the requirement to open their books to outsiders. Their contracts simply specify levels of production and commitments to ship given amounts on specific dates.

When Sears is considering entering into an agreement with a supplier, it asks a lot of probing questions. Next to its aversion to returns, Sears dislikes refunding customers' money because it does not have the goods it has advertised. That is why the company feels it must know how well a supplier will perform.

A Sears order inevitably means that a supplier will step up its production and sales by a significant amount. The company wants to know if a potential source is able to realize savings on account of this increased volume because it wants the benefit of such savings. The manufacturer must be willing and able to establish a production cycle with a relatively constant output rather than with peaks and troughs, as may have occurred in the past. Even if a company can meet Sears's requirements at the time an order is placed, it may not measure up to later demands. Sears wants to be able to cut prices and increase its order, so it must be assured that a possible supplier can further reduce its costs if it later increases its sales to Sears.

Sears will probably not enter into a supplier-customer relationship when its purchases will not represent a significant part of the company's production. It reasons that if Sears is not vital to the supplier's future success, that company may fail to deliver what it promised.

Just how dependent suppliers are expected to become is demonstrated by Sears's requirement that they be willing to build up big inventories far ahead of an order from the giant retailer. That allows Sears to stage national or seasonal promotion campaigns, secure in the knowledge that if these stimulate demand, the company will be able to meet it. A supplier also has to be able to shift gears both to meet increased demand and to respond to changes in the general market for its products. Finally, Sears wants to work with companies that know how to keep a secret. Inevitably, it will reveal to its suppliers how it plans to market products and when it will stage promotional campaigns. It hardly wants that information passed on to its competitors.

Some suppliers have been with Sears for decades. Rather than drop a supplier that begins to slip, Sears may lend it money, take on some of its manufacturing or product engineering, develop quality control procedures, and offer it advice.

Despite all of the conditions it imposes, Sears insists that its suppliers sell to the general market as well. It believes that if its suppliers continue competing in the marketplace, they will remain efficient. The supplier will stay up-to-date on what is happening in the market and can thus provide useful information for Sears. The prices the supplier obtains in the competitive market will be an indicator both to it and to Sears of just how efficient a producer it is. Finally, sales to others than Sears help balance a company's production schedules, which may lower its costs. With more revenues from more sales, it will be able to devote more effort to research and development, which also works to Sears's benefit. Of course, many suppliers would not want to be totally dependent on Sears, in any case. By diversifying, they insure their survival. And chances are that they grew strong enough to be of interest to Sears because of their selling abilities, which they would want to continue to use.

From time to time, Sears has invested its own funds in the stock of its suppliers, notably the Whirlpool company, which produces washing machines. But it has always been reluctant to get into the production end of the business. Even today, the man in charge of what Sears calls its "factories" insists that "we are merchandisers not manufacturers."

But the 1936 Federal Trade Commission ruling, banning the sale of Goodyear tires under Sears's Allstate name, propelled the company into more extensive ownership of its own suppliers. Although Sears was able, at that time, to find other suppliers of Allstate tires, it was forced to take a closer look at investing in its own tire maker as a way of being assured of a steady flow of one of its most popular products.

The company's 1938 annual report stated the rationale for owning stock in its suppliers, a policy it has followed ever since: "In cases where the volume of a particular sort of merchandise is large and the sources so limited that dependence on them might be hazardous from the point of view of continuity of supply, the company has from time to time acquired partial stock ownership in such sources which strengthens its merchandising policies." Sidney Boyar, who has headed Sears's relations with its factories, insists that "we don't put money in for investment or capital gain. We're here to serve a merchandising need."

"The companies Sears keeps," as *Fortune* magazine once called the suppliers in which Sears is a part owner, provide almost 30 percent of the products the company sells. The equity that Sears holds in its "affiliated factories" may range from 1 or 2 percent to 60 percent. In most cases, Sears does not own a majority of the stock.

Of course, there is no better way to keep tabs on supplier efficiency than by ownership, so that is another incentive to invest. In addition, Sears has sometimes been forced into creating its own suppliers by manufacturers who refuse to sell to it. They fear that they would end up helping Sears compete with their own brand-name goods.

Yet another spur to getting into manufacturing has been the inability of potential suppliers to meet Sears's needs because they were so busy trying to keep up with booming demand. That happened when television sets were first coming on the market, and the only alternative for Sears was to open its own company.

Despite its reluctance to become its own supplier, Sears has now become one of the major manufacturers in the United States. In September 1975, the *Chicago Tribune* studied its affiliates to determine just how big they are. At that time, they employed about 114,000 people in 278 plants and 74 freight terminals. In turn, the affiliates had interests in 27 foreign firms. Not bad, for a company that is reluctant to get into the manufacturing business. Dividends alone from these affiliates, to say nothing of the savings they meant in purchasing, amounted to $6.2 million in black ink for the Sears balance sheet. Their total sales were $4.2 billion.

Sears, the reluctant investor, has also done pretty well in ringing up capital gains because it does not always hold on to all the stock it owns in a supplying company. For example, in 1956, it sold its paint and wallpaper factories to DeSoto Chemical Coatings and got in return 92 percent of the common stock and 55 percent of the preferred. By 1974 Sears had reduced its ownership to a 32 percent stock interest in DeSoto, which had become the largest wallpaper maker in the United States. Sears had, of course, made money on the sale of its stock holdings.

Some of Sears's holdings date back to the company's early days. In 1910, it bought a piece of the David Bradley Manufacturing Works and sold farm equipment under that name. Later David Bradley was merged into the Roper Corporation along with two other Sears investments, E-Z Way Stove Works and the Florence Stove Company. It now owns a major interest in the firm, based in Kankakee, Illinois, and buys more than two-thirds of its production for sale under Sears's own brand names. These products include ovens and ranges, rotary mowers, snow throwers, garden tractors, chain saws, drapery hardware, and luggage. That makes Roper one of the biggest national suppliers of these items, yet few consumers are even dimly aware that there is such a company.

Perhaps the best known of Sears's investments and one that dates back to the days of Julius Rosenwald is the Whirlpool Corporation. Today, Sears holds only a small part of Whirlpool's stock, but it takes the lion's share of the refrigerators, home laundry appliances, freezers, and vacuum cleaners that it turns out. Of course, Whirlpool also markets under its own brand name. The Sears-Whirlpool association is one that is likely to last as long as either company. Together they have invested in production facilities in other countries where Sears has retail operations. But, even as close an associate as Whirlpool is subject to continual Sears scrutiny to see if it is competitive. For example, Sears recently ordered dishwashers from a competing supplier because it could beat Whirlpool's price.

Sears also owns a big chunk of the Sanyo Electric Company, which Sears acquired when the Japanese outfit bought the U.S. supplier of television sets Sears had owned jointly with Whirlpool. Sanyo is Sears's prime supplier of console sets. In addition, Sears gets a lot of its television sets from abroad, enabling it to undersell the market. Other American retailers complain that the Japanese and other foreign suppliers are actually dumping—selling to Sears at prices below what they get at home.

What about Allstate tires? Sears owns about 10 percent of Armstrong Rubber, which also sells its tires under its own name. Sears takes about 39 percent of that company's output, yet is not completely dependent on Armstrong. When it decided to introduce radial tires under its own brand name, Sears went to the company that had first mass-marketed the radial, Michelin of France. While it already had some sales in the United States, Michelin's arrangement with Sears allowed it to boost sales tremendously.

Just how Sears gets drawn into investing in a supplier is illustrated by the case of Globe-Union. That company produces the Die-Hard battery, one of Sears's most popular products and one that is heavily promoted. Sales were going so well that a few years ago Sears went back to Globe-Union and asked it to step up production on a year-round basis. The supplier said that it could not handle any more Sears business and did not have the resources to open another plant. So Sears looked around to see if there were other companies that could come up with the same battery. It could not find one. Faced with a shortage that would have forced it to stop advertising the Die-Hard, Sears went back to Globe-Union. Usually Sears waits for the supplier to ask for an infusion of capital before it considers the possibility. But this time Sears asked Globe-Union if it would build the needed facilities with a Sears investment. The company agreed. Sears put in $8.5 million in return for preferred stock, and two new plants were built. Sears buys 46 percent of the batteries that Globe-Union sells.

In the post–World War II period, Sears built up supply relationships with 15 small companies, which provided almost 90 percent of the retailer's requirements in their lines. For example, one man came up with the idea for hard-sided luggage made of polypropylene but lacked the capital to produce enough to meet Sears's demand. So Sears became his partner, holding less than half of the voting stock, although it had contributed more than half of the working capital. Just like the luggage company, most of the other small producers were firms dominated by a single man. As these people neared retirement age, Sears was faced with the real possibility that it might lose some of its most important suppliers. So it sponsored the merger of all 15 of these firms into the Kellwood Company in 1961. Boyar recalls the entire process with some satisfaction: "On the day of the merger, we made several men millionaires." These entrepreneurs were amply rewarded by Sears for their commitment over the years. Kellwood, in which Sears is a major shareholder, is one of the largest manufacturers of wearing apparel, home furnishings, and camping equipment, and Sears buys almost 80 percent of what it produces.

Although Sears likes to get at least 20 percent of the stock and to place a man on the board of its affiliates, it may sell all or most of its holdings at any time. Rarely does it seek to get control of more than half of the stock of any affiliate.

And not all the companies Sears deals with are big. In fact, Sears may select a small company to produce a new line that it wants to carry, which can turn out to be a bonanza for the small firm. In 1963, Sears decided that it wanted to carry its own line of baby supplies instead of selling those made by other manufacturers. The reason was simple: It could snare only a small share of the market selling other people's ideas. It picked Hanks Craft of Reedsburg, Wisconsin, to produce its new line. One of the biggest innovations was the Sears-designed baby bottle, which indicates the contents and the day of preparation. That nurser has just about driven similar products under other brand names right off Sears's shelves.

Department 820 at Sears, "Affiliated Factory Relations," looks after the companies in which Sears is involved. There is no doubt that however small the Sears investment may be in any company, it expects to play a major role in how that company does business. Yet its greatest leverage with all suppliers, including those it owns in part, results from its enormous buying power.

It is 820's job to keep the affiliated factories healthy, and that means they have to be increasing sales. "We'll sell to anybody," says Sid Boyar, the former vice-president in charge of factories, "including J. C. Penney." As a result, the drive for profits and efficiency may mean that a Sears-owned company may use some of the skills it has learned from Sears to sell to a Sears competitor. That is something to ponder when you are shopping at Penney. Sears may have a grip on your consumer dollar even then.

Factory Relations keeps an eye on companies that might need a Sears investment and evaluates those that ask for help. When Sears is thinking about an investment, the final decision is made by a Factory Committee and the Sears chairman, based on 820's investigation. Once the decision is made, Department 820 handles the negotiations.

Of course Department 820 supervises the companies Sears keeps, following most of the same procedures as are used for any company that serves as a supplier. Perhaps the most important addition to the checklist is Sears's concern that "management has the right personnel policies, with regard both to paying going wages in the vicinity and to having good programs for employee benefits," according to a corporate description of 820's functions.

But part ownership and board membership get Sears more directly into the management of their affiliates than is the case with their other suppliers. Company officials maintain close contact not only with the top executive who sits on the board but also with staff members whose judgment they want. In particular, Sears advises companies where to locate plants on the basis of its own research and lets management know what is happening in the industry as a whole, on the basis of its obviously unparalleled network of contacts. Within 820 is a factory personnel division that is trained to help out in handling labor problems, union negotiations, and employee benefit plans. Just as the company has been extremely careful, if not to say conservative, about its own labor relations, it does not want its affiliates running into labor problems or strikes that will hinder the steady flow of goods to the stores. Obviously, given the kind of close relationship between Sears and its 31 affiliated factories and 12,000 other suppliers, the company has to tread a fine line to avoid running afoul of antitrust laws.

Almost inevitably, Sears ends up being a major source of supply of executives to its "factories." The people in Department 820 often get to know more about how a partially owned company is managed or ought to be managed than do many of its own executives. So it is not surprising that some of them are picked to become top officers of the affiliates, although Sears certainly does not force them on their factories. Boyar notes that some of his former aides have moved on to positions that have made them quite wealthy. For example, one former Sears retail store manager later found himself at the head of Whirlpool.

Department 820 works with the affiliated factories on a corporate basis; it does not handle Sears's purchases from them. That is up to the National Merchandise Managers. But having 820 certainly makes the merchandisers' jobs a lot easier. They have to know if a supplier will be able to come through on a steady basis, and they need constant reassurance that they are placing orders at the best possible prices. The 820 people can get information from affiliated factories that most retailers cannot obtain from their sources. And the factories people can analyze the whole company to let merchandisers know if it has the stability and staying power to be around later when it is needed either to produce more or to supply spare parts for its products. Merchandisers also want to know a lot about the insurance, tax, and accounting situation of suppliers, and obviously the factories people are in an excellent position to provide it.

Of course, Sears's merchandisers do much more than deal with suppliers, whether partially owned or not. To see just how vital they are, take a closer look at one product line—what Sears calls the Women's Store. Actually, it involves some 14 departments selling 144 lines, ranging from wearing apparel to vitamins, lingerie to luggage. The people who buy these goods represent an enormous share of the total retail market, four times as many as those who buy tires. At Sears, it is the fastest growing retail sector and brings in a good profit.

Women's Store merchandisers are located not in Chicago, where most of their colleagues work, but in New York, closer to fashion trends. They also have branches in Los Angeles, Dallas, Atlanta, and Miami and in 18 cities abroad, including London, Paris, Frankfurt, New Delhi, Mexico City, Tokyo, and Hong Kong. Still, New York is the Mecca for fashion and 70 percent of the women's wear that Sears buys in the United States comes from that area. Normally, department store buyers have to worry about a lot more than simply picking out what the company will sell. They must handle reorders, advertising, and even sales supervision. Sears has personnel for each of these tasks, so the New York merchandisers are expected to be out in the market every day. By continually "shopping," Sears people know the trends in style, color, and textiles. Some 43 Sears stores are also feeding them information constantly about sales patterns in the lines they handle. Finally, there are Sears comparison shoppers in 27 big United States markets, like New York, Chicago, and Los Angeles, to check on prices and displays of the company and its major competitors.

Buying women's apparel for Sears is a typical of the company's other purchasing operations in one respect: About one-quarter of what the merchandiser selects comes from the open market. In most other lines, little is bought that does not come from long-term suppliers. Under so-called "specification buying," Sears gets exactly what it wants. But, even with all its research, it may not be able to forecast accurately what will happen in the volatile world of women's fashions. So it retains its flexibility by buying new styles in the open market.

In most cases, though, the suppliers, or "vendors" as Sears tags them, come to call on the merchandisers, who make the decisions on the styles that Sears will handle. But that is just the beginning of the process. There is a design laboratory in New York where sample garments are sent. If they have been made to Sears's specifications, they are checked. Selling tens of thousands of an individual item, Sears has to be sure that size standards have been met so a size 8 gown in Boston is the same as one in Los Angeles. The lab also looks at the garment to see how it has been produced. Perhaps it will be possible to simplify production methods and thus lower cost without actually changing the item. In order to protect the company's reputation for the durability of its goods, the lab may suggest that the garment actually be strengthened. The lab and the merchandiser will also decide whether to use fabrics provided by the manufacturers or to supply Sears's own yard goods. Sears encourages its merchandisers to order garments in a limited variety of colors. That helps keep down costs and overstocks of wild patterns that turn out to be flops.

By the time it has finished studying a garment, Sears may know more about how to produce it and how much it costs than the original manufacturer. The merchandisers and lab people can advise the supplier on cutting manufacturing costs, and if significant savings can be realized, Sears gets a share of them. Of course, some manufacturers are unhappy with this arrangement, which they feel simply builds Sears's profits. They say that buyers tend to exaggerate production savings, while "billing" Sears stores at high prices that do not reflect the supposed savings. (Each store is assigned a cost for each item it sells so that its profits can be determined.) These manufacturers imply that Sears is making a bigger profit by paying as little as possible, claiming that production savings must be passed on, but then actually withholding those savings from customers. One investment advisory report says, "This, however, is difficult to substantiate and would be in conflict with management's definition of appropriate buying policies."

As its early experiences with the Lady Duff-Gordon line showed, Sears had a lot to learn about selling fashions. Its position as the largest seller of appliances in the United States provided some useful lessons, particularly in maintaining quality and durability standards. But the company has been involved in a continuing effort to combine fashion and reasonable prices, which some in the garment business think are mutually exclusive.

Charles Harper, a merchandising man, explained to a group of securities anaylists several years ago the kind of problems that Sears faces. The buyers had foreseen a strong demand for prewashed denims and had a good supply on hand. But so many people wanted them that Sears and other retailers could not keep up with nationwide demand. The hitch was that prewashed denim fabric was in short supply. Some retailers took stocks of indigo jeans and washed or bleached them in order to meet consumer demand. But Sears found that washing caused shrinkage, throwing the sizes off, and bleaching weakened the seams. With a reputation for reliability on the line and the threat of many returns under its guarantee, Sears declined to follow that course and undoubtedly lost its share of the market to others that season.

A great many people still think of Sears as the store where you go to buy a washing machine or a sump pump but not a fashionable dress. In order to get women to think of Sears as a department store, the efforts of merchandisers had to be backed up by other departments. Just where apparel was placed in the stores and how it was displayed was stressed, and strict instructions went out from Chicago to the field. It was felt that, with proper displays, people who came into the store for something else might end up buying a dress. That is probably why dress racks are often found near the display of Toughskins jeans for children. While Mom is in the store to buy a pair for junior, she may be tempted to pick up something for herself. Advertising has also been redesigned and increased. Traditionally, the company's ad campaigns are aimed at selling a selection of products during a specific period. But to become a more popular fashion store, Sears had first to run an image-building campaign.

Sears will never be a national fashion leader because it cannot afford to take the risks imposed by such a role. A department store in New York may be able to absorb an error on 50 dresses, but Sears might find itself with 50,000 bad guesses on its hands if it got too far ahead of the pack. But merchandisers are given fairly specific goals related to how the company plans to expand its share of the market. For example, Sears wants to be able to offer some fashion wear at lower prices to attract young people whose incomes are still low. At the same time, it recognizes that department stores make their greatest volume of sales in apparel items priced somewhat higher than what is normal at Sears, and it will try to meet these outlets on their own terms. That means merchandisers must slowly widen the variety of fashion goods they order. The process must be gradual because the company does not want to frighten off its traditional customers by suddenly taking on the image of a high-priced fashion house.

One way for Sears to increase its fashion appeal has been to use and advertise its own brand names. Some of its women's apparel brand names have gone from obscurity to general national recognition in just a few years. For example, Sears always makes a major effort to sell to women wearing large sizes, a market often avoided by other retailers. It came up with a specially designed "Ah-h Bra" for large women, which ended up giving the company a strong image as one of the developers of the seamless bra. As a result, Sears now sells one-sixth of all bras sold in the United States. Fearlessly, Sears also attacked the problem of most girdles, which flatten what the company decorously calls "the derrière," while holding in the tummy, the job for which they are intended. Sears found "Pretty Natural Shapers" would do what was desired, and not do what was not. This may not seem like high fashion, but this kind of product development has helped Sears do battle with traditional national brands and become competitive in lines in which it was previously not much of a factor.

What "Women's Store" merchandisers do to get the goods in their lines is repeated in every merchandising department. It is sophisticated and responsible work, and they are given considerable decision-making authority. The company has come a long way from the days when Julius Rosenwald called the company "a federation of merchants," where merchandisers were free to learn by trial and error with little central control. Now, the merchandiser benefits from decades of experience, and the company coordinates their efforts. Still, they are the front line, when it comes to buying.

CHAPTER 11

MERCHANT TO THE MILLIONS

At least once every year, three out of every four American adults enter a Sears store. Few other American institutions can claim such a magnetic appeal. Getting these people into the store is the first step in turning them into customers.

It may be the company's venerable reputation that brings the people in, but more likely they come because of the company's advertising.

Just about the only thing that is obvious to anybody, whether a customer or not, is that Sears is the largest advertiser in the United States. Everybody is regularly exposed to Sears's commercials on television, magazine ads, and a veritable blizzard of newspaper supplements. In 1975, not including spending for catalog sales and Allstate, retail advertising cost Sears $378 million. Some 40 advertising agencies were kept busy churning out the copy to sell Sears's products.

It was not always that way. Sears learned about advertising by trial and error and by what its own 1940 annual report actually called "torment." The answer, at least for General Wood, was the newspaper. By 1940, the company was spending more than $11 million on newspaper space, making it the largest purchaser of such advertising.

Newspapers by their very nature are local. Anxious to promote its image as a local store, rather than as a national chain, Sears found newspapers the obvious medium. Using them also let Sears vary prices around the country to reflect shipping and operating costs, which could differ widely. Actually, almost all of the ads themselves were prepared in Chicago, but they were inserted in newspapers by local stores, and prices were adjusted to meet local conditions. Because of their professional preparation, Sears's ads were generally of a higher quality than those placed by competing retailers.

The only other form of advertising aside from a small amount of radio used in the Wood era was display windows and other in-store exhibits of goods. Sears products were expected to sell themselves, while salespeople simply handled the paperwork. This notion would not work very well as more and more people did just as the General had forecast and had to be induced to drive to the store. That's why newspaper advertising was the obvious relief for the company's "torment."

Yet the national media offered a rare and more economical way of reaching more customers. After World War II, Sears was under less severe attack from local retailers and could afford not to be so concerned about its image as a local store. An increasingly sophisticated and mobile American population knew better anyway. Not until General Wood retired, however, would Sears start testing the national waters.

The first step was a limited number of magazine ads. Still concerned about making a final break with advertising designed to maintain the local image, the first big push came in boosting Allstate Insurance. Other insurance companies were already using national media, and there was no need to try to convince people that Allstate was just a local outfit. In fact, customers were more reassured when they knew they were buying insurance from a reputable national company.

In 1962, Sears began a corporate identity campaign, but it was not until five years later that management felt confident enough to let Sears's advertising overshadow Allstate's. Not that Sears did not spend enormous sums on advertising, but it continued until then to concentrate on local newspapers and radio. Obviously, this conservative policy was actually denying Sears the full benefit of its national merchandising system. Unless the company spoke out nationally about products that it distributed nationally, it would miss out on the very economies of scale that were supposedly its strong point.

Now, millions of dollars are spent on tires ($8.7 million in 1975), batteries, men's and children's clothes. The success of these campaigns is demonstrated at the cash register. The Sears Die-Hard battery, for example, is undoubtedly the most well-known auto battery in the country.

One of the obstacles to more efficient national advertising was the company's policy of setting prices on a local or regional basis, with the retail store manager having considerable freedom in making adjustments to meet local conditions. That prevented the company from setting and advertising a national price. The stagflation of the 1970s forced a change in that policy, and by 1974 Sears had begun price promotions in the national media. The 1976 organizational changes made it possible to expand price-oriented ads. Just a year earlier, Sears had launched its major corporate identity campaign: "Where America Shops." Instead of simply pushing specific goods, this campaign was meant to leave the impression that Sears had something for everybody, no matter his or her economic standing. It was yet another indication that, without abandoning its local identity, Sears was finally unafraid to be known to its customers as a major national retail chain.

With such a huge commitment to advertising, Sears puts enormous effort into each campaign. One of the more successful has been the Great American Homes Paint Campaign. It shows historic American buildings being given a fresh coat of paint—Sears's, of course. Every aspect of the campaign is designed to convey two messages. On one level, Sears is showing itself as a good citizen by painting these buildings. At the same time, it reminds potential customers that if Sears paint is good enough for John Paul Jones's house, it is good enough for theirs.

"The development of the commercials for the campaign is a complex process," says national retail ad manager Robert Kissel. "On the average it takes about eighteen months to select a home, paint it, write and produce the commercial. Usually four new commercials are produced in a year, two on exteriors and two on interiors. They are then integrated into the television schedule the year after they are produced and run for about two years." Selecting homes is not as easy as it might seem. The ad agency must find them in all parts of the country to demonstrate that the paint is mixed to suit the climate. Then, a story line must be created that weaves the story of the historic home owner with praise for the paint. That means that copywriters have to be careful not to cross the line into sacrilege, all the while they are selling their relatively unglamorous product. Perhaps the biggest coup of the series was being offered the chance to paint Boston's Old North Church. "As a happy bonus," says Kissel, "the Vicar of the Old North Church was able to play a major role in one of the commercials." And now the master stroke. On April 18, 1975, President Ford spoke from the pulpit of the Sears-painted Church. That same day, the first Old North Church commercial was aired on national television.

After initial hesitation, Sears had scored again. Its advertising program, both local and national, is generally rated by the industry as one of the most effective in the country. Sales figures bear out that appraisal.

The company has become unafraid of using its advertising clout. It insists that its television commercials "should not appear in programs containing excessive violence or anti-social behavior." Because it purchases such large blocks of commercial time, the company found that occasionally its commercials were being scheduled on programs to which it objected. In 1976, it wrote to the networks and its advertising agencies and insisted that its guidelines be followed. "We have been assured of their full cooperation, and have been gratified by the public response," the company reported. It concentrates its ads on news, sports, and family programs.

But a conflict between advertising and retailing led to one major incident that Sears, Roebuck and Company wished had never happened. "Bait and switch" is an old if not very honorable retailing game. A store will offer an appealing bargain in its advertising as a way of attracting customers to the store. Once there, the customer will find that the heavily promoted item is mysteriously out of stock, or a salesperson will begin playing it down and suggest that the customer would really prefer a higher-priced item. If you have been thinking about buying a washing machine and see an ad for one at a good price, you are now in the frame of mind to make the purchase. You even see the new appliance in your home in your mind's eye. So it may not be too difficult for the salesperson to convince you to spend more than you had originally planned. After all, the added features are probably worth the extra money, although they may be hard to afford.

"Bait and switch" is hardly a technique that ought to be associated with Sears. A national company can lose a reputation carefully built over decades if there are a number of complaints about its advertising and sales methods. Besides, ever since Julius Rosenwald came to the company, it has put itself on a pedestal of corporate morality that could easily crumble if people begin to think of Sears in the same terms as any fly-by-night retailer.

In 1959, the Federal Trade Commission warned American retailers that it was watching for "bait and switch" violations. In response, the company issued a directive stating: "Sears does not tolerate under any circumstances bait advertising or any other unfair or deceptive selling practice. Sears has developed a substantial reputation with the American public for fair dealings, and cannot afford to have that good will jeopardized."

Then, on September 17, 1974, the FTC issued a formal complaint against Sears. Although some people at the company grumbled that the charges had been brought because a disgruntled former employee had gone to the FTC, the complaint was a detailed indictment of classic "bait and switch" tactics.

For example, here is a Sears ad that was cited:

Portable Zig Zag Sewing Machine

From Sears . . .

    $58

- Sews on buttons, sews buttonholes;
  Does zig-zag or straight stitching

- Monograms, appliques, other fancy work
  For household linens, gifts

- Sews forward and reverse for her
  convenience

The FTC discovered that when prospective customers came to Sears stores to buy this machine or other major home appliances, they would find salesmen who disparaged the advertised item and who would sell them higher-priced models. In the case of the sewing machine, salesmen would say that they were noisy and would not sew straight stitch, zig-zag stitch, or in reverse, and they could not sew buttonholes. The salesman would also mention that the advertised models did not have as long a guarantee period as more expensive machines. They might remark that the customer would probably find it difficult to sew over seams or fabrics of different thicknesses. Finally, they would shrug and tell the customer that, in any case, the advertised machines were not in stock, and there would be long delays in delivery. In the face of all that discouragement, you would have to be a pretty determined customer to insist on the appliance advertised.

The FTC carried its charges a step further. It claimed that Sears had advertised low-priced products with the specific plan of having its salespeople resort to "bait and switch." It also asserted that Sears compensated its salespeople better for selling higher-priced appliances and "deters said salesmen from selling the advertised sewing machines . . . and other major home appliances."

Sears was stung by the charges, but there was no doubt that the FTC had documented cases. Finally, in 1977, a consent decree was negotiated with the FTC, which bound Sears to take remedial action. It promised to sell anything it advertised and not to disparage any advertised item in any way. Salespeople could not demonstrate an appliance in any way that might make it appear defective. In addition, Sears was to have adequate supplies on hand and was to be able to deliver merchandise ordered within a reasonable period. For three years after the FTC decree, Sears would have to keep detailed records on stocks of every advertised home appliance. And, both in its ads and in the store, Sears would have to state that "each of these advertised items is readily available for sale as advertised."

Throughout the case, Sears had maintained that "the violations of Sears policy and FTC standards which came to light in the recent FTC hearings were isolated incidents." To some extent, the company was vindicated in its claim that its policies were not responsible for the use of "bait and switch" tactics. In its original complaint, the FTC said that it would prohibit Sears from setting sales quotas that discriminate against low-margin, advertised items, and from using employee discipline or retention programs that discriminate against sales of advertised merchandise. In the consent decree, these prohibitions were absent.

Even if the company itself was not responsible for "bait and switch" tactics, their occurrence was a sure sign of something wrong at Sears. Top corporate officials claimed that local stores might be cutting their inventories too close. One salesman grumbled that "management wants to keep inventories down but sales up, so you always have a potential out-of-stock situation." He claimed that such policies "depressed" salesmen. "The thing Sears fails to realize is that a salesman gets so mad he doesn't care if he sells or not," he said.

Perhaps it was the traditional Sears effort to keep inventories as low as possible that caused "bait and switch." But appliance salesmen get a 6 percent commission and obviously find more in the pay envelope if they sell more expensive items. So, even in the absence of a corporate "bait and switch" policy, Sears has to be careful that its sales personnel do not ignore the company's advertising and press too hard for the big sale. At the very least, the unhappy incident was a sign that the Chicago headquarters was not keeping close enough watch on what was happening in the field. It was a mistake that Sears cannot afford to repeat too many times.

One major strength of the company's advertising image is the use of Sears's own brand names for almost everything on its shelves. One company official says that only Marks and Spencer in England is like Sears in attempting to get as much as possible of what it sells under its own label. While that policy has commercial advantages, it also imposes a heavy responsibility on Sears to stand behind what it sells.

In the beginning, Richard Sears had sold his goods without mention of brand names; they were all Sears items. Gradually, as he wrote the catalog, Sears would attach specific names to each product. For example, the famous cream separator was dubbed the "Economy." By the early twentieth century, some companies were advertising their wares across the country under their own brand names, and it had become evident to Richard Sears that such identification helped to sell goods.

Once Richard Sears got going, Sears produced a blizzard of brand names for just about everything it produced. Employees obviously delighted in dreaming up their own names and applying them to the company's merchandise. Some ideas came from outside the company.

Hans Simonson, a draftsman in Bismark, North Dakota, wanted badly to go to art school. In fact, he worked at sketching plans in

Richard Sears, when he began selling watches in 1886.

Alvah C. Roebuck, the watchmaker who joined Sears in 1887.

Arthur M. Wood, the lawyer who heads the largest retailing organization.

Gen. Robert Wood (l.) and Julius Rosenwald, the men who built Sears, Roebuck and Co., pictured in a moment of elation in 1929.

The original Sears Tower on Chicago's West Side.

Sears Tower, company headquarters,
the world's tallest building.

How it all began: selling watches by catalog.
1902 catalog.

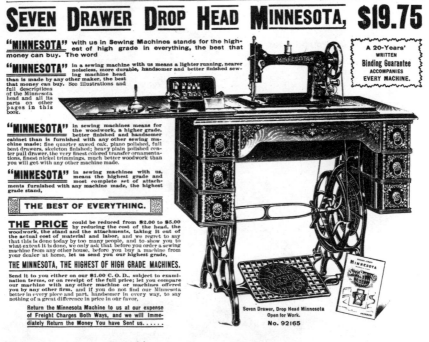

Richard Sears' moneymaking prose.
1902 catalog.

A catalog sales desk. There's one in every Sears store.

Mailing room of a catalog distribution plant.

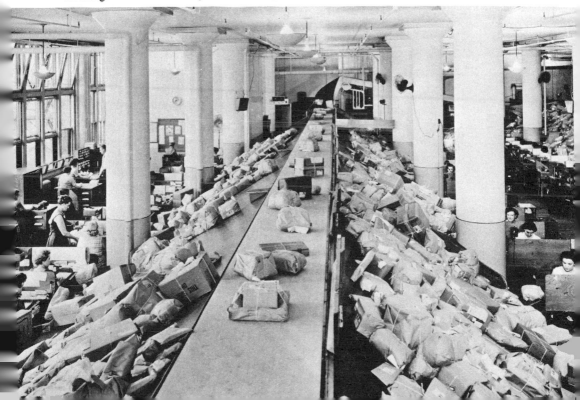

Inside the first Sears retail store in Chicago.

Sears branches out. An early retail store in La Porte, Indiana in 1929.

A Sears store with plenty of parking. Westwood store in
Los Angeles about 1936.

Inside a Sears shopping mall, built by Homart.

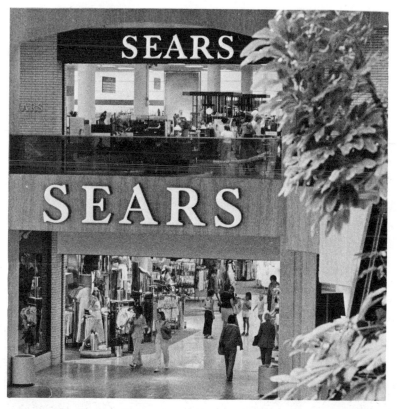

The Sears Army. A catalog plant crew is addressed by Dean Swift, the company president.

order to save up the money he would need. Then, one day in 1926, a Sears ad caught his eye. The company was replacing its old "Justice" line of tires and was looking for a new name. Whether Sears actually expected to find a suitable one among those submitted by the public is doubtful, but the contest made for a good publicity campaign. Hans was one of 937,886 people who submitted some 2,-253,746 names for the tire. The Sears folks liked his suggestion and gave him the first prize of $5,000, enough to get him off to art school. The name he suggested was "Allstate," still used 50 years later for tires and other automotive equipment, to say nothing of Sears's insurance companies.

Sometimes, the Patent Office would refuse to register Sears's names, but, even so, there eventually were hundreds or even thousands of them. With so many brand names, the advantages that were supposed to be gained through advertising were severely undercut. As a result, the company began a policy of pruning the names, constantly reducing them and making sure they were protected by law.

Besides using brand names for product lines, Sears began to use an idea developed by Boston's E. A. Filene: price lines. He had calculated that it was wise to sell products at just a few price levels rather than sell different versions of the same type of item at a wide range of prices. Sears settled on three, which it labeled "Good", "Better," and "Best". Of these names only "Sears Best" has survived, but the basic idea is still used.

Thanks to its own research, Sears has also come up with its own trademarked processes for processed fabrics. Perma-Prest is a registered mark for no-iron merchandise, Perma-Smooth for wrinkle-resistant goods requiring only light ironing, and Sani-Guard for fabrics chemically treated to control odors and enhance cleanliness. Sears even has a Perma-Prest room (strategically located on the same floor as its public relations department in the Sears Tower), where the company says it examines laundered merchandise to see if it comes up to the firm's standards.

Of course, getting the potential customer into the store through advertising is only half the job; Sears wants to sell something to all of them.

The front line for selling is what Sears calls "the field"—the retail stores. Just as the buyers are given sufficient scope to try to come up with the combination of quality and cost that will bring in the profits, so, too, are the retail store managers the shock troops of sales.

The company plans every store carefully, decides on the product lines to be handled and even their placement. The way the store looks, down to the last detail, is decided at headquarters. But each retail store must meet local conditions, so the store manager, who holds one of the most coveted positions in the organization, is given ultimate responsibility to change the plans made by higher-ups. As a result, the merchandisers must not only select the goods and determine just how much should be placed on the shelves, but they must also convince the store managers of the wisdom of their decisions.

Only the store managers can be fully aware of the competition. Ask one who his competition is, and he will ask you for which product line. He may have to face off with a local tire merchant, a discount house, another chain, or even a Sears store in a neighboring market. In the past, managers could make price adjustments to meet the prevailing conditions in his local marketplace, but national pricing is putting an end to that kind of discretion. For the local store manager, the bottom line is the bottom line. One manager tells of taking over his first store, only to find that it was badly overstocked. On his own, he marked down the overstocked items in order to get rid of them in one month. "I destroyed the store's profitability," he remarked later, and he would have destroyed his own future with Sears if he had not taken the advice of higher-ups who payed a quick visit. They told him that if he tried to get rid of overstock quickly by cutting prices too deeply his store would stay in the red. They counseled patience in trying to reduce inventories. He learned his lesson and went on to bigger and better things at Sears. But he never lost his right to adjust prices as he saw fit because what Sears wanted from his store was profit, not merely a sense of control. If he could use unorthodox methods and make them work, the company would be satisfied.

Yet this same man, now in charge of a large Sears store, cannot convince management to put in a lawn shrubbery department. "Sometimes getting this company to accept a suggestion like that is like turning the *Queen Mary* around in the middle of a river." But he is undaunted. He thinks he will get his shrubs if he keeps at it. And he probably will because he would not have gotten to be a store manager if he were not a good salesman.

Every month each store manager gets his report card showing how his departments stand in comparison to those in other Sears stores. He studies these reports with an intensity bordering on passion, if for no other reason than that a company formula will increase his salary if he increases the company's profits. Higher echelons pass down to the manager sales and profit goals. A graduated scale of salary increases is tied to the amounts by which he or she tops the store's target. If you do not exceed it, you do not get a raise.

The manager may exercise considerable flexibility in laying out his store, despite the directives coming from Chicago. For example, one manager finds that Sears cannot beat the local competition in the fence business; so there is no point in giving up a lot of space to that line. Or C.B. radios are coming into the market quickly; so he gives it as much as he can by cutting back on furniture and luggage, two lines that sell nowhere as well as C.B.s. He can even buy merchandise directly from a source that does not usually do business with Sears. One manager found a very successful bathing suit in Florida, and it did well in his Maine store. But Sears would not stock it elsewhere, and he had to stop handling it when the manufacturer refused to adhere to Sears's standards requiring it to guarantee its merchandise.

In his quest for profit, no store manager can depart from Sears rules. He must have a catalog sales counter in his store. He must offer Sears products at advertised prices. Once, a mistake in a Sears ad showed a C.B. radio at a far lower price than was intended. Still, the manager had to sell the radio at the advertised price. Managers will even sell goods at the lower prices advertised in Sears stores in other parts of the country, unless the price differential with their own market is way out of line. And, of course, the guarantee must be observed. Once a manager in Cortland, New York, took an unusual return, a muumuu that had been purchased in a Sears store in Hawaii. Not able to sell it in the chilly clime of northern New York, he finally gave it away for a church bazaar.

Ask any Sears store manager if he likes his job, and it is almost a certainty that he or she (there are now a few women in charge) will beam. Sears lets them play store—with real money. They have all the challenge and satisfaction of running a retail store without having to put up the capital. To a great extent, the fortune of Sears, Roebuck and Company depends on the approximately 4,000 people who man the front line running retail stores. Of course, with all their freedom, Sears is always in control. Says one manager, "We don't do it by the seat of our pants."

Tucked away, out of sight, in every Sears store is an office that helps the store manager sell his goods. In fact, this office, which handles all the purchases made on credit, is not even under his direct control. But he must be glad that it is there.

"Credit is not seen as a profit center at Sears," says Fred Weimer, one of Sears's top money managers. "We just meet the competition." In simplest terms, Sears would not offer credit unless it had to do so in order to attract customers. By now, the company ought to be pretty happy with credit. It usually returns a good, if not spectacular, profit. Of all Sears sales, some 53 percent are made on credit. In other words, without credit, Sears might only be half as large as it is now. With it, Sears is probably the third largest single source of retail credit in the United States, after the financing operations of General Motors and Ford. Credit arrangements, like Master Charge, actually are made on behalf of each individual participating bank, but even if you lumped all Master Charge credit together, Sears's credit would be just as large.

It was not always that way. At first Richard Sears was opposed to credit. In the 1899 catalog, he wrote: "We sell for cash, having no bad debts . . . no expense for collections, we can sell at a far lower margin of profit than any other dealer and when you buy from us you are not helping to pay all such useless expense." Yet Sears had used most effectively the slogan "Send No Money" as a way of attracting customers. The Send-No-Money promotion allowed skeptical farmers to examine the product before paying. Even this slogan was dropped in 1902, however, mostly because the company found that a great many items were being returned. Obviously, some customers placed orders frivolously, without intending to make the purchase. After that, the company did so well that it continued to spurn credit and to claim that it was at a competitive advantage because it did not offer it.

Sears confused the growing demand for credit with what it

thought was a desire on the part of its customers to take a look at a major purchase before paying for it. It offered to send durable goods on a 30-day trial if the purchaser would put the price of the item in a bank account and send the company a deposit certificate. But that is not what the people wanted, and they kept up their requests for credit. Other retailers began offering it more frequently, and, in 1910, the company realized that competition required extending credit. One big factor in the company's decision was the discovery that some people were buying cream separators from Sears for cash and then reselling them under expensive credit arrangements. In the catalog, Sears responded, "We want your cream separator order and will meet or beat any and all competition."

Sears got busy offering credit terms on many durable items. Meanwhile, Ward was once again slow in responding and did nothing while Sears experimented. Sears promised sales with "No Money Down" and, in a major breakthrough, began inserting credit forms in the catalog. Previously, the absence of a form had led people to believe that credit sales would have to be secured by a lien on some form of property. By making clear, as early as 1917, that it was extending credit, pure and simple, just on the basis of four pieces of information—length of time at present location, occupation, and two references—Sears attracted many middle-income and professional people, a new clientele.

In later years, the form might grow longer, but the approach remained the same. In 1975, for example, one man received an "invitation" to open a credit account. Tired of repeatedly filling out background forms, he provided the same information as had been required 60 years earlier and crossed out the rest of the form. Across it, he wrote, "Special offer . . . Sears can get me as a credit card customer if it acts now." Sears gave the man an account. (In a 1977 test with J. C. Penney's credit questionnaire, he got the same result, showing both the acceptance of Sears's practices and why Sears worries about Penney's catch-up prospects.)

The flu epidemic of 1918, the economic slump of 1921–1922, and casual methods of checking upon the ability of customers to pay led to loan defaults in 6.4 percent of the cases where the company gave credit. So, it tightened up its questionnaire and took some products off the "No-Down-Payment" rule. Yet it kept right on promoting what it now called its "Easy Payment Plan." By the 1920s, Ward was openly offering credit, and Spiegel limited itself entirely to installment mail-order selling. The rising tide of credit meant that 85 percent of all furniture, 80 percent of phonographs, and the great majority of many other durables sold by Sears were being sold on credit. By 1927, 15 percent of all Sears goods were sold on installments.

When the depression hit, Sears had to decide quickly if it should restrict credit, especially in the face of possible massive defaults. But, unlike the situation in 1921, Sears had been running its credit operations conservatively and found no need to tighten its credit terms. In fact, it even made buying easier. It contacted good cash customers and offered them credit. For those who had been paying their loan bills promptly, Sears suggested that they add on still more purchases. In 1934, the Sears Finance Corporation was set up to lend money for home modernization, the loans being backed by the Federal Housing Administration. But people kept demanding more credit, especially on the smaller, soft goods, which had always been considered cash merchandise. As the company included more lines under credit arrangements, the share of its total business handled this way rose rapidly.

Where does Sears get the money to "lend" to its customers? It must still pay its suppliers, even if it is willing to wait for customers to settle on an easy payment plan. At first, the company simply financed credit operations out of working funds. Although this may not have adversely affected profits, Sears was denied the use of its own money for further expansion. During the 1930s, the situation became critical. Sears was faced with the choice of increasing its capital, keeping the lid on installment sales, or financing credit sales with outside help. Adding capital seemed an expensive way to proceed, and nobody seriously wanted to limit credit sales, which would, in fact, have limited the growth of the company.

Sears officials had noticed that banks were increasingly backing finance company operations. The banks themselves did not want to make consumer loans, but they would lend money to finance companies for that purpose. When Sears went to the banks, it was told that they would purchase credit contracts from the company at a discount if Sears promised to accept what was called 100 percent contingent liability; that is, if anybody failed to pay off the note, Sears would make good on it to the bank. This was hardly a bargain, since there were very few defaults by that time; moreover, Sears already could borrow at the best rates, probably the same or better than the discount it would have to pay, from banks without all the rigamarole of the sale of credit agreements. So Sears turned the offer down.

Instead it developed its own proposal to take back to the banks. It would sell credit contracts to them and would then, in effect, serve as their collection agency. The company would immediately be paid 90 percent of the value of the contracts, with the remainder kept by the bank as a reserve. The money held by the bank would always equal a 10 percent share of the total contract value. At first, the idea was not popular with the banking community. But Sears was too good a customer to ignore, and, in 1935, New York's National City Bank agreed to the Sears plan. That broke the jam, and soon more than 200 banks in all parts of the country had similar arrangements with Sears. Other retailers picked up on the Sears plan, and it was widely used.

By 1956, installment sales accounted for more than 41 percent of all sales, with outstanding accounts valued at $920 million at any one time. Clearly, Sears was big business for banks. But it had gradually occurred to company officials that Sears ought to get into the financing business itself. It was now big enough to borrow money expressly for use in financing credit purchases, and it had the model of other companies, notably the General Motors Acceptance Corporation. That year, the Sears Roebuck Acceptance Corporation (S.R.A.C.), a wholly owned subsidiary, was created.

The purpose of this new company was to borrow, directly from the public through the sale of notes, the funds needed to finance installment sales. Sears issues notes to S.R.A.C. to cover credit purchases. By January 31, 1977, S.R.A.C. held $4.1 billion in such notes. It, in turn, borrows by selling its own debt obligations, called commercial paper, to investors, banks, and custodians of trusts. S.R.A.C. is a giant in the financing field, although it still ranks behind General Motors and Ford. It has made Sears less dependent on banks. Although Sears continues to borrow significant amounts from them, they are almost never asked to buy Sears credit agreements. Sears had been cautious about getting into the business of financing the installment purchases of its customers, but the results have been heartening. At the end of January 1977, credit operations yielded a modest annual profit of $12 million. In short, even on a service it maintains merely as a way of being competitive, Sears makes money.

Today, Fred Weimer and his colleagues preside over some 21.6 million active charge accounts. Sears, Roebuck and Company has put its credit cards in one out of every three households in the United States.

Sears now offers two basic credit arrangements. The first is the traditional installment loan. The now famous "Sears Easy Payment Plan" allows for repayment in 18 months on any item purchased from the company. Customers can take six months longer on specific durable goods and on any merchandise whose cash price less a down payment is at least $350. Finally, the Easy Payment Plan allows as long as 36 months for a select list of durables, among them Sears's most popular products. Although interest rates vary from state to state, Sears usually charges an annual rate of 20 percent under this plan. Under its installment loan operations, Sears also offers its "Modernizing Credit Plan" with a lower interest rate, usually 14.75 percent. It covers a specific list of items to be used for home improvements and provides for loans of $100 to $5000, with repayment taking as long as five years. The chief advantage of either of these installment plans is that Sears requires no security. A customer might well be able to do better at the bank, but some kind of security could be required there.

The arrival of the bank credit card on the financial scene prompted Sears to begin a new form of credit: the Sears Revolving Charge Account. The bank credit card even offers people the opportunity to borrow money by using a credit line. That made the traditional installment account less important. Sears had to be able to compete with credit arrangements at other stores that accept Master Charge and Visa and that allow customers to charge their purchases and then pay a minimum monthly amount. Actually Sears had used such "revolving" charge plans in the past but began to push its own card aggressively in the face of competition from the bank cards and in recognition of its own customers' preferences. Now some three-quarters of credit sales are made under this plan, with the rest still relying on the more traditional plans. Bank credit card plans report that about one-third of the customers never use the credit feature of the revolving plan, but pay their bills within 30 days. At Sears, a far higher percentage actually use the credit, so that only 15 to 20 percent pay their bills soon enough to avoid having to pay interest.

The usual interest charge under the revolving plan is 18 percent annually, or 1.5 percent each month. The rate is set in each state, and, in some cases, Sears says that it has a hard time doing business when ceilings are low. Through retail merchants' associations, Sears has been a vigorous lobbyist for high ceilings. In fact, credit legislation is probably the most important single area for Sears's political efforts. In recent years, it has succeeded in raising the ceiling in Iowa from 9 percent to 18 percent and in Wisconsin from 12 percent to 18 percent annually.

In South Dakota, where a low rate still applies, Sears attempted to withdraw from the credit business. If you asked for a charge account, you could still get one, but no effort was made to promote credit. If that policy hurt Sears customers, it damaged the company even more. It was an open invitation to competition, which forced Sears to get back into the credit business with both feet. Weimer laments that by offering credit at low rates, Sears must force cash customers to subsidize credit operations because the company raises all prices somewhat to cover its credit losses.

The revolving credit plans are almost always governed by consumer credit laws in the various states. That kind of legislation is needed to protect the consumer, but, so far as Sears is concerned, it causes problems. Each year, the company is the object of lawsuits, alleging that it has violated credit laws. At any one time, cases may be pending in as many as 15 states. Although the amounts involved are usually not great, the mere presence of the suits indicates the complexity of running a modern credit operation.

Keeping track of almost 30 million active and inactive accounts, more than in any other credit system, is obviously complex. Customers may open an account in any store or catalog office, which means that there is always at least one trained credit-office person in every Sears outlet. When a purchase is made through credit, Sears relies on the computer to handle most of the transmission and record keeping.

Let us say you hand the clerk your revolving charge card. In most cases, it will be inserted into what is now called "the point of sale terminal," the successor to the old-fashioned cash register. One number on your card indicates the Credit Center—where the computer lives—that keeps your records. Your number and other information about your purchase are kept in the store's minicomputer until after the close of business. The store computer can tell the salesperson if the customer has used up his or her credit allowance, but frequently sales are made without reference to the current balance so long as payments have been made regularly. The big computer at the Credit Center later calls up the store's computer and takes the information that the latter has accumulated. At the Credit Center a daily tape is made, showing what was purchased and by whom and what commissions are due to salespeople. Information from the daily tapes is the best way Sears has of monitoring credit and other sales operations.

The Credit Center computer looks for another number on your card, one indicating your billing cycle. Sears sends out bills at ten different times each month. The rest of that five-digit number further indicates the location of your account within that cycle. The computer at the Credit Center, of which there are 15 in the United States, keeps track of the limit on credit allowed to you, how close you have come to it in the past six months, and how well you have paid your bills during that period, together with information on recent purchases. This is the computer that will actually print and mail your statement once each month.

In addition, twice a month the computer will send a report on your account to the office that actually handles your account, known as the Credit Central. There are about 400 of these units in the company, and although they do not like to be called collection agencies, collecting is one of their main functions. Each Credit Central serves a group of stores. For example, the one in Portland, Maine, handles six stores, six catalog sales offices, and three catalog sales merchants. A staff of 19 people there deal with 61,000 accounts.

If you fall behind in your payments, the Credit Center computer will send a delinquency notice to your Credit Central. Then you are likely to hear from them by phone or by mail. Each customer is handled in line with the information showing their credit record over the last few months. As a result, the people in the Credit Central know if you usually keep up with your payments, or if you usually pay the full amount rather than use the revolving charge feature of your card. Actually, very few Sears customers fail to pay their bills. The write-off, the percentage of accounts that go unpaid, is about one-half of 1 percent, well below the national average for credit purchases.

The Credit Centrals also handle customer complaints and inquiries. Most complaints, actually a tiny number, come from people who are rejected when they apply for a credit card. Though Sears wants to get its card into as many hands as possible, some people simply do not have good enough credit records. (Of course, some do not have any record, but they get Sears cards if they have some income.) Naturally, they do not like to learn that they have been turned down. But Sears has conducted studies over the years that show that few customers stop buying at their stores simply because they have been turned down for credit. As a result, the company keeps to its standards but insists that its credit personnel go out of their way to be courteous to those who are rejected.

The billing cycle itself can be a cause of complaints. Let us say you are to be billed on the fifteenth of each month. In fact, the computer cuts off transactions a couple of days earlier. So, if you have made a purchase on the thirteenth, it will not appear on the statement sent two days later. It will be held for a month and then appear on the next statement. You may end up paying for your purchase as late as seven weeks after you made it. Nobody complains about that. What they do complain about is a similar delay in credits for returns being made to their accounts. Sears tries to get credits into the statement right up to the last minute and will enter them even after it has stopped entering additional sales. But if you return an item on the fifteenth and receive your statement on the seventeenth, the charge will still be on it. That causes most of the complaints the company receives about credit, except for outright rejections.

Although there has been no scientific survey published about consumer attitudes toward Sears, it is a fair bet that there is a lot of grumbling about credit. Nobody is overjoyed at having to meet monthly payments or at finding that "some dumb computer" is keeping a charge on their account that should be wiped off. So credit operations, even when they are well run, come in for a big share of consumer unhappiness. Actually, since most of the problems are caused by delays in the system, they solve themselves.

The handbook given to new employees in Sears's credit operations makes it clear that the company's antidote is to handle customers with care. It explains in great detail the way that Sears credit personnel are to deal with customers over the phone. "Mentally try to put yourself in your customer's place. Instead of responding in Sears terms . . . answer your customers in their own kind of language."

With people more secure about their incomes, thanks to a generally sound economy and government income support plans, credit has become increasingly popular. In addition, buying with a credit card makes it easier to keep financial records. So selling by credit has become vital to Sears. As a single source of credit, Sears deals directly with more credit customers than any other commercial organization.

Just like the credit operation, Sears's service organization provides a major boost to sales. And just as Sears does not seem to make a big fuss about credit, it does not about service.

In the middle of the yellow index pages in the Sears catalog is a page entitled "You can count on Sears for Service." That is about the only public mention the company makes of its parts and service operation, a large unseen network that backs up both catalog and retail sales. Sears could easily claim that "we service what we sell— or what we have ever sold" because that is, in fact, the company's policy.

The name of the game is to keep the customers coming back to Sears. The company sells many major appliances, and it is inevitable that sometimes they will break down. That is where the service operation comes in. If it can make the repairs, all in the family, the company figures the customers will be more inclined to buy their next appliances from Sears as well.

Of course, many repairs are simple. All the customer needs is the right part. So Sears stocks the parts for all products it sells, as long as the cost of the replacement does not make it more economical for the user simply to buy a new item instead of repairing the old one.

Every Sears retail store has some kind of a service operation. In small stores at remote locations, service work may be done by local people on a contract basis, or appliances may be shipped to area service centers. But in most cases, customer service means on-the-spot repair work by trained company personnel.

In each of the company's five territories is a training center where service personnel are taught the ins and outs of the products Sears sells. Some people may come back again and again to the center to learn how to handle different kinds of appliances. Then, when they go back to the field, they will get refresher and update courses so they can handle new items added to the company's inventory.

Walk into the Sears Training Center at Pennsauken, New Jersey. Today's class is on washing machines, and about 20 service people are sprawled on the floor and draped over the machines, trying to jockey their motors back into place. Service "people"? Yes, because one of those pitching in with the boys and fiddling with a machine is a woman. She looks up at you from under the works with an engaging smile, then goes back to wiring the motor. More and more women are getting into the repair business, and, to judge by the workday atmosphere of the repair class, Sears is making the adjustment easily.

These people at the Training Center not only learn about the company's latest models, but also take a course in the fundamentals of repairing electrical equipment or appliances. Because Sears will fix a washing machine it might have sold 20 years earlier, service people have to know enough about the basics to handle unexpected situations and unfamiliar models. In fact, the company would probably not have to operate such an extensive training program if it were not committed to handling anything it had ever sold. It would be a lot easier just to pass out manuals for the latest model.

Down the hall from the classroom is the most modern of automotive garages. Its three bays duplicate the standard auto service center that you are likely to find near most Sears stores. Sears does not sell cars, but it aims to do everything else from insuring them to repairing them. As a dealer in automotive spare parts, the company has hired the service personnel to install them for the vast majority of Americans who do not know the manifold from the muffler. Today, the "professor," an auto repair man with decades of experience, is going to take his crew under the car for the first time. But to do that, he has to show them the proper way of getting it up on a ramp, and they cluster around as he glides the car into place. They are impressed by the apparent ease with which he does his work, and the old mechanic obviously enjoys basking in their admiration. Later, he hauls out all kinds of diagnostic equipment because the shop is fully equipped with the latest gadgets they will find later in the auto service centers. There is always talk about whether the women's lib movement means that there will be women auto mechanics. At Sears, that is an accomplished fact, and more of them are going through this program every year.

When the service people get back to their stores, they will be expected to form part of a team that can handle anything from sewing machines to sump pumps. The Pennsauken operation also houses a so-called central service operation, similar to those in many stores. When a customer calls to report trouble with an appliance, an operator can call up from a computer complete information on every product that person has bought from the company that is under a guarantee or a maintenance agreement. The computer display allows the operator to read when the item was purchased and if it has been repaired before. That saves the customer time in reporting the details. Perhaps even more important for Sears, the operator can appear to be personally familiar with the customer's purchases. That personal touch is always sought by Sears, which wants its customers to be impressed by the economies available because of its size, but not intimidated by it. The operator glances up at a blackboard indicating the service schedule and makes an appointment with the customer for a repair person to call. Once confirmed, the appointment is added to the information in the computer, which automatically prints out a service order.

Smaller items can be taken directly to any Sears store, although the actual work will be done at a central service. Television sets are probably the items most frequently brought into the service centers, if for no other reason than that so many are sold. At this center, the T.V. repair people have their own department, but so do those who work on stereo equipment and electric guitars. Sometimes the place can get pretty hectic. "Good Friday is usually our biggest day," says the center's chief. "Don't know why."

At this center, Sears tries to get the goods back out to the customer as quickly as possible. If they bring a small appliance to the center, they will get an estimate while they wait. On the phone banks, somebody is on duty about 14 hours a day, with an answering service covering the rest of the time. Occasionally, that is not enough, especially if your oil burner has stopped in the middle of the night. Or if you are the fellow who tried to assemble a miniature kitchen set on Christmas eve and found himself totally lost at four o'clock on Christmas morning. Unable to get any help, he fired off an angry telegram to the president of Sears. The hapless fellow even had trouble with his wire because he still grouses that he never got an answer. The story has a happy ending. As dawn rose, he finally got the present for his daughter fully assembled.

If you have bought an appliance from Sears, it was sold under a guarantee, generally good for a year. You will be hearing from Sears again before that guarantee expires because the company will want to sell you a maintenance agreement. At each central service, a battery of operators does nothing but make calls to Sears customers, trying to sell them these agreements. Even if you turn them down once, they may try again to sell you the agreement. Often the agreement is a good deal since it is actually an extension of the guarantee and covers parts and service. But the service people sometimes push too hard and have, on occasion, exaggerated local service charges in an effort to put the Sears agreement in the best light. All of this sales effort is not motivated just by a desire to protect customers. Sears has made a big investment in its service operation, and it wants to cover it by making sure it takes on all the repair work it can. Even more important, the company makes a good profit on maintenance agreements, although it refuses to say just how much.

Perhaps the most dazzling aspect of the whole back-up operation is Sears's handling of spare parts. Near the Pennsauken service operation is a 109,000 square foot warehouse that stocks the spare parts for Sears's Eastern Territory. There are four other similar warehouses in the United States, which serve both individual customers and the service organization. All a customer has to have is the serial number of the Sears product and an idea of what the part looks like and where it fits. Each customer service desk at retail stores is provided with microfische cards of the inventory at the parts warehouse. The customer is shown the diagram of the appliance and can pick out the part. For the careful customer, who keeps the parts list that comes with each appliance, the job is even easier.

The New Jersey center keeps a record of some 800,000 parts, with about half that many actually in stock. In many cases, a newer part will fit into an old Sears model. Each part is stocked in line with actual demand. In one bin, there are only four small screws, hardly enough, you would think, to supply Sears stores in 11 states. But a supervisor assures you that the supply is adequate for the demand. By contrast, one corner of the warehouse is piled with washing machine parts. They are not even put on storage shelves because they move out so quickly. According to one warehouse official, Sears sells two washing machines out of every five these days; so their spare parts are a major item for the warehouse. But even if you brought in your old cream separator, it is likely that Sears would find some way to scrounge a spare part for it. "We consider twenty years as the period during which we have to have the parts," says a warehouse manager, "but maybe we can handle something fifty years old." That kind of thinking puts the whole operation into a Sears perspective. What is more, the people who handle the parts business are not just backstage operators. Most of them come from the retail business and expect to return there. That is why people in the parts department never think of themselves as being in a backwater.

Ambrose Bierce, the prince of American cynics, once defined a merchant as "one engaged in a commercial pursuit. A commercial pursuit," he continued, "is one in which the thing pursued is a dollar."

At Sears, all aspects of sales—advertising, store management, credit, and service—are devoted to the pursuit of the dollar. The company even calls itself "the merchant to the millions." They know what Bierce was talking about.

CHAPTER 12

INNOCENTS ABROAD

"We moved abroad because of the vision of General Wood," says John Gallagher, the man who now heads Sears's international operations. Once again, the fine hand of the General is responsible for a Sears innovation. Yet, unlike so many other of the Sears schemes he hatched, this one began small and has remained small. Sales in all of Sears's foreign operations now amount to less than 1 percent of the company's total sales.

Why did the world's largest retailer refrain from the kind of overseas expansion, the creation of a multinational corporation, undertaken by other major American corporations? Here, too, the answer seems to be the policies of General Wood and the peculiar nature of Sears, Roebuck and the retail business.

Ever since he had worked on the Panama Canal, Wood had strong emotional ties to Panama. His links to Central America and the Caribbean area were strengthened by his having a cousin who was a successful businessman in Mexico City. Wood felt that he understood something about Latin America. What is more, having spent some time there, he had dabbled in his hobby of demography and believed that the area was on the verge of major economic growth.

Wood's interest in Latin America was a reflection also of his disdain for Europe, which he believed was in the process of economic decay. When it came to Europe, his pleas for political isolation were interwoven with his business judgment. America should not get involved with Europe, and neither should Sears. In the late 1930s, the company had set up an international subsidiary with the purpose of exporting Sears merchandise, but the experiment was a somewhat costly failure. Obviously, with the world sliding rapidly into world war, this was no time to start an export business. Wood must have felt, on the basis of that venture, that you could not sell refrigerators to Europe, Africa, or Asia, when these continents were dominated by powers who were more concerned about the impending war than the growth of commerce. Latin America, closely tied to the United States, economically dominated by it, and likely to be protected from the war by the great 3000-mile Atlantic moat, was a more likely prospect.

The first timid step came in 1942, when Sears opened a small store in Havana. After the losses suffered in the 1930s, Sears was not about to do anything on a grand scale, but Cuba, still reliant on the United States, was safe for a start. Once the war was over, Sears was ready to increase the pace of foreign expansion. Even before the war ended, detailed plans were prepared for entry into the Mexican market.

In Mexico City, most of the large stores were owned and managed by French interests, perhaps the vestige of the brief reign of the Emperor Maximilian in the nineteenth century. These were stores in the grand and somewhat antiquated European style. Their clientele was essentially the small, wealthy upper class. Sears calculated that a broader market existed, a market for those of middle income, the group with the greatest purchasing power. By using the same merchandising and buying techniques that had worked in the United States, Wood believed that it would be possible to bring this group into Sears stores, while attracting the same clientele as patronized the French department stores.

Mexico was "an almost immediate success," says a Sears international official. "There was pent-up demand." That may be an understatement of the first order. When the store opened, Mexico City crowds almost stormed it. The company had to issue passes to admit customers to the store. That is probably the dream of all retailers— so many customers that they must be given tickets of admission.

The secret of the success was in Sears pricing. Although prices were higher than in its American stores, they were below those of the Mexican competition. A sophisticated formula was used to determine just what Sears could charge. For example, almost any appliance would have to be bought on credit since few Mexicans could be expected to have the full ticket price. Generally, an appliance would be paid for in 18 months, and Sears calculated that most customers would not be able to handle more than a $10 monthly payment. Conclusion: An appliance ought not to cost more than $180, including any carrying charges. Then, back to the supplier to come up with a refrigerator or washing machine that would be attractive in the Mexican market, but still priced below $180.

In one important way, Sears did not go native. It put the price tag on an item, and it meant it. Many people had been used to haggling. One American magazine later told the story of just how the Sears system worked, with something of a wry touch: "A Mexican rancher who seldom visits the city stopped at Sears' Chihuahua store last month and asked the price of a .22 calibre rifle. '590 pesos, marked down from 750,' said the clerk. 'I'll give you an even 500,' said the rancher. Informed that the old Latin custom of haggling did not apply at Sears, he stared unbelievingly for a moment, [then] glumly produced the cash."

One other homegrown touch proved instantly popular: "Satisfaction guaranteed or your money back." The guarantee had been a key to Richard Sears's success and worked like a charm in Latin America. In Mexico and elsewhere, the concept of product liability or standards was far less deeply rooted than in the United States; so a company that promised to honor a guarantee and actually meant it was a rarity. The guarantee provided an enormous commercial advantage.

In Mexico and in other countries where Sears opened its stores, it imported its principles of merchandising. Local personnel were sent back to the United States to learn how to buy for Sears. Store organization techniques came from Chicago, based on decades of experience. Sears found that merchandising worked pretty much the same south of the border as in the United States. Adjustments for income level, cultural differences, and climate did not alter their basic workability.

Initially Sears had planned to stock its Latin American stores with merchandise from back home. In some cases it was able to bring its goods into the new markets with relative ease, but the original plan soon had to be changed. Balance of payments problems were a frequent obstacle, as the Latin American countries balked at seeing dollars leave to pay for American-made goods. Transportation and import duties could also drive Sears prices up to the point where they were no longer competitive. As the company saw these trends developing, it would make local buying arrangements. If it could find a local manufacturer who could handle the production of Sears products, American patterns and tools and dies would be brought to that firm, and it would get the contract. Sometimes no local producer could be found, and American investment was needed to get a company off the ground. In Brazil, for example, Sears purchased 17.5 percent of an appliance company in partnership with Whirlpool and Brazilian interests. Once it was in full operation supplying Sears stores, the company gradually reduced its holdings. In Colombia, Sears and Whirlpool built and sold an appliance factory to local people, giving them seven years to pay for it and continuing to operate it for them. In the process of finding and helping its own suppliers, Sears sought to avoid the old custom of haggling. As in the United States, it needed sure and constant sources of supply at predictable prices. By insisting that local business adhere to that principle, Sears changed some commercial practices; but nobody seemed to miss haggling if they could get an assured market for their production at Sears.

The store planners had to recognize that their market was different from back home. Their experience told them where to place the various departments and how to build their stores, but the sprawling A stores of the American suburbs would have been ill-suited to the initial foray into Latin America. So stores were smaller, and, in sharp contrast with Sears back home, they carried a much higher percentage of soft goods, more affordable in developing countries. From the outset, personnel were recruited locally, with few people from Sears's American operations being sent in. Typically only a handful of top executives were sent from Chicago. Although local people might assume positions of considerable responsibility in the Latin operations, they could not very often expect to enter the Sears career ladder with a view to later assignment in the United States.

There is one big difference between the way Sears got started in the United States and its establishment in Latin America. The core of the parent company was the mail-order operation that began with Richard Sears. It all started with the catalog, and the big book still produces a large share of Sears's total sales. Not so in Latin America. Instead of being a Wish Book for rural people, the catalog there is used mainly in urban areas. The obvious reason for the difference is literacy. There is usually a higher literacy rate, essential for using the catalog, in cities than in rural areas in developing countries. In addition, catalog distribution depends on the postal system, which can be rudimentary in the countryside there. To make payment by mail, customers have to purchase postal money orders, often an inconvenience. Checking accounts are not widely used outside of the cities. In fact, even there, most payments are made by people coming into the store or by itinerant Sears collectors. All of these factors combined to make it far more difficult to start up catalog operations than to open retail stores.

Eventually Sears would enter 11 Latin American countries, counting Puerto Rico. Of course, the Havana operation was swallowed up by the victory of Fidel Castro. But, by 1976, Sears had some 73 stores of various sizes in operation in these countries. The company established in each country is independent of all others and of the parent, except for the ties of ownership. This allows Sears to adjust to conditions in each country and to alter its ownership share to reflect those conditions. With a totally expectable touch of paternalism, General Wood decreed, when the first store was opened, that he would permit Mexicans to own the company at the right time. He did not want to enter into a partnership with those who could then invest because he was "not coming to Mexico to help rich Mexicans." Now, Sears's Mexican employees own 20 percent of the original operation.

In recent years, Latin American governments have cracked down on foreign ownership of local companies. As a result, Sears has had to adjust. A new store in Mexicali is owned 49 percent by Sears Mexico and 51 percent by Mexican nationals. In Venezuela, the company had to reduce its ownership share from 80 percent to 20 percent. Probably, Sears has done well enough in the developing markets of Latin America to afford to divest itself of majority ownership and still come up a winner.

Even today, General Wood's stamp on the choice of countries in which to do business is evident. Altogether Sears has had stores in 13 countries in Latin America and Europe. Six of these countries are in Central America, where Wood had the strongest ties, and a seventh is Puerto Rico. The countries where Sears would establish subsidiaries were carefully chosen, after detailed research. For example, why pick Peru, probably one of the poorest countries on the continent? Sears found that 80 percent of the population is Indian and outside of the market economy. Their presence in the population pulls the country's per capita income down. Sears looks only at the other 20 percent of the population. "Peru is actually not that poor," says a Sears international man. "And it has a free market type of economy." When one Peruvian regime freed business of government controls, Sears knew the time had come to enter the market there and eventually opened two stores. Of course, conditions change. "We would not go there today, if we weren't already there," says the Sears man. Peru now has a military regime. But by now, Sears is a Peruvian store. One of its biggest competitors was a traditional department store. Twice each year, its buyer would visit New York and Europe, where she would select the store's stock. Then, when the balance of payments situation deteriorated, the store found itself actually cut off from its sources of supply because it could not export the hard currency needed to pay for its goods. Meanwhile, Sears had built up local suppliers, so that 70 percent of its goods were produced locally. "When balance of payments problems came, we were not in a serious situation," the Sears executive reports, with the smile of self-satisfaction in which the company's top people occasionally indulge.

In short, Sears will enter a country where competitive conditions are reasonably similar to the way things are done back home. It takes a careful look at the local political scene before taking the plunge. That is why there is no Sears store in Argentina or Chile, although both seem to be attractive markets.

"There's a real middle class with a European background in Argentina," the Sears man notes, "but we never went into business there. The General visited Peron and asked for some indication that the company would be governed by commercial law." Wood did not want Sears to be under some special rules that would make it particularly vulnerable. Sears even established the necessary legal structure to go into Argentina. The Sears man shrugs, "Every time the government seemed about to have the economy under control, something happened."

Chile presented another problem. The country had a democratic political structure, but the government controlled the economy. "We would have had to accept the government as a partner, and Sears would not have had management control of store policies," the official reports. So Sears stayed away.

In Latin America, where economic conditions are often typical of those prevailing in developing countries around the world, Sears's biggest problem is inflation. "It's absolutely impossible to make a profit if there is a continuing high rate of inflation," says an official, who sets anything above 10 percent as unacceptable to the company. Sears must count on selling on credit in these countries. In effect, it is loaning money to its customers at a fixed interest rate. The company can end up as a very cheap lender if other interest rates are allowed to climb. Then, Sears cannot borrow in that national market at a rate that allows it to make a profit on its credit sales. It ends up paying more for the money it lends than it is receiving in interest.

Inflation can also eat away at the profit margin on merchandise. As costs spiral, Sears has to raise its own ticket prices. Yet it may often run into government-imposed price controls, which are aimed at stemming inflation. "There's no way you can keep up," says an official who once headed the Sears Venezuelan operations. A period of three or four years of high inflation can just about wipe out a foreign subsidiary. Rising prices in recent years have made it a lot tougher for Sears to do business abroad, and top executives readily admit that inflation has discouraged the company from expanding any more rapidly abroad. Still, in 1975, Sears netted $23 million on $399 million of Latin American sales.

General Wood also looked north as Sears's foreign operations expanded. Canada had the stability and market characteristics of the American market, but it also had a developed economy with strong retailers. Sears was reluctant to plunge into Canada on its own. Instead, Wood looked around for a suitable partner. He had known the top people at Simpsons and found their business attitude similar to his own, although the Canadian firm was not used to Sears's style of merchandising. What was the same, in the words of a Sears official, was "their ethical concern with how to do business and how to treat people."

Sears might have tried to buy Simpsons out but would have run the considerable risk of a strongly negative reaction from the Canadians. Instead, the net worth of Simpsons's stock was determined, and then Sears put in an equal amount of money. The companies were to be equal partners, each holding 50 percent of the voting stock. Today, they each own 41 percent of all stock, with the general public holding the rest. As a result, Simpsons-Sears, the company's biggest foreign operation, is the one in which it has held the least equity.

The new venture in Canada started off by opening small appliance stores but soon found that the market needed the larger A-type stores that were so important to the American retail operation. Few Sears, Roebuck people were added to the Canadian executive staff, although many provided initial help in mastering the company's merchandising methods. Now there is only one American representative of Sears, the number two man in Simpsons-Sears. Increasingly, merchandise has been obtained from local businesses because Sears has found that Canadians are even willing to pay a slight premium in order to buy from their own producers. Cooperation between the Canadians and Americans has been a whopping success. Simpsons-Sears is the largest merchandiser in Canada and operates a mail-order house that would make it one of the largest were it in the United States. In 1975, Simpsons-Sears showed a healthy net income of almost $31 million.

So long as the General dominated Sears, it would expand no further. In the postwar economic expansion of Europe, there might have been a place for Sears. But the company did not go there then because Wood continued to believe that Europe was in a process of constant economic decay.

Yet it was almost inevitable that, soon after Wood had left the scene, Sears would begin exploring the European market. By that time, however, many doors were already closed. Local department stores had emerged, renewed and ready for business, from the rubble of the war. Competitive opportunity in a country like Germany was simply not apparent to Sears officials. Some thought was given to forging agreements like the one with Simpsons, but few retailers were worthy of consideration, and, in any case, none was eager to share its perch atop European economic recovery.

Still persuaded that there was a place for Sears in Europe, the company shifted its focus to smaller countries, more similar to the nations of Central America than to the United States or Canada. The first choice was Spain.

The link between what Sears was already doing in its foreign operations and Spain was obvious: the language and culture shared by the former mother country and her colonies. It appeared that many of the techniques learned south of the border could be exported to Spain. In fact, some of the executives in Sears's Latin American companies had originally left Spain because they felt a lack of economic opportunity. The Spanish economy, with a growing middle class, looked ripe, and Sears was attracted by the relatively low investment that would be required to get started. Finally, Sears believed that Spain would one day be admitted to the European Common Market, allowing the company to gain a foothold within that grouping's tariff walls.

In the late 1960s, Sears moved into Spain. Many of its calculations were wrong. Perhaps the biggest mistake was seeing Spain as an underdeveloped country and treating it as though it were in Latin America. "The competition responded very vigorously," Arthur Wood, the Sears Chairman, reported years later. "It took us the better part of three years to get our first store open. And at the outset, we had the wrong merchandise. So we had to change our product mix and pricing and develop a whole new promotional program."

It was not Mexico all over again. The crowds did not need to be held back, nor did the competition fold in the face of Sears merchandising techniques. The company did not make money immediately, plunging instead into a relatively long run in the red. Still, sales grew remarkably each year, and as Sears learned about the Spanish market and business methods, it began to show a profit. In 1970, it lost almost $2.2 million there, with only two stores. By 1973, it showed a $3.1 million net income. By early 1976, it was operating three big retail stores and 17 retail sales offices in Spain. Its favorable profit picture was, however, being hurt by losses on foreign exchange, thanks to the devaluation of the peseta. In short, Spain was a success, but not on the grand scale to which Sears is accustomed.

If Spain presented unexpected problems for the company, the next market it tried turned out to be a disaster, although a relatively minor one for a company of Sears's size. Still searching for a small country in which it might be competitive, Sears chose Belgium. It settled upon Galeries Anspach, a 74-year-old company, which operated a shopping center, two department stores, and six small retail outlets. Sears sought only a minority share of 20 percent, but the family that owned the Belgian company wanted out and insisted that Sears take over the whole operation. Although it was just turning its Spanish chain into a profitable operation, Sears decided to acquire the Belgian stores as well, if for no other reason than that the land under one store in Brussels was worth $10 million.

Sears knew that Galeries Anspach was a loser but hoped to turn it around by opening more shopping centers, just then becoming popular in Belgium. Under Sears ownership, losses continued to mount because of the costs of expansion.

Then, almost everything turned sour. The worldwide combination of inflation and recession hit Belgium hard. Though the company had been willing, if unhappy, to wait out inflation in Latin America, it ran into a situation in Belgium in which it felt trapped. "There's no way you can stay in business in Belgium," said a top Sears official as the company inspected its wounds and decided what to do next. What was unusual about Belgium, at least so far as Sears was concerned, was the role of the national government. Closely tied to the labor unions, it ruled that Sears and other companies could not simply lay off people as a way of cutting expenses. Payments would have to continue to unemployed staff over a three- or four-year period. As a result, the sales force represented a steadily increasing cost because their wages were "indexed"; that is, they rose at the same pace as the cost of living. The same was true of the rents paid by the stores.

At the same time, Sears and other large department stores were running into the age-old ire of the small merchants. They are particularly strong in Belgium, where a so-called Ministry of the Middle Class looks out for their interests. The small storekeepers, working through the government, brought all shopping center development to a halt for at least four years. Unlike in the United States, where Sears had joined with other chains to counteract lobbying by small merchants, it was unable to wage an effective campaign in Belgium. All around it, major department store chains were falling, forced into mergers in order to survive. Their prices, like Sears's, were under government control while their labor costs continued to rise because of indexing. Even credit zoomed out of sight, with interest rates rising from 8 percent to 17 percent in just a couple of years.

Finally, Sears went to the government to ask for help. Inevitably, the company was turned down. In the face of what it called "state socialism," the company felt, in the words of one executive, that it must "get out as gracefully as possible." It finally hit upon the plan of selling Galeries Anspach to its Belgian manager with a Sears pledge to cover his losses for another two years. Just as soon as the government gave its approval, the Belgian took up his option, and, in late 1976, Sears was gone from the Belgian market. It took a $54 million loss there that year.

Maybe the General had been right. Perhaps the Sears way of doing business was simply not suited to Europe. Certainly top Sears officials, confronted with what they viewed as excessive government intervention, had experienced feelings of distress and frustration as they had tried to keep their Belgian subsidiary afloat. With real sadness and some deep bitterness, Sears retreated. In the view of its executives, it had not been given a fair chance because its growth was totally dependent on a free market system, which no longer existed in Belgium.

As those responsible for international operations surveyed the world, they concluded that almost any country could turn into another Belgium. South Africa might work, but the company did not want to appear to be supporting the regime there. Elsewhere, Sears would have to come up with a new approach, or else it would have to stay home.

As result of their investigation of the rich Japanese market, Sears came up with that new approach. Corporate structures and financial arrangements were rigid in Japan, and Sears knew that it could not hope to break up such practices in order to do business in its traditional manner. The company had gone a long way toward eliminating the middleman in its American operations. But, in Japan, the wholesaler or middleman was essential to the functioning of the economic system. In addition, the Japanese had unusual limitations on the size of a retail establishment, which required even the big department stores to go through the elaborate fiction of claiming that each floor of the store was in fact a different store. Yet the Japanese market was large and rich. Sears knew it could not cope with the system, but it wanted badly to sell in Japan.

The answer was to sell what Sears could do best: its merchandising. For a fee, it would provide the technology it had developed and loan its personnel to a foreign retailer. In short, it would wrap into a neat package of management services the fruits of its decades of experience. It might also invest in the foreign enterprise that was using Sears techniques in hopes of realizing a capital gain. If possible, it would have the foreign retailer stock Sears products. In the case of Japan, it arranged also to sell from the Sears catalog, using the Los Angeles Catalog Merchandise Distribution Center as its base of operations. If demand merited, an inventory of catalog merchandise could be kept in Japan.

In Japan and other developed countries like Australia, where it made an arrangement with the Walton's chain, Sears would remain behind the scenes. Obviously, management had deep doubts about the company's ability to adjust to the quite different conditions of competition that existed abroad. So Sears would run a foreign aid program for retailers, and, of course, it would be run for a profit. The financial risk in such undertakings would be slight compared with actually building and operating Sears stores abroad. Yet it could acquire an equity interest in foreign firms if it felt they had a good chance of success. That decision would depend on just how carefully they followed Sears advice.

Nowhere more than in its international operation is Sears a typically American institution. It has a distrust of foreigners and their ways. It feels comfortable only when it can engage in all-out, open competition. Perhaps the foreign experience even made Sears appreciate the American economic system a bit more, to judge from all the complaints about government interference.

Here, then, was one giant American corporation that would never become a multinational. It would stay at home, and its future would be wholly determined by how well it performed in the American market. The world might change some day, and, if it did, Sears would be ready to take the plunge again. In the meantime, its new Japanese-style arrangement and its subsidiaries in Latin America and Spain would continue. Even on a restricted scale, Sears made a tidy profit of some $25 million on those foreign operations in 1975. Whatever one thought about General Wood, his successors might pause and reflect that, after all, his judgment had again been vindicated. Just as Dorothy in *The Wizard of Oz*, Sears could awake safely from its foreign ventures, repeating faithfully, "There's no place like home."

CHAPTER 13

GOOD HANDS, BIG MONEY

In one respect, at least, General Robert Wood was an ordinary man. Every morning he would board the Chicago Northwestern 7:28 train from Highland Park to get to his job—as head of Sears, Roebuck—in the Chicago Loop. He was no man to catch an extra 40 winks on the train, and he had probably already glanced at the newspaper; so he engaged in the commuter's vice: playing cards.

One day, early in 1930, Carl Odell, an insurance broker, won the morning's hand. As he played, he casually tossed a suggestion to the General. "Why don't you fellows over at Sears start an auto insurance company and sell by mail?" Obviously, Odell had dropped the idea in passing without thinking that anything would come of it, at least not as the country was sliding into an economic abyss after Black Thursday just a few months earlier.

But Wood saw that the proposal was not simply one to add another item to the catalog inventory. His demographic studies had convinced him that most Americans would soon have automobiles, and that the motor car would bring a revolution in the United States. Already he was planning the location of Sears retail stores to take advantage of America's increased mobility. But what about the car itself? Sears sold tires, spare parts, tools, and, for a short period, even the whole car, and Wood wanted to wring every bit of economic advantage he could from people's passion for the automobile. So he chewed on Odell's suggestion. But not for long.

Odell was asked to prepare a memorandum on how selling insurance by mail order, an untested scheme, might work. After a quick course in the insurance business, given by experts in the field, Wood concluded that selling insurance drew upon many of the same merchandising techniques the company had already developed. Insurance companies needed to keep overhead down and to cut prices, while still offering a quality product. He thought he had the key to the cost-price problem in Odell's idea of direct selling to the public without going through an agent.

Perhaps without even realizing it, he had already decided to go ahead. He knew that Sears could count on the same customers coming back year after year and reasoned that if insurance policy holders did the same, the cost of getting clients would be low, making a reduction in premiums possible. His guess was that he could beat the competition by about 20 percent.

Despite his optimism, Wood was careful because he knew that most companies had contracted as the depression deepened and were not planning new and untested operations. In October 1930, he started his consultations. He called together those members of the Sears Board of Directors who were company officials. After he had laid out his plan, one after another questioned going into this new business during the depression, and some, noting that none among them had experience in the insurance business, wondered if the new venture could ever earn a profit. But Wood was convinced and convincing. Finally, the officers acquiesced. Undoubtedly, some of them left the board room that day wondering if they had agreed to another of the General's imaginative and profitable schemes or an embarrassing fiasco.

In November, he had a company official prepare a short memo to the full board, outlining his arguments for the plan. Then, a few days later, he took the train to New York to complete the final step: convincing the outside members of the board. The meeting took place in the offices of Goldman, Sachs, the people who had been the earliest backers of Sears. He stressed that the top officers had already given their approval. "When I sprung this bombshell on them, though they were old friends and old associates, their reception . . . was pretty frigid. However, I won them over . . . ," the General remembered later. Back in Chicago in November, the full board gave its approval, leaving Wood a chance to back out at any time before the insurance business was begun.

But there would be no last minute doubts, and in April 1931, barely more than a year after Odell had come up with the idea, Sears's own insurance company was in business. For its name, Wood selected Allstate, which had been used for the company's popular auto tires. Odell was hired as the first general manager. A top Sears executive was assigned to the new company to make sure that it operated according to Sears's traditional methods, particularly those resulting from economies of scale.

The entry of this brash newcomer into the insurance business was greeted with hostility from established firms. It was the same reception that Sears had faced upon its entry into the retail business. At first, the rest of the industry was merely wary. Insurance could be written in any state without a license, as long as the business was conducted entirely by mail. Allstate was licensed in Illinois. However, the company could not send an agent to solicit business or an adjustor to settle claims without getting approval in other states as well. Outsiders also thought that Sears would not be able to invest enough money, during the depression at least, to cover the heavy start-up expenses of the insurance business.

To get started, Sears put up a healthy $700,000. Costs were kept down by offering the automobile insurance through the catalog. Customers could simply clip a coupon and mail it in. They were sent an insurance quotation and an application form, which, when returned with the premium, made them Allstate policyholders. At the company's office in Room 124 of the Sears Administration Building in Chicago, a staff of 20 waited for the first replies to the more than 500,000 circulars that had been sent out. A man in Aurora, Illinois, wrote first and got policy number one. In all, some 40,000 inquiries were received, a very high response to such a business solicitation. Then, one day, a man walked into the Allstate office with an automobile door handle in his hand. It had been broken off his car during an attempted auto theft that morning. All members of the staff sprang into action in their eagerness to settle the company's first claim. But there was one small hitch: Nobody had bothered to plan or to print a claim form. That would have to be the next task. In the meantime, the amount of the loss was determined, and the client got his money.

Meanwhile, the stock market continued to fall, reducing the value of Sears's original investment. At the same time, the company experienced the inevitable first year underwriting losses. By the end of 1931, the company had 4,217 cars insured, but a $70,000 loss. During the next year, when Sears's sales were down and the depression reached its bottom, Allstate boosted sales and showed a profit. Even as the company got into gear, it became evident that it would be held back if it could not obtain licenses to do business in states other than Illinois, where its headquarters were located. Gradually it began to expand into other states. But first it had to overcome yet another obstacle. Some states prevented it from offering fire insurance on cars. That, it seemed, could only come from a fire insurance company. As a result, before the first year was out, the Allstate Fire Insurance Company had been organized. Still, the rest of the industry watched carefully, not yet feeling challenged.

Just like the parent company, Allstate had started out as a mail-order operation, designed to gain the benefits inherent in that way of doing business. But the call of the retail world was strong, especially since Sears had so many retail outlets, natural locations for Allstate offices, already in operation. Even as early as 1931, the insurance company had studied the possibility of placing salesmen in the stores but, for the time being, contented itself with placing advertising leaflets on the counters.

By early 1933, Odell received reports showing that many Sears customers were coming into retail stores to ask about Allstate insurance. Interestingly, the small rural stores reported a far higher number of inquiries than larger ones in cities. The reason was obvious: The insurance had been promoted to catalog customers, and most of them lived in the country. So, the company was missing an opportunity to sell to the cities, where most of the people were. Then, a staff study reported that the company could boost sales if it had its own agents who actively promoted Allstate policies.

Since Allstate was already licensed in Illinois, Odell decided to try an experiment. On the Midway of the 1933 Chicago "Century of Progress" Fair, the company set up a card table in the corner of the Sears exhibit. The test was a success, and soon Allstate had a permanent location in a Sears store in downtown Chicago. From being a "direct writer," selling insurance directly to the public without agents, Allstate was becoming an "exclusive agency," selling to the public through agents representing that company and no other. This was a sharp break with the prevailing custom, according to which most insurance was sold by independent agents who might handle policies from several companies. Companies selling this way usually belonged to a "bureau," which studied the insurance market and set premiums that were charged by all members. Because there was no rate competition, the companies battled for the favor of the agents by offering richer commissions. Only a few "mutual" insurance companies operated outside this structure. They used their own agents and offered lower premiums by returning a dividend to policyholders at the end of the year.

Although Allstate was not a mutual insurance company, it used the exclusive agent system and set its own rates. Now, the rest of the industry was alarmed. Sears was selling insurance over the counter, not in an agent's office, and was turning its back on the industry's conventions. Independent agents had prided themselves on being members of a full-fledged profession, offering advisory services as well as salesmanship to their clients. One independent wrote Wood, "As insurance brokers licensed by the state to engage in that profession as are doctors, lawyers and other professions, we believe that the buyer of insurance can best be served by personal contact with a person properly fitted to engage in the profession by long experience if necessary or intensive schooling of shorter duration and I for one am 'fighting it out' along that line." The General was obviously unimpressed and forwarded the letter to Odell with a short memo. "Please note." Odell, a longtime insurance man himself, was similarly unmoved, particularly because Sears was, in fact, training its own salesmen and not simply putting them behind a counter.

The Allstate people allowed themselves a bad pun and proudly called their merchandising breakthrough the "counter-revolution." But they resented the charge that their salesmen were nothing more than ribbon clerks. In fact, under the independent agency systems, the salesman was forced to handle a tremendous volume of paperwork before forwarding the completed insurance contract to the issuing company. At Sears, all the administrative details were handled centrally.

Less expensive merchandising was not the only reason why Sears could sell at a lower price. Independent brokers depended for their entire income on the commissions paid by the insurance companies. They, and not the companies themselves, maintained direct contact with the client. The obvious result was that the agents were tempted to accept doubtful business. The biggest part of the commission was earned at the start of the policy period, so the salesmen were not overly concerned if the policy lapsed soon after. Of course, if a client submitted many claims because he had not been properly investigated by a salesman, the company was the loser, and its loss was translated into higher premiums for its policyholders. At Allstate, although salesmen were paid by commission, they were also employees of the company and were made to feel that they had a stake in keeping costs as low as possible. What is more, they had to follow company guidelines in accepting risks.

In later years, still another major difference between the way Allstate and the others did business became apparent. Because the commissions were higher at the start of a policy period, some independents tended to shift their clients from company to company without any real reason. Each time a customer began a policy with another company, the salesman was able to collect the big initial commission. Obviously, Allstate and other exclusive agency companies wanted the customer to come back again to the same place. Repeat business kept the companies' costs lower than they would have been had it been required to pay big commissions continually, as policies were started, allowed to lapse, and then started again.

Admittedly, an Allstate agent is paid less than an independent for the same sale of insurance. But the independent must pay rent and administrative costs. Because Allstate agents can devote more of their time to selling, they may end up among the best paid in the industry. All of this was not calculated to please the independent agents or the companies whose insurance they sold, and they fought back. In some states, Allstate was banned from offering insurance at prices below bureau rates. But the obstacles were not enough to slow the steady growth of the company.

Within a couple of years of its founding, Allstate was experiencing the Sears success: steadily growing sales and profits and the ready sense that the company had uncovered a big, new market. The next step was to expand, just as Richard Sears had gone from watches to men's suits. In 1934, two major Illinois life insurance companies

were put into state receivership, and other companies were asked to
bid on reinsuring their business. Allstate won the right to reinsure
the policies of the National Life Insurance Company. While National's investments were weak, most of its insurance was strong. But
Allstate needed some time to reorganize it. The court order required
Allstate to keep on National's agents, which created something of a
problem. What were these agents supposed to do while Allstate was
reviving their company? Naturally, they were given Allstate policies
to sell. Most of these agents were located in urban areas, the market
that Allstate had not yet cracked. As these agents began working out
of Sears retail stores in the bigger cities, they became the core of the
over-the-counter sales force.

Meanwhile, Allstate had renamed the old company Hercules Life
Insurance, after the brand name then used for Sears work clothes.
Although the company's life insurance had been sold mainly by
agents, under Allstate control the major selling was still through the
mail. After all, Allstate had gotten off to a solid start that way.
Hercules was, in fact, a far larger company than Allstate, but that
only meant that when it suffered a loss, as it did, the profit made by
the original Sears company was completely wiped out. It did not take
long for Wood to act, and Allstate quickly unloaded Hercules. The
General did not try to hide the reason for the failure. "We can't sell
life insurance from a catalog."

Relieved of this burden, Allstate continued its expansion without
interruption. Branch offices were established in major cities around
the country. Even World War II could not slow its growth. Gasoline
rationing and a resulting cut in auto insurance rates seemed to have
no effect on Allstate's fortunes. Though In 1943 there was only a
limited increase in premiums, more importantly, between 1940 and
1945, the number of policies written rose from 138,000 to 327,000.
Perhaps the big reason for the company's ability to weather the war
was the requirement adopted by many states in 1944 that a driver
would have to prove that he could pay for injuries or damages
resulting from his driving in order to get a license. Allstate began
advertising aggressively for this business, and its greatest asset was
its convenient and well-known location in Sears stores. Many people
would wait to buy their required insurance until the last minute and
then hurry down to the Sears store. One night, on the eve of a new

law's going into force, people lined up in one major Sears store just as it was due to close. The manager decided to keep it open a couple of hours longer but finally told the Allstate salesmen that he could not keep the entire retail operation open for just their business. With that, the insurance salespeople borrowed some card tables and moved onto the sidewalk in front of the store. They took applications far into the night, until every person on line had been served.

But Allstate also had something of an advantage over other companies. Officials immediately recognized that the war would strip the company of most of its sales forces. In 1942, it began hiring and training women as insurance agents to fill each vacancy as it was created. Previously, insurance had not been considered women's work, and even Allstate's new staff were told that they had been hired only "for the duration." They would have to give up their jobs when the men came back home from war. Some women stayed with the company after the war, allowing returning servicemen to staff the company's expansion. Gradually, however, the women were phased out and replaced by men. Despite Allstate's wartime success with women, the stereotype died hard.

General Wood was accurately forecasting the continued expansion of the postwar American economy, on the basis of the increased popularity of the automobile. So it stood to reason that Allstate should ride the crest of the wave. But the old merchandising techniques would not be good enough. The decision to push expansion as hard as possible led to one of the most dazzling examples of growth in the insurance industry. Less than three decades later, Allstate would be the second largest insurance company in the world.

Sears had never been much for national advertising until 1952, and it started slowly. In fact, most of the company spending on national ad campaigns in the early years would go for Allstate. The insurance company's research had revealed that many people did not actually shop around for insurance. The success of the direct-mail selling effort was adequate proof of that. Allstate could add policyholders if it would reach out to them, management thought. One way was to send agents from behind the counters to make house calls. But a far more important way was to advertise the product.

In the summer of 1951, Allstate officials set to work on a major advertising campaign. Obviously, it would be impossible to explain coverages in detail in ads. Instead, the company must try to give people a feeling of confidence in Allstate's policies and service. Easier said than done. A lot of slogans were "run up the flagpole," but nobody "saluted." Then Dave Ellis, a longtime Allstate executive, began searching his own experience in hopes of coming up with an idea. He remembered his own concern a few months earlier when his youngest daughter had fallen ill with hepatitis just before her high school graduation. When she was taken to the hospital, he had hurried home, concerned about her condition. But his wife had reassured him. "The hospital says not to worry. We're in good hands with Dr. _____." When Ellis told the story, the case-hardened admen jumped at the slogan, which was to become one of the most famous in the annals of Madison Avenue. Ellis also suggested that the phrase be illustrated by a pair of hands cradling a car. Later, a home and figures of people were added as the company expanded its coverage. The advertising campaign using Ellis's idea is over a quarter of a century old and still serves to identify Allstate.

Mail order was just the first of many innovations by Allstate, some of which would become the focus of the ad campaign. As early as 1939, it had established a rating plan permitting a far more sophisticated appreciation of the risks inherent in each driver. This allowed the company to lower some rates that had been set artificially high because some people were placed in overly broad classes. Another service, begun in 1946, authorized agents to arrange auto financing through banks and to sell Allstate insurance in a single package. The "Illustrator Policy" was an early attempt to make the arcane language of insurance understandable to clients. Each phrase in the policy was accompanied by a drawing and a simple caption. For example, the policy read, "To pay for loss or damage to the automobile, hereinafter called loss, caused by collision of the automobile with another object, or by upset of the automobile, but only for the amount of each such loss in excess of the deductible amount, if any, stated in the declarations as applicable hereto." The caption read: "When your own car is bumped or smashed-up." Perhaps the short form was hardly a paragon of full disclosure, but it was a step in the right direction, and it helped sell policies.

In 1952, the company had created the Allstate Foundation. One of its major programs was backing college courses to train high school teachers as driving instructors. Some $1.2 million was spent on this program, which, before it was over, had aided 15,000 teachers. The object of these grants was to improve driving by young people and reduce their accident rate. Some 6.5 million high school students went through courses taught by Allstate-trained people. As part of its attack on the problem of young drivers, Allstate began offering in 1953 a 15 percent discount on premiums for policies covering young drivers who had completed approved courses. Seven years later, Allstate began a good drivers plan, which allowed discounts for drivers who had avoided accidents.

This attempt to regard those who had better training and fewer accidents helped attract customers. And, of course, it reduced the claim payments that the company would be forced to make. Gradually Allstate was evolving a corporate image as it tried to find ways of reducing its claims burden. It began to promote publicly new devices and programs that would reduce accidents. Often its proposals would cause a collision—between Allstate and the automobile manufacturers in Detroit.

"We cultivate the maverick image," says an Allstate official at the company's sprawling, modern headquarters in Northbrook, Illinois. As he gazes out of his window overlooking one of the Interstates speeding motorists into Chicago, he admits the image is in the company's self-interest. Reward safety and you pay fewer claims or at least less expensive ones. And this policy also makes Allstate a good citizen. If drivers ask for equipment that makes them safer drivers in order to pay lower insurance premiums, the company is actually using them to put pressure on Detroit and on the rulesmakers in Washington. Competing companies are forced to follow suit or risk losing business to Allstate.

As part of this program, Allstate began offering a compact-car discount in 1959. This saving now amounts to 15 percent for owners of small American and foreign cars. When it was introduced, relatively few American-made cars qualified, and Allstate's action was seen as pressure on Detroit to step up production of compacts. Even more important, Allstate was taking sides in one of the debates that has become an institution among drivers: Are small cars safer, or are damage and injury more likely in them whenever they are involved in an accident? By offering the compact discount policy, Allstate as much as said that its experience showed that you were likely to be safer in a small car because you would less often be involved in accidents. Detroit groaned.

In its extensive advertising campaign, Allstate also took after drunken drivers. Company officials had to insist on going ahead with this program over the objections of Allstate's own ad agency. The Madison Avenue men argued that the company was gratuitously interfering with people's private lives; that by such meddling, Allstate would turn away prospective customers who, although they did not drink to excess, would resent the company's telling them how to conduct their personal lives. Allstate was undeterred and became a major promoter of the use of alcohol tests for possible drunken drivers. Eventually, of course, the use of breath tests and other devices became commonplace, as did advertisements cautioning against mixing driving and drink. The company seems never to have suffered a backlash, despite the worries of the admen.

Research at Allstate indicated that the cost of low-speed crashes was out of proportion to the repair expenses on higher-speed collisions. As a result, the company began lobbying for the installation of bumpers that would sustain impacts at low speed and simultaneously prevent any damage. In 1970, it introduced a 20 percent discount for cars that could sustain an impact of 5 miles an hour on either the front or rear bumper. Auto manufacturers saw this campaign as a way of forcing them to build more elaborate bumpers and boost the price of their product. The federal government was in the middle, and, a year after Allstate introduced its discount, it required that all 1973 model cars be able to take some stress, although not up to the company's standard. In the end, car manufacturers began to produce bumpers that met or exceeded the federal standard, and Allstate, although its own goal had not been completely met, could take credit for the improvement.

When the energy crisis struck in 1973–1974, Allstate, through its national advertising, became a major promoter of car pools. A policyholder might save as much as 22 percent on his or her premiums by joining a car pool. Clearly, that would save gas, but it would also reduce the responsibility for an accident of any person who joined.

Repeatedly, Allstate had clashed with the automobile makers. Every conflict had put Congress and the United States Department of Transportation in the middle. Allstate was a profit-making business, hardly a do-good consumer group. Yet it kept pushing for tougher safety standards and was not easily dismissed by Washington. With its sizable corporate wealth, Allstate had access to the media in a way most consumer groups never will, and that, too, could make Washington uncomfortable. Its advertising budget is huge. In addition, it conducted tests on bumpers and air bags and then provided film clips for use on television news broadcasts. At the same time, the auto makers, sometimes with the help of the United Auto Workers, were able to mount a major counterattack in an effort to keep things as they were or at least slow developments that they opposed.

The ultimate conflict came over air bags, devices that inflate almost instantly on impact to cushion the driver and front-seat passenger in case of accident. The air bag is what is known in the business as a passive restraint, a way of holding back the passengers without their having done anything to protect themselves. It contrasts with the seat belt, which many people do not use, although their cars must be equipped with them. The federal government moved to force people to use belts through an interlock system that prevented cars from starting unless the belts were fastened, but many Americans rebelled and had the interlock dismantled. As a result, the government began looking around for a passive restraint whose installation it could reasonably require.

Some 60 percent of all auto accidents involve frontal collisions, with four-fifths of all deaths and injuries resulting from them. The Department of Transportation has already mandated the use of head restraints, which protect against most of the injuries from rear-end accidents. One safety engineer admits that side-impact accidents are "the Achilles heel," and protecting against injury from them will require structural changes in cars. Air bags offer protection against collisions over a 120-degree range in front of the car. They are deployed whenever the car decelerates suddenly by 12 miles per hour, thus providing some protection from all kinds of impacts. Although they do not require the use of a seat belt, a lap belt does insure added protection in the case of a roll-over or when the impact causes car doors to spring open. Air bags are not the only kind of passive restraint. Some experimentation has been conducted on three-point seat belts, which are attached to the door and go into place without any help from the passenger. The government has focused much more attention on air bags, which are more unobtrusive and are less likely to meet consumer resistance. But it is one thing to develop the concept of the air bag and quite another to get it into cars.

According to Allstate officials, the auto industry had acquired the technology to begin introducing air bags as early as 1972. But fearing that they would increase the cost of the cars they were trying to sell, they kept coming up with words of discouragement about their use. Ford actually ran tests, but it was hard for crusader Nader and others to obtain information from either suppliers or users about how well the air bags actually worked. Although Allstate people do not come right out and say it, their complaint about the reluctance of auto companies to introduce a workable safety feature leaves the implication that the auto makers fear that all the talk about safety will discourage people from driving.

Then Allstate conducted the first test of the air bag, using a real driver rather than a model. Its tests indicated that the air bag would not fire accidentally when the car went over a bump or sustained an impact other than a collision. Company officials were invited to appear on network television news programs, but when Allstate sought to purchase commercial time to explain its case for the air bag and show the film of its tests, it was refused on the grounds that the issue of air bags was "controversial." The company offered to pay for an equal amount of commercial time for those who opposed air bags, but the networks still refused. Obviously, nobody was going to step forward into the glare of publicity to oppose the safety device. Then, in early 1973, an event brought the case home. A man in an air bag–equipped car was driving in Chicago and suddenly blacked out. His vehicle hurtled into a police car, and the air bag inflated and then deflated as planned. The driver sustained almost no injury from the crash. The story was nationally covered.

Meanwhile, the Department of Transportation was conducting more studies and estimated that 9,000 to 15,000 deaths could be prevented annually if air bags were used. Perhaps half a million injuries could be avoided. Yet the automobile manufacturers claimed that the air bag would drive up the cost of their already expensive product. Allstate openly sneered at that judgment. "It would cost less than a vinyl roof or mag wheels," said one executive.

In late 1976, William Coleman, the Transportation Secretary in the Ford administration, decreed that two American auto makers should test the air bag in a limited number of cars to see just how much consumer resistance there would be. After that test, the government would make a new decision on requiring their use. Allstate was pleased that Coleman had accepted their arguments about how well air bags work but chafed at the delays before a final decision. One insurance industry official noted, "They came to all the right conclusions and made the wrong decision."

Brock Adams, the Transportation Secretary in the new Carter administration, apparently held the same view. A few months later, he said that auto makers would have to provide air bags or other passive restraints by 1984. Allstate lost no time in taking the credit, calling Adams's ruling "a victory and the culmination of seven years of dedicated support for passive restraints by Allstate."

In 1973, the company had begun a whopping 30 percent discount for cars with air bags. By the time of the Transportation Secretary's decision, other companies had begun to follow suit. The potential savings were likely to be greater than the added cost of putting the air bag in cars. So Allstate was confident about the ultimate outcome. But, as one official said with a trace of pride, "Detroit hates us."

In dealing with claims, Allstate has also found itself the center of controversy. Instead of sending cars involved in accidents to two or three estimators, Allstate uses its own claims adjusters. They are authorized to send insured cars to certain shops that guarantee their work and make repairs at an agreed price. A company official admits that, in handling 3 million auto claims, adjusters can make bad decisions, but he defends this system against the attacks of local shops who complain about the favoritism and who charge that Allstate people must be getting kickbacks from the preferred shops. Recently, they have had more to complain about because Allstate has begun operating test repair shops to improve management techniques and, more important, to gain practical shop experience as a way of checking on escalating shop charges. Some repair garages fear

that Allstate is preparing to go into the body-repair business or to
bludgeon them into lowering their charges. The company answers
that it is simply conducting research, but it is obviously trying to
bring repair charges under control.

This is the kind of controversy on which Allstate thrives. But the
company also finds itself the target of criticism that it would just as
soon avoid. Potentially the most damaging was the finding by Consumers Union that Allstate was the worst major automobile insurance company in the United States.

Periodically, *Consumer Reports,* the monthly magazine published
by Consumers Union, reviews the auto insurance business. In 1969,
as part of its membership questionnaire sent to more than 1.4 million
subscribers, it asked about auto insurance and received 230,871 responses. On the basis of the answers, it rated some 24 companies. The
ratings covered their activities over the preceding five years. The
verdict on Allstate was dismal.

Each company was rated on the basis of several aspects of the
insurance business. One of these was first-party claims, those made
by the insured against his or her own company. The consumer
organization suggested that most companies would provide good
service on these claims in order not to lose customers. That means
promptly settling the claim, as well as making what the customer
regards as an adequate payment. But Consumers Union found that
Allstate had a "much poorer than average handling of first-party
claims." From time to time, someone will make claims against the
insurance company of the other person involved in an accident. This
is a so-called third-party claim. Here, insurance companies may
provide less satisfaction because they are not dealing with their own
customers. Allstate's handling was rated "poorer than average."

Beyond looking at claims, the Consumers Union report selected
policy cancellation, refusals to renew, and big increases in premiums
as factors entering into an evaluation of the auto insurance companies. Allstate guarantees that after a policy has been in force for at
least 60 days, it will renew the policy for five years. That pledge gave
it a "much lower than average incidence of refusals to renew policies." But the study showed that Allstate had a "much higher incidence of policy cancellations," probably in those first 60 days. During that time, the company could investigate the background of new

policyholders, and, if it found they had an unsatisfactory record with their previous insurer, it could still cancel. In other words, the no-cut clause was extended in practice to the better risks. For those who got the five-year guarantee, the company would, according to Consumers Union, introduce "big step-ups of premiums." In other words, you were sure to be covered, but you had no protection against big price increases, other than cancelling the policy yourself. By contrast, State Farm was top-rated by Consumers Union and got an excellent comment for each phase of its handling of policies. State Farm is the largest automobile insurance company and Allstate's biggest competition.

When the consumer study appeared in June 1970, there was "a great deal of indignation" at Allstate headquarters, according to a spokesman. He said that the report was "like rating Babe Ruth, Lou Gehrig, and Stan Musial." The meaning was clear: A bunch of heavy hitters were being compared, and each had its own strong points that far outweighed the negatives. Allstate's sharpest attack was reserved for the way Consumers Union had built its sample. The company would have preferred a statistically representative sample of the American people to the self-selected sample of *Consumer Reports* readers, admittedly an elite group. It also claimed that too many *Consumer Reports* readers were located in the East to give a fair national picture.

But the report was "a matter of concern," says one official. "We checked our system out. We couldn't find that much difference from the other companies." Allstate concluded that State Farm had done better on settling claims because it had given its agents, rather than adjusters, the right to make small settlements. Allstate maintained, however, that State Farm had lost money handling claims in that way.

For Allstate, the bottom line was whether consumers themselves indicated any lack of confidence in the company. Sales continued to grow at a steady rate, despite the report. The obvious implication, for the company at least, was that if policies were not good, a company the size of Allstate would experience some loss of consumer confidence. "If what they said were true," said one Allstate man, "we wouldn't be able to grow."

Despite the company's continued good sales after the *Consumer*

Reports article, no conclusion that the findings were untrue can be drawn. The article cannot be used in advertising; so Allstate's competitors could not mention it, and obviously a great many people are simply unaware of the findings of Consumers Union. Perhaps even more significant is the amount of advertising done by Allstate. Massive ad campaigns could obviously sell policies, even in the face of a negative comment by Consumers Union.

Allstate had made some valid criticisms about the selection of the sample. Even *Consumer Reports* seemed to be on the defensive in an article accompanying the ratings, entitled "How Reliable Is This Survey?" In 1977, as the magazine was preparing a new survey, its representatives met with Allstate officials to discuss their sampling technique and other aspects of the study. The company was somewhat more reassured about the study and professed confidence about the expected results, not yet available.

The company's advertising may be the source of some of its troubles. Take a 1977 ad for Allstate's "Circle of Life" plan, a policy issued by Allstate Life, which was founded in 1957, when the company was ready to attempt the life insurance business again. "Circle of Life" advertising is mailed to Sears credit card customers. The policy provides a decreasing level of protection over time for a fixed $7.50 per month premium. This is the reverse of many traditional policies, which increase the premium as the policyholder grows older in order to maintain the same level of death benefits. But Allstate makes a virtue of not increasing the premium. It also makes payment convenient by charging the premium to the credit card, although it must be paid each month and cannot be financed. However, for a person buying a life insurance policy, a most important purchase, Allstate provides too little information. The promotional material makes vague reference to the cash values built up under the plan, but nowhere does it list them, as it does the death benefit at each age. Because the material also fails to mention whether the policy may be canceled or paid up at any time, the prospective purchaser is left with the impression that he or she will be paying premiums forever. The credit card holder is asked to complete a simple application form, and then the policy will be issued. "But to give you every possible 'consumer advantage,' we offer a TEN DAY FREE REVIEW PERIOD!" This review period is now a standard feature of Allstate policies and at first glance looks like the old Satisfaction Guaranteed policy. In fact, it is a good merchandising technique because the company knows that once a policy has been ordered, relatively few customers are going to wade through the fine print and then return the policy. As an example of contemporary direct-mail selling, the material sent on the "Circle of Life" plan is outstanding. Whether that is the proper way to sell as important a service as life insurance is likely to be open to question, especially for consumer advocatess.

Over the years Allstate has expanded its services to include virtually all major varieties of insurance. Its "full circle of protection" includes fire, personal theft, homeowners, personal health, and boat owners, plus commercial coverage. It also writes group insurance. In addition, the company has taken on a host of other activities: a motor club, a financing operation, savings and loan, mortgage banking, insurance inspection, safety engineering, and a mutual fund. The "little" Sears subsidiary begun in the depths of the depression is now just about as big as two of the parent company's competitors: Montgomery Ward and J. C. Penney.

The Allstate subsidiaries cushioned the company from the shock of the 1973 recession, the worst economic decline since the depression. But because the company is still essentially an automobile insurer, the recession hit hard. Allstate, like other auto insurance companies, found itself facing rapidly escalating claims costs, while state regulators attempted to hold down premiums. The result was huge underwriting losses in 1974 and following years. Allstate, which sells nearly 20 percent of the auto insurance in New Jersey, actually threatened to withdraw from the market there unless it were allowed to increase its premiums. It got a 25 percent boost. Some state insurance regulators want to take Allstate's investment income into account in calculating premiums, but the company is strongly opposed. It claims that without this income as a cushion, the underwriting losses on auto insurance would have caused the company as a whole to sustain a loss in the wake of the recession.

One analysis by an investment house found that "the year 1975 was by far the worst in the history of the casualty industry, particularly in automobile insurance underwriting." But it also reported that, despite its troubles, Allstate did better than the industry as a whole and increased its market share to 13.5 percent.

The recession was a major scare for Allstate, and downtown at the Sears Tower, the skidding insurance earnings complicated an already bad situation, the recession also having hit retail sales while inflation kept pushing costs up. But even during these trying times, you could not have found many at Sears who regretted General Wood's early decision to go into the insurance business. Over the long haul, the "good hands" company had brought in big profits. However, because of its sensitivity to economic conditions, its reliance on state insurance regulators, and its constant perusal by consumer advocates, Allstate will always represent something of a risk for Sears. Too bad Allstate does not have a policy for that.

CHAPTER 14

THE SEARS ARMY

Tom Biczak says his mother cried when he went to work for Sears. Having put him through Seton Hall College, after which he had spent two years in the army, she thought he should aspire to more. He was throwing it all away, just to be a storekeeper. Worse, his first job, as a management trainee, was on the receiving dock. It was enough to break a mother's heart.

When Tom left the army post at Fort Dix, New Jersey, for his job interview, he had never set foot in a Sears store. A city boy, he had always thought of Sears as a store for farmers. Tom got four job offers at the end of his army career. Montgomery Ward, Du Pont, and Federal Telephone all wanted him to come aboard. But he took the offer from Sears. Why? "Nobody talked about their company the way Sears people did."

So Tom went to work on the loading dock. He must have wondered if his mother were not right when Sears sent him to the toy department next. "Nobody wanted to run it," he says, so the new boy got the job. Then, he started climbing the executive ladder: housewares manager in Patterson, New Jersey; hardware manager in a succession of larger stores; customer service manager, assistant store manager, hard-lines manager, and at last, about 10 years after he had joined the company, he was given his own store. The people at territorial headquarters had been keeping an eye on him. To be given his own store in that short a period was a sign that he was a good Sears man. Two more store assignments came, with Tom finally in charge of a fairly large outlet.

As far as Tom is concerned, the story has a happy ending every payday. "I'm doing very well," he says, and to add extra emphasis he tells you, almost daring you to ask how much he makes, that the job is "extremely lucrative." Mrs. Biczak was wrong, after all. All of Tom's friends were becoming engineers, a job she would have liked for her son. But now, Tom makes more money than any of his old friends. And he obviously gets a big kick out of running a Sears, Roebuck store.

Tom Biczak's story is like that of most other store managers, indeed like that of many of the men who run Sears. Most are from humble backgrounds, graduates of colleges that will never play Harvard in football. They are the kind of people who can appreciate just how far they have come and, perhaps even more important, who can understand the value of their customers' dollars.

If you ask a current member of the Sears executive suite where the chairman of the board twenty years from now is working today, invariably the answer is that he is currently managing a retail store. In the army, you do not get to be a general unless you have had a battlefield command. It is just the same at Sears, and running a store is like leading an infantry company into battle.

Sears promotes from within. So many executives wear 10-year pins, 20-year pins, and 30-year pins that those without them stand out. That means there is no need to indoctrinate top executives in the Sears way of doing things. More important, store managers have been given considerable freedom to act for Sears, and if they have done well on the front lines, they are likely to do well in headquarters. The appealing result of this process is that the executive suite is not populated by a group of slick corporate types. It is easy to imagine most of them running a store.

The way Sears decides whom it wants to hire for the officer corps and who gets ahead is not left to chance. Tom Biczak remembers that he "took a test." Some people do not pass that "executive battery," which rates "personal character" as well as mental ability. And some who do are discouraged by a full description of the retail business that Sears dishes out before a job offer is made. Those that are hired may find themselves spending a week now and then pretending they are a store manager in an elaborate game organized by the company. In some situations, a group of young executives are given a problem to solve. No leader is designated, and no guidelines are handed out. But the company watches closely to see who will take charge and what methods are used. The cream gets to be store manager—in real life—before the rest of the crop.

In short, if you like the retail business, being an executive at Sears is not a bad life. In many positions, your earnings are determined by how well you do for the company because Sears does not want its best people leaving for places where they feel they would have more opportunity.

Being an employee, a "time-card" person rather than a "checklist" person, is quite different. Sears has 433,000 employees and most are on a "time card." The nature of the retail business dictates a relatively high turnover of these people and relatively low pay. Old-time retailers will tell you it could not work any other way. If Sears or any retailer offered high pay to its foot soldiers, it might be able to hold on to them longer, but its operating costs would skyrocket.

Julius Rosenwald knew this and, despite his many charities, offered no such largesse to the company's employees. His target was always to do just about what the other fellow was doing. Loyalty was a fine thing to cultivate among the people who ran the company, but to J. R. and his successors it was a luxury where the rest of the employees were concerned.

Because of his private generosity, Rosenwald was often under pressure to do more for Sears people. In fact, as a result of such pressure, one of Sears's most distinctive employee benefit programs was created. Faced with charges that low wages were driving Sears women to prostitution, Rosenwald decided to introduce a profit-sharing plan. This program was begun more than 50 years before employees' stock ownership plans would bloom and at a time when only Procter & Gamble, among the larger firms, had instituted a similar program.

The Sears profit-sharing plan has served as the company's basic retirement program. As late as 1977, *The New York Times* called it "revolutionary for its day." The most striking characteristic of the plan, one that has attracted considerable and sometimes sensational publicity for it, is that the size of Sears's contribution is a function of how much profit the company has made.

In the days of almost phenomenal company growth, average workers could retire as wealthy people. Perhaps the most well-known case and probably the wealthiest participant was a man who worked for Sears for over 40 years and retired in the 1950s with a $538,000 chunk of the fund. Although he was not a typical beneficiary of the profit-sharing plan, his golden handshake from the company was not the result of his having been a ranking officer either. In fact, there is a $15,000 ceiling on the salary base that can be used for contributions. The purpose of this limitation is to prevent a raid on the fund by the best-paid people.

Smaller, yet significant amounts, have been built up by today's workers. Although the company will not discuss individual participants, it will describe how the fund works for individual members at different levels. Each employee who has worked for the company for at least a year (or for two if he or she is a part-timer) contributes 5 percent of his or her salary up to a maximum of $750.

The company's contribution for each member has been more complicated because it depends on both the age and the length of service of each individual employee. Group A members have less than 5 years of service, whereas the most senior group D includes people with 15 years or more of service and who are over 50. A contribution by a member of group D is matched by an amount four times what a similar contribution by a member of Group A would get. In 1975, for example, a junior member got a thirty-six cent contribution from the company for each dollar deposited, and the most senior people got $1.44 for each dollar.

The company determines the amount of its contribution by taking the overall contribution to the fund each year and dividing it according to a formula that reflects the contributions and number of people in each group. The gross amount has been 11 percent of consolidated income—income before deduction of dividends, federal income taxes, and contributions to any pension plan.

Let us take a look, then, at how a typical employee would fare. A woman with four years of service earned $8,560 in 1975. She deposited $428.02 that year, and the company put in $154.09. To this was added $23.61 in earnings on the profit-sharing fund's investments in stocks of other companies and $20.66 in dividends on Sears stock held for the woman. The total income of $626.38 was invested in Sears stock for the most part, although some went into "general investments." In four years, she had put $1,340.67 into the fund, and her account was valued at $1,795. These results, while respectable, were not as spectacular as those in the fund's earlier years because the value of Sears stock had actually declined somewhat during the period this woman was participating in the profit-sharing fund.

Another employee, one with 25 years of service and 1975 earnings of $14,267 had an account worth $69,379. In 1975, some $6,563.14 was deposited to his account (including $2,606.36 in the increased value of his general investments), of which he had contributed only $713.33.

Obviously, the profit-sharing program is intended to have two incentives built into it. Employees are encouraged to stay with Sears and stay in the program because the amount of the company's contribution rises the longer they work for the company. And the bigger the company's profit in any year, the more money there is to share. In fact, these incentives do not mean much. Some 47 percent of participants have five years of service or less. Short tenure is characteristic of the retail business, and clearly the profit-sharing plan has not done anything to alter the pattern. Moreover, it is arguable that many Sears employees are prompted to redouble their efforts to help the company make a bigger profit just so their retirement account will grow more quickly. On the contrary, it would be natural for most of them to believe that their efforts were too insignificant to make any difference. Ask Sears employees how important the profit-sharing plan is to them, and most seem to shrug it off. Even the man who runs it admits that "it was never that great a factor" in attracting people to work for Sears.

As a retirement plan, Sears's profit sharing has worked reasonably well. Fund officials estimate that for people who stay with the company during their full working careers, profit sharing, coupled with social security payments, results in retirement pay of 75 to 125 percent of their pay in the last year. Upon withdrawal from the plan, an employee may be given shares of Sears stock, the stocks' cash value on that date, or a single premium annuity, an insurance policy guaranteeing the employee or survivor a fixed income. The value of investments in other companies' stock is paid over in cash. Although most retirees have little experience with the stock market, the vast majority of them take the Sears stock, probably in the belief that it will appreciate during their retirement years. Profit-sharing officials will help advise them on how to handle the stock so as to assure themselves of the necessary retirement income. Until August 1975, the company made a standing offer to buy back its own stock from retirees at the market price on the day the request was made. This feature was designed to save the retirees any brokerage expenses. But such a buy-back was made illegal by the Employees Retirement Income Security Act, the law some employers sometimes call Every Ridiculous Idea Since Adam.

E.R.I.S.A., as the law is known, caused big trouble for the Sears profit-sharing plan. It was not that the plan was doing anything wrong, but Individual Retirement Accounts (I.R.A.), do-it-yourself retirement plans made possible under E.R.I.S.A., were a temptation for Sears employees to drop out of profit sharing. (Under the I.R.A., a person whose employer does not have a formal retirement plan can start his or her own program and contribute up to $1,500 a year to it. The contribution can be deducted from income in calculating income taxes.) In fact, a rumor ran through the company that because of the new law, Sears was going to end profit sharing. Some long-time employees withdrew from the profit sharing plan, and newer employees refused to join, attracted by the advertising for the I.R.A. It was an unusually trying time for profit sharing, which Sears had always touted as obviously better than any other plan, and the fund had to wage its own countercampaign to hold its members.

Perhaps the challenge of I.R.A. was the last straw because, by 1977, the company recognized that, at 61 years of age, the profit-sharing plan was itself ready for retirement as Sears's main pension program. Social security payroll taxes had continued to climb, and, together with the 5 percent employee contribution to profit sharing, they took a big bite out of take-home pay. In addition, profit sharing did not cover many part-time workers, so that about 100,000 Sears employees had no retirement program at all. Under profit sharing, employees were allowed to make partial withdrawals before retirement under certain circumstances, but if they made a total withdrawal, they were not eligible to rejoin. All of these circumstances combined to make profit sharing much less attractive to employees and much less adequate as a retirement plan than when Rosenwald had first created it. In 1916, there had been no social security and no I.R.A. In the intervening years, both government and private programs had caught up with and, in many cases, passed Sears's profit sharing.

In addition to profit-sharing, which covers only salary and wages up to $15,000, Sears has operated a pension program for some 19,000 employees with salaries above that ceiling. This is a more usual pension plan, to which the employee makes no contribution. In 1977, Sears decided to expand this program and to establish a regular pension program for all employees. Unlike the profit-sharing plan, whose return was based on the performance of Sears stock, the principal fund asset, the new pension plan would provide a more certain retirement payment. In effect, the company was admitting that it could not promise continued steady growth in the value of Sears stock and recognized that it had an obligation to provide more retirement income security.

The new plan would deal with most of the major problems arising under profit sharing. Since Sears will now provide a regular pension program, most employees will not be able to set up I.R.A. More part-time employees should be able to participate in the pension plan because of somewhat eased eligibility rules. And changes in profit sharing itself will allow for even complete withdrawals, without preventing employees from later rejoining the plan.

Sears's contributions to the pension plan will amount to $69 million more in its first year of operation than it otherwise would have spent on retirement benefits. This was the price it had to pay in order to keep its retirement program on a par with American business. In later years, its added costs will decline because of major changes in what remains of the profit-sharing plan.

Rosenwald's original substitute for a retirement program is being transformed into a savings plan. Employees can choose to contribute nothing to it or amounts equal to from 2 to 5 percent of their compensation up to $15,000. The company will now provide 6 percent of its consolidated net earnings rather than the previous 11 percent. Gone are the classes of employee contributors. Instead the company's contribution will be divided pro rata on the basis of employees' contributions in a given year.

In the days before Sears announced these changes in its retirement program, rumors raced through Wall Street that the company was going to abandon profit sharing entirely. Employees of another corporation with a pension fund that had invested heavily in that firm's own stock had brought a suit complaining that the value of their pensions had been reduced because of a decrease in the value of the stock. If they were successful, that company, and perhaps Sears, could be forced to diversify the stock holdings of the pension plan. If Sears's profit sharing had been forced to sell company stock, the effect could have been serious because the fund is the largest shareholder in the company. By installing a new pension program and transforming profit sharing into a savings plan, Sears avoided a situation in which it might have had to divest itself of an enormous block of company stock.

At the beginning of 1976, the profit-sharing fund held 31 million shares of stock representing 19.6 percent of all outstanding shares. (Five years earlier, before I.R.A., the fund had owned 32.8 million shares, representing 21 percent.) At one time, this huge block of stock could be voted by Sears management, which composes the board of trustees of the plan. Some economists say that, in a widely held corporation, controlling 20 percent or more of the stock means controlling the corporation. Although this control never became critical, it offered management a good deal of reassurance, and it denied participants in the plan one of the supposed benefits of owning stock, the right to vote on corporate matters. In 1958, the company decided to extend voting rights to its own employees in the plan, about 291,000 people. Each April a "Voting Week" is held in all Sears units. Each participant receives a "Confidential Voting Instruction Form," which allows him or her to vote on issues coming before the company's annual meeting. The votes are sent to an outside accounting firm for tabulation and weighting according to the number of shares each participant holds. A profit-sharing fund committee, no member of which is a company officer or director, casts the votes in line with participants' instructions. The company has no way of knowing how each person voted. It has been argued that there is really no such thing as corporate democracy, that how shareholders vote makes little or no difference in how companies are run. That is probably true, but to the extent that stockholder voting has any meaning, Sears employees now have at least a theoretical say in how their company is run. Some other corporations use stock purchase plans that allow their employees to vote, but probably none in Sears's league gives such a high proportion of the total vote to its employees.

The profit-sharing plan is limited to incomes up to $15,000, but Sears has something special for employees with higher salaries: "incentive compensation." Perhaps even more important, however, it offers a stock-option plan to leading employees as a way of boosting their retirement kitty.

In addition to its retirement and savings programs, Sears has a stock-option plan. Certain top employees are given the right to buy a specific amount of company stock at the price prevailing on the offer date, determined from time to time by Sears directors, at any time for the next ten years or so. The expectation, of course, is that the value of the stock will increase during that period, and the favored employees will be able to realize a nice profit on the transaction. Since they will probably buy the stock from the company at the time they intend to sell it in the open market, the stock option plan amounts to a direct subsidy at the time the transaction is made.

But what happens when the value of the stock declines? In the early 1970s, when Sears stock was trading as high as 123.25, options for 2.4 million shares were granted at $116.44 and $101.13. Thereafter, however, Sears stock began falling as the company entered a crisis resulting from inflation and its rough competition from discounters. In late 1974, it had fallen to $41.50 per share. In order to cushion its key employees from the shock, the Sears board gave them the opportunity of cancelling their outstanding options and taking new ones at a lower purchase price. Among the major recipients of these moves were the top people in the company. For example, Chairman Arthur Wood was given 33,750 shares, and President Dean Swift got 41,250.

Murray Cohen, who owned 22 shares of Sears stock did not like what he saw as corporate favoritism. In March 1976, he and his wife sued Sears, attacking the validity of the stock-options exchanges. Said their lawyer, "The stockholder who paid his money and took his risk doesn't get these benefits." Cohen had the right to be peeved. Options that had been granted before February 1971 had brought company officials, some of them members of the board of directors, a net profit of $9.2 million. If Cohen had bought his stock and held on to it, he might actually have lost money during the same period.

In the face of the Cohen lawsuit, the company had to scramble. Top officials stoutly asserted "that no violation of federal securities laws occurred." But, just to be on the safe side, a special shareholders meeting was called for October 1976 to ratify the directors' decision. As *The Wall Street Journal* wrote, ". . . the company currently is in the unusual position of asking its stockholders to ratify actions of its directors well after the fact." Cohen had charged that the original options had been authorized by stockholders; so any change had to receive similar approval. Some 66 percent of the shares voted supported the directors' action, and the furor appeared to have been quieted.

Despite its notoriety and the clear implication that there are two classes of Sears employees, the stock-option plan is relatively minor compared with profit sharing. And, even though that plan is far less lucrative than stories about rich retirees imply, profit sharing is a worthy legacy of the Rosenwald days at Sears.

General Wood left no such gift to the company's workers. Like Rosenwald, he believed that Sears should offer employees no more than did its competitors, for to do otherwise would be to hand others an unwarranted advantage. But he went even further. Under the General, for all his professions of support for Roosevelt's New Deal, Sears became a union-busting company. If there was one piece of legislation that Roosevelt championed and Wood hated, it was the National Labor Relations Act. That was the law designed to give employees of any company the right to organize and to demand a union representation election. Under that law, management is banned from coercing workers, firing organizers, or refusing to bargain with a union selected by its employees. Under General Wood, Sears did all of these things.

In the annals of the American labor movement, one of the most hated names is that of the man *Fortune* magazine labeled "Nate Shefferman, Union Buster." In 1935, Shefferman first went to work for Sears, Roebuck and Company, but it was not until 22 years later that his activities became public. That was the heyday of the McClellan Committee on Improper Activities in the Labor or Management Field, the select committee that would uncover many of the illegal activities of the Teamsters Union. What Shefferman had done was equally shocking to many, even in the business community. Here is some of what *Fortune* wrote.

Of the many tales of flimflammery unfolded in the McClellan Committee's investigation, one in particular should give businessmen pause. . . . Nathan Shefferman was perhaps the most effective manipulator of industrial-relations problems in the retail field. . . . Through a variety of ingenious techniques he strove to single out, isolate, buy out, or discharge pro-union 'troublemakers' in a company, organize anti-union task forces of employees, and, if unionization seemed inevitable, to bring in a compliant union, usually Beck's Teamsters. . . . Neither Shefferman's rise nor subsequent influence would have been possible without the extraordinary encouragement of Sears, Roebuck and Co., the largest general merchandise chain in the country.

Shefferman started out as a small-time businessman, but his little schemes turned to dust during the depression. He had acquired some experience in personnel management, and when the National Labor Board was created under the National Recovery Administration, he wangled a job as mediator in the Philadelphia office. It was not long before he met Lessing Rosenwald, then the chairman of Sears. He was hired and moved to Chicago to begin his long and profitable relationship with Sears. At first, he would report to Thomas Carney, one of the key men at the company, who would later become president. Then, he would be responsible to C. B. Caldwell, a director and vice-president in charge of personnel. There was plenty of work for Shefferman because unions, in the heady days of the New Deal, were eager to organize. But Nate had his ways. He would encourage employees to air their complaints, so he could find out who the troublemakers were. He kept up a steady barrage of anti-union propaganda. When it looked as though a Sears unit might be organized, he would set up an employees council, a company union, instead.

But Shefferman was not good for Sears's image, and he was not as effective as he might be on his own. So the company encouraged him to set up his own firm, called Labor Relations Associates or L.R.A. Although Shefferman would remain a Sears employee until 1948, working for L.R.A. at the same time enabled him to undertake union-busting activities that might have embarrassed the company and even offended union customers. What is more, by working through L.R.A., Shefferman could provide his services to Sears suppliers as well.

The McClellan committee would gradually strip away the cover for Shefferman's operation. As *Fortune* later wrote, "It was at the Sears Boston stores that Shefferman's varied techniques came into full play." Sears had made a serious error in pulling out all the stops in Boston. One member of the McClellan committee happened to be the junior senator from Massachusetts, John F. Kennedy. Even worse, from Sears's viewpoint, the chief counsel was Robert Kennedy. Key staff members were Pierre Salinger, who in just a few years would be presidential press secretary and, briefly, United States Senator, and Walter Sheridan, the man whose investigations of the Teamsters resulted in convictions of top union officials for everything from tax evasion to jury tampering.

The troubles in Boston dated back to 1938. Harold Roitman, a clerk in the retail store, decided to try to organize his fellow workers in the Retail Clerks Union. He circulated among them, asking them to sign union membership cards. Although he met with some success, he gradually found that some people were quitting soon after signing up. Sears had been calling them to warn that they and other members of their families would lose their jobs if they held union cards. This kind of company coercion was possible at the time because the National Labor Relations Act had not yet been extended to the retail business.

Then, the company moved to set up its own Employees Council at the Boston store. Unfortunately, the personnel department tripped over itself and induced two company supporters to run for president of the local. They split the procompany vote, and Roitman found himself the head of the company union. Roitman took his job seriously and, with other members of the executive council, drew up bargaining demands to take to management. But Sears refused to deal with its own Employees Council, saying it would talk with its workers on an individual basis. Under Massachusetts law, a bargaining election was held, and the company was told it must negotiate with Roitman and his people.

Because the organization of the company union had not produced the desired results, Sears shifted over to outright union busting. The mail-order warehouse people, located in the same building as the store, had been organized by the Teamsters, and they went out on strike. Throwing up a picket line, they prevented other Sears employees, also Teamster members, from driving delivery trucks up to the plant. To get around this stalemate, Sears simply set up another company, which of course had no collective bargaining agreement with the Teamsters to handle its trucking operations. Suddenly the drivers were no longer Sears employees. (Today, much of Sears's trucking is done in this way.) The Teamsters Union offered no objection, and drivers felt themselves free, now that they no longer technically worked for Sears, to pass the picket lines. Just to be on the safe side, Sears arranged for shipments to be made in the middle of the night.

Meanwhile, the crumbling facade of union solidarity was also being undermined on the retail side. Roitman was told by the company to meet with Nathan Shefferman, who had just arrived from Chicago. The union man later recalled, ". . . throughout the conversation he made it clear that, if I was willing to give up the union activities that I was then engaged in, there would be a bright future for me, both in Sears, Roebuck, or, if I was interested, in his separate labor-relations activities." Roitman refused. So Sears transferred him, moving him from the main retail store, where he could be in contact with the workers, to an auto accessories shop some 50 yards away. Asked why he had been shifted, Roitman related that "the boys in the service station were going to take care of me, both by keeping me under surveillance and, as I recall it, there was a very active rumor that they were supposed to beat me up in the process." Roitman found out about the plan from the service station men themselves. Before Roitman left the company to go on to law school, he was able, working as an individual, to negotiate some improvements in working conditions. But the company always refused to bargain with its Employees Council, and there matters would rest for more than 10 years.

Roy Webber, a salesman in the furniture department, replaced Roitman in the frustrating job of president of the Sears, Roebuck Employees Council. Gradually, he came to the conclusion that the group would have to affiliate with the Retail Clerks Union, if it were to deal with the company effectively. In 1950, he told John Lind, a Retail Clerks organizer, that his people wanted to join because they were being "pushed around" by the company. But just before an NLRB election, Webber changed his mind, and the union lost. Webber had been given a $20-a-week raise. Within three years, he would regain his conscience. He again launched an organizing drive, and again Sears tried to buy him off. One company official offered him a job in South America, but he refused. Then, Vice-President Caldwell suggested to him a transfer to the Midwest. Again, he refused. The company stripped him of his $20 weekly increase, and soon after the workers voted to affiliate with the Retail Clerks, he was fired. Webber took his case to the NLRB, which ruled that he had been discharged for his union activities, a violation of the law. Even then, Sears, working through L.R.A., tried to convince him to take a $2,000 settlement instead of insisting on reinstatement. Again Webber refused. Two years later, Sears fired him again, and this time Webber gave up the fight. Because of his organizing activities, his sales performance had declined, and that was the pretext used by Sears to get rid of him.

By the time of the 1953 vote in favor of the Retail Clerks Union, Sears was worried. They had been unable to get their own people elected to head the union or to convince known union sympathizers to come over to their side. It was time, past time, for Shefferman to bust the union. He assigned James Neilsen to do the job. Mr. Neilsen was an unpopular fellow in labor circles; so he almost always used aliases: Fred Warren, Jim Edwards, Jim Neil. This time, he was "James Guffy." His first step was to upset the vote that had already been taken by encouraging and financing a group of workers to claim that they were the real Sears, Roebuck Employees Council, and that the pro-union forces had usurped the name. That was one way to sow confusion and, Neilsen-Guffy hoped, prompt a new election. In the next two years, Shefferman's people wove intricate schemes all devoted to the single end of driving out the Retail Clerks.

One ploy, the most obvious, was to reinvigorate the company union. Angelo Giammasi, an employee in the parts and service department, had never wanted to sign up with the Retail Clerks; so he was a natural ally for Neilsen-Guffy. The Shefferman man began funneling Sears money to Giammasi for the express purpose of influencing employees to vote for the company union. The parts man could either put the money in his own pocket or use it to bribe his fellow workers. It is not clear what he did with the money, but he knew that simply by accepting it he was breaking the law. The

L.R.A. man admitted to Giammasi that what he was doing violated the Taft-Hartley Act.

Then, the Webber case went to the NLRB, along with other complaints by the Retail Clerks Union about Sears practices. Instead of leaving town, Neilsen simply changed hotels and names. Now he was Fred Warren. But Neilsen-Warren, who had a prior criminal record, knew that the NLRB was looking for him in Boston, and his days there were numbered. He had to be replaced by another L.R.A. man, Lou Jackson.

Sears worked closely with Jackson. When Giammasi complained that he was short of funds, Jackson arranged for Paul Rohrdanz, the personnel director that the company had sent in to work with L.R.A., to slip the company-union man an extra pay envelope. Giammasi sincerely believed in what he was doing. He wanted a return to the old company union. But Jackson had other ideas. L.R.A. merely wanted to talk up the company union as a way to strip away support from the Retail Clerks. Suddenly, Giammasi found he was having trouble getting the unaffiliated labor group on the ballot for the NLRB election. Just three days before the scheduled election, Jackson withdrew his support of Giammasi's efforts. When Giammasi went to see Jackson, the union-buster gave him a letter that had been drafted for his signature. It called upon Sears workers to vote for "no union." Giammasi balked. He had worked hard for the idea of a company union, and he resisted going back on his word. He had even written a letter in longhand to circulate among the employees urging them to support his position. But Jackson would have nothing of it. Instead, he had Sears mimeograph the letter L.R.A. had written, ostensibly from Giammasi, claiming that the company had been steadily improving conditions and calling for a "no union" vote.

Later, L.R.A. and Sears would try to get rid of Giammasi. Jackson said Sears would give him $1,000 if he would quit and start a printing business of his own. But Giammasi, a long-time Sears employee, was reluctant to go out on his own unless the company would guarantee him business for the next five years. Sears refused, and Giammasi stayed on.

The crowning blow to the organizational effort was arranged by Shefferman himself. John Lind, the man who had been an organizer for the Retail Clerks Union, shifted over to the Laundry Workers

Union, thanks to Shefferman's help. Apparently, he would have no more to do with trying to organize Sears. But he was actually to work for the Teamsters, which soon started an organizational drive in competition with the Retail Clerks. This use of a former Retail Clerks man to organize for a competing union, sure to confuse the workers, was "dirty pool" in labor circles, but the Teamsters were, at that time, on their way to expulsion from the American Federation of Labor. Lind approached one Sears worker, a James R. Donoghue, and got him to work on behalf of the Teamsters. Donoghue was paid $125 to put together a committee on behalf of the Teamsters. Then, just prior to the union election, Lind worked out a deal with Donoghue. The Teamster wanted to wreck his car and make it seem that the Retail Clerks had done it, in order to discredit them. Donoghue agreed on the condition "that nothing would happen to any of the people that were organizing that worked in the store for the Retail Clerks, and that agreement was accepted." Donoghue's car was left in the lot across the street from the Sears store, and Lind's agents ice-picked the tires and put a brick through a window. Donoghue's insurance took care of the window, and Sears, Roebuck and Company replaced the three damaged tubes. Donoghue was not charged for them. Instead Shefferman paid and was, of course, reimbursed when he submitted his expenses to the company.

Obviously, Shefferman had ways of getting the Teamsters to back his union-busting activities. It was clear that the Teamsters had no real interest of their own in organizing the Sears Boston retail clerks but were acting at Shefferman's request. In any case, they had no chance of winning an election because of some worker antipathy toward them, and because their effort was sufficient to disrupt the election but not enough to win it. How could Shefferman orchestrate another union in this way? It seems that Nate Shefferman was the great and good friend of Dave Beck, the head of the Teamsters.

Beck and Shefferman had met in the 1930s and had developed a mutually beneficial arrangement. They got along well personally, Shefferman's jokes and trinkets setting off the abstemiousness of Beck. "He always had a conversation piece," one Teamsters union official recalled. "And if you were interested, he would offer to supply one at a discount." Eventually Shefferman became Beck's personal buying agent. They also set up an informal partnership, which, among other deals, supplied the furnishings for the new Teamsters' headquarters building in Washington. Much of the work was done through Shefferman's Union Merchandising Company, and the biggest share of the profits of that company went to a cousin of Beck's wife.

As Beck's personal purchasing agent, Shefferman would cater to his friend's every whim. After the goods were shipped to Beck, Shefferman would send the bills to the Teamsters Union, which paid them through a public relations account. A lot of the goods came from Sears. Between 1948 and 1956, Shefferman bought $478,451.79 worth of merchandise from the company. Actually, because Sears gave Shefferman a big discount, the retail value of these items was even higher. Of this amount, some $94,000 worth was for Beck and his family, and another $19,600 was for another top Teamsters Union official. But Sears did not stop at providing merchandise to Shefferman for Beck's pleasure. It also covered his entertainment expenses for Beck and other union people. The company found itself reimbursing Shefferman for everything from air trips to deep-sea fishing excursions. No wonder that Beck was willing to lend his Teamsters to Shefferman for a few minor union-busting activities. And from Sears's point of view, it was a lot cheaper to buy Beck's help than to pay higher wages to the Boston employees.

Ultimately, Beck was indicted for defrauding his own union and for income tax evasion. One of the counts in the Beck indictments also charged Shefferman with participating in tax fraud. When Beck was packed off to prison, Shefferman was finished, discredited by the public disclosures of the McClellan Committee. Sears, Roebuck and Company was unscathed.

As for the Boston Sears's union election, Shefferman's L.R.A. was completely successful. The employees voted overwhelmingly in favor of no union, apparently because they were confused about the Retail Clerks (which many thought had withdrawn its active interest in organizing the store), the Teamsters, and the Sears Employees Council. In the end, Sears came out ahead. Even the company union it had been forced to tolerate since Roitman's time was swept away. It was a classic coup for Shefferman.

But how involved was Sears, Roebuck itself in Shefferman's operations? One executive did not like them at all. Thomas McDermott was manager of the Sears stores in the Boston area. When he learned what Neilson-Guffy was doing, he protested to the Sears territorial personnel officer. At the McClellan hearings, Robert Kennedy asked him why he did not approve of Guffy. "Because, No. 1, I didn't know what he was telling our people, and No. 2, I didn't care for the man personally, and I just didn't like him," McDermott replied. "I didn't think he was the type of individual who should be representing Sears, Roebuck and Co."

Obviously, Sears, Roebuck and Company had other ideas. They assigned Paul Rohrdanz to handle personnel matters in the Boston stores as a way of circumventing McDermott. At the McClellan hearings, Rohrdanz admitted, "Any request that Mr. Guffy might have, I was to fulfill, and report to the company what the requests were." Rohrdanz also worked with the Teamsters' organizing effort. Rohrdanz's help included putting a private investigator on the tail of union organizers, getting some of the most active union people transferred, and charging one of them with being a sexual deviate. In short, Rohrdanz, on behalf of Sears, played the same kind of hardball as Shefferman.

It was only when the Internal Revenue Service came around asking questions about Shefferman and Beck that Sears began to get nervous about its association with L.R.A. Although Shefferman continued to be paid, his services were no longer used. This was a major loss for Sears because the McClellan investigation had revealed that he had been active not only in Boston but also in a number of other cities, usually working through local retailers' associations, which in turn received financing from Sears. The hearings also revealed his anti-union efforts at Whirlpool, a partially owned Sears supplier.

Wallace Tudor, who had succeeded Caldwell as vice-president for personnel, repudiated Shefferman before the McClellan Committee.

> I want to state, with the utmost candor and conviction, that many of the activities engaged in by Labor Relations Associates and certain company personnel acting with them were inexcusable, unnecessary, and disgraceful. A repetition of these mistakes will not be tolerated by this company.

Later, committee investigator Sheridan would write of this statement:

This was in sharp contrast to the much less candid statements the top officials of Sears, Roebuck had made to me and Pierre Salinger during our investigation. They had also tried unsuccessfully to persuade Bob Kennedy not to hold hearings. Faced with public disclosure, they had finally severed their connection with Shefferman shortly before the hearings after having paid his organization $239,651.42 during the previous four years.

In view of Sears's attitude, counsel Kennedy was not willing to accept Tudor's repudiation without further probing.

> Mr. KENNEDY. It just occurs to me that you have seen the light awfully late, 1955 or 1956. . . .
>
> Mr. TUDOR. . . . I must say that it is evident that Mr. Caldwell gave Mr. Shefferman too much latitude and relied too much on his judgment and suggestions.
>
> Mr. KENNEDY. Is this all Mr. Caldwell's fault, then?
>
> Mr. TUDOR. . . . Well, Mr. Caldwell and Mr. Shefferman will have to assume their fair share of the responsibility for the situation in which we find ourselves today.
>
> Mr. KENNEDY. . . . I can't understand why somebody at the top of Sears didn't do something about it.
>
> Mr. TUDOR. An officer of the company, in Sears, as large as it is, has great latitude and great authority. It rested in Mr. Caldwell's hands. However, I am not convinced at all, in fact, I am certain that Mr. Caldwell was not aware of the intrigue that was going on in Boston.

It was convenient to make Caldwell the scapegoat because he had suffered a coronary, making it impossible for him to defend himself. Without his testimony, everybody else in the company could claim that they knew little about what he was doing.

Kennedy, however, was able to produce Raymond Holmes, a Sears employee, and the written report he had made to Caldwell about Boston in October 1953. The report makes it clear that Caldwell was aware of the union-busting activities there. Perhaps the most damning information in the report related to the need to circumvent McDermott, Sears's own man in charge.

In all, it was a sorry page in Sears's history, but it turned out to be no more than that. Even McClellan committee members treated the company gingerly. It remained for *Fortune* magazine to deliver the verdict of the Sears-Shefferman association, concluding that

> the record cannot be so easily expunged, nor the problem of responsibility so quietly evaded. Nor can one answer easily the baffling question as to why a company so extraordinarily self-conscious about its organizational structure welcomed such backstairs operations.

The answer seems obvious. Sears did not think it would be caught. Shefferman had operated freely for almost 20 years before his association with Beck and the McClellan committee investigations brought him down. What is more, Sears could always rationalize its actions by comparing them with what other retailers were doing.

Of course, the company would have to be more careful in the future. There were legal ways to accomplish its ends. One man sat through all of the hearings for Sears: Arthur Wood, then the company's general counsel. Chances are that, even after he became chairman of Sears, Roebuck and Company, he never forgot those uncomfortable days in the fall of 1957, in the caucus room of the Old Senate Office Building.

The kind of battles that Sears had fought under the General to keep unions out of the retail business have continued. Unionization has penetrated only certain Sears operations, particularly those relating to trucking and warehousing. These occupations are heavily unionized throughout the country; so Sears concedes no competitive advantage by letting unions, mostly the Teamsters, into these operations. But it continues to fight against the organization of its store employees by the Retail Clerks, as do other retailers, and it has been remarkably successful.

In only a few cities did Sears negotiate union contracts for its retail store employees. Such accords were usually signed in places where trade unionism was strong and the company ran the risk of losing an appreciable number of customers if it failed to deal with the Retail Clerks, an affiliate of the AFL-CIO. But the number of such contracts has been steadily declining because Sears does not want to bear the added expense that results from collective bargaining agreements.

San Francisco was one of the few locales where Sears had a contract with the Retail Clerks. Signed in 1937, the agreement covered only two downtown stores. The contract came up for renegotiation on August 1, 1972, but the union claimed that Sears failed even to make a proposal. The union demanded that Sears employees receive treatment equal to that of employees of other department stores in the area, a principle that the company was unwilling to accept. Discussions continued under an extension of the old contract, but no agreement was in sight.

Then, on August 21, 1973, a Teamsters local at Sears went out on strike, and other unions honored the picket lines. Soon the Retail Clerks, the Retail Store local, representing shoe department employees, the tv technician's union, and the servicemen's union, ended the contract extension with Sears and joined the picket line. Later, some Retail Clerks officials would feel that they had been betrayed by the Teamsters, who went back to work before the busy Christmas season. That move dashed the Retail Clerk's hopes of getting a contract requiring Sears to meet prevailing local conditions. But the strikers were getting to Sears, and, in January 1974, it offered a full proposal. The union argued that the offer was so bad that it was meant to be rejected, as a test to see if the Retail Clerks could survive in the Sears stores. Some union officials believed that Sears was attempting to retaliate against the union over an incident that had happened 14 years earlier. At that time, 262 union members had refused to cross the picket line thrown up by the Machinists and had been fired by Sears. Only after going to court was the union able to prove that such action by the workers was permitted under the existing contract. Sears was forced to reinstate the workers.

The 1974 strike attracted wide public attention. Mayor Joseph Alioto offered to mediate, but Sears refused. Local social action organizations and other unions backed the Retail Clerks. At stake was the survival of the union at Sears. It depended on just how long the company could withstand the unfavorable publicity.

W. J. Usery, the head of the Federal Mediation and Conciliation Service called both parties to Washington, but, even then, they could reach no agreement. Finally, Usery flew to Chicago and told Sears officials that they must come to some kind of an accord. The combined pressure from Usery and the San Francisco community was irresistable, and Sears and the union settled. On May 6, 1974, the new agreements were initialed.

But the battle was far from over. On January 31, 1975, while the new contract was still in effect, Sears closed its Mission Street store, one of the two that was unionized. Before the store closed, Sears and the union entered into talks concerning the placement of the Mission employees, and the company conducted interviews with the clear implication that workers would be given other jobs. Sears had offered to put the union people on a preferential hiring list for six months, but the union demanded a one-year period because the six-month offer would expire in July, well before the season when Sears usually added full-time personnel.

In fact, only one union member was offered a job by Sears. It was in a catalog sales office some 40 miles from the Mission store. Not only was the location inconvenient for the man, but he also had no chance of maintaining his income, which had been based on the amount of his sales.

The logical place for the Mission store employees to find work was at the nearby Geary Street store. Between January 1 and September 2, 1975, at least 64 new employees were hired there, but not one was a union member. According to one temporary worker, a student from Belfast, Ireland, all he had to do was walk in off the street in order to get a job.

Geary Street was the last Sears store under union contract in the San Francisco area. The Retail Clerks thought they knew why no union employees had been hired when, on September 2, a nonunion employee petitioned the NLRB for a decertification election, a procedure under which the employees can vote not to be represented by the Retail Clerks or any other union. Had Sears been hiring union personnel from its Mission store, the chances are good that there would have been no move to displace the union at the Geary store. But with the addition of new nonunion personnel, who the union claimed had not been given a copy of the union contract to examine when hired, as required in the agreement between Sears and the Retail Clerks, it was virtually certain that the Retail Clerks would be pushed out of their last foothold in the Sears San Francisco stores. By failure to show new workers the union contract, Sears, in effect, denied them the option of joining the union. In fact, just as soon as the decertification petition was filed, Sears stopped negotiating with the union on a new contract and refused to provide it with the names of new employees, as was required under the existing contract. In short, Sears began treating the union as though decertification had already taken place.

The Retail Clerks Union complained about Sears's tactics to the local office of the National Labor Relations Board. Without stating its reasons in detail, the NLRB turned down the complaint and complimented Sears for doing a good job in trying to place its Mission store employees. The case went to the NLRB in Washington on appeal, a procedure that has dragged on ever since.

Of the three cities where the Retail Clerks organized Sears stores —Seattle, San Francisco, and Detroit—it seems clear that they will retain a foothold only in Detroit, which is strongly union. The Retail Clerks have just about given up. Says L. O. Heilson, for 24 years a Sears employee and now an official of Local 1100 of the Retail Clerks in San Francisco, "We can't organize a retail store today under the law."

Current NLRB rules permit part-time help to vote in a union election on the same basis as full-time employees. The Retail Clerks claim that, if there is ever a threat of a union election, Sears can take on more part-time people who have no particular interest in the union. Sears can put them on three-hour shifts, so the company can avoid providing facilities and benefits for those workers.

Retailing is characterized by a high turnover, perhaps as much as 30 percent a year. Sears and other chains work their hardest during an organizational drive, when enough workers are signed up to demand an NLRB-supervised election, to discourage employees from joining the union. It is just at this point when violations of the law are most likely. But the NLRB may take from three to five years to issue its ruling, by which time almost all of the original employees have left. At that point, the whole process must be begun again. By this time, the union must give up, simply because its resources are limited.

The Retail Clerks understand why Sears pursues its anti-union policy. They calculate that a union contract would cost the company an additional $64 million a year to do business in California. So the union does not look to Sears to ease conditions for organizing. The union wants Congress to change the NLRB rules to limit voting by part-time personnel and to speed up its procedures. Walter Johnson, head of Local 1100, told a congressional committee, "Meaningful change in NLRB procedures would free more slaves than did Lincoln's Emancipation Proclamation."

If government rules on labor relations have allowed Sears to keep unions out of the retail business, other rules have forced Sears to make a radical change in its hiring and promotion practices. In the late 1960s, the Equal Employment Opportunity Commission (EEOC) began pressing Sears and several other large national corporations to improve their performance in employing women and members of minority groups. In 1973, the EEOC began considering a charge that Sears was violating the 1964 Civil Rights Act. The resulting reaction by the company would probably have disturbed and amazed the General.

The Sears affirmative action program began in 1968. By 1973, the company was ready to publish in its annual report what *Business and Society Review* called "the most complete disclosure ever made by a corporation on female and minority representation." That report showed an increase in black personnel from 7.6 to 11.1 percent since 1969. While the percentage of women working for Sears did not increase much during this period, at the top "officials and managers" level, it went from 19.7 to 27.6 percent, and at the "professionals level" it went from 14.7 to 48.7 percent.

In 1974, Sears stepped up its affirmative action program by instituting what it calls "Mandatory Achievement of Goals," or M.A.G. This system, administered out of the Sears Tower, requires unit managers at every level to meet specific hiring and promotion goals. The company has informed them that "they will be evaluated, compensated and promoted based on their performance in affirmative action as well as sales and profits." In fact, these are the only two measures of success at Sears: profits and affirmative action performance. The basis of M.A.G. is that every vacancy caused by the departure or promotion of a woman or minority group person must be filled by somebody from the same group. All other vacancies must be filled on a one-for-two basis: A woman or minority group person must go into one out of every two vacancies that occur.

Each unit manager is given a confidential affirmative action manual with his or her marching orders for the year. The manual puts M.A.G. into practical application, taking into account the actual availability of women and minority group personnel. In the 1976 book, for example, the company required that one out of every five appointments in "non-traditional job classifications for women," like automotive repairs, had to be filled by a woman. Interestingly, the reverse was true for positions usually held by women; in one out of five cases a man had to be named. In either situation, one out of two replacements had to be from a minority group. The manual indicates just what the company has in mind: "Example: you anticipate 6 full time commission sales openings. However 2 of them are minorities and women, with the remaining four being white men. MAG requires that the 2 be replaced 'in-kind' prior to making any other assignments to that job classification and *then* the one out of two (50%) rule applies to the remaining 4." As a result, the manager could end up with four minority employees and two white men. Managers are to report monthly on their progress. In that way, they follow the same data-gathering and monitoring system used effectively for operations.

Obviously, minority group goals have to reflect the local labor market. Wherever a minority is more than 2 percent of the population, it must be represented. But the manual is clear that if a store is located in a 100 percent black area, it must nonetheless have some white personnel. The company looks at a fairly wide "hiring area" for each unit. The manual requires managers to bring people in from fringe areas. "The fact that few if any of present employees come from these areas or that public transportation is poor or non-existent cannot continue to be used to excuse the absence of minority employees. Like their white counterparts they will have to be hired into our well-paid jobs such as commission sales and technicians so they can either afford the cost of transportation to that area or the cost of housing in that area."

The results of M.A.G. are impressive. By January 1977, women represented 35 percent of "officials and managers." In the "professionals," they held steady at 48.6 percent of the jobs, up from about 15 percent in 1969. Blacks had been moved into 13.4 percent of the jobs, up 5.8 percent from 1969, and held 6.4 percent of the top-level posts as "officials and managers" and 11.9 percent of sales positions.

This performance has not been exceeded by any other large American corporation. And the M.A.G. program is permanently installed at Sears.

To be sure, not everything went smoothly as M.A.G. was introduced. The company reports that "several members of management have been dismissed, and others have been disciplined as a result of the program." Ray Graham, the man who heads the affirmative action program in Chicago, recalls visiting balky store managers in the South and telling them they would have to accept the program or leave.

Graham says he gets good support from a top-level management committee whenever he wants to push harder. The program to involve minorities and women in Sears's operations has been extended beyond hiring. Graham's office has prepared a guide to serving as a Sears supplier in hopes of doing more business with minority-owned firms. Sears also funds Tower Ventures, a Minority Enterprise Small Business Investment Company created by the Commerce Department. Both Sears and the Small Business Administration channel funds to minority-owned businesses in hopes of getting them on their feet. Some of them become Sears suppliers. Increasingly, Sears puts its cash into minority-owned banks.

Some white men have left Sears, grumbling that they have lost their opportunity to advance because of the preference given to women and minority group members. Graham knows he is not the most popular man at Sears. He recognizes that he "may be in a career assignment." That is a tactful way of saying that he may never again be promoted. But he has already managed three Sears stores, and the conviction that he is doing something worthwhile for the company is etched into everything he says. His family spurs him on. His daughter is a young Sears executive, and she doesn't hesitate to report to him about her own experiences at the hands of patronizing bosses. Graham visibly bristles as he recalls the latest indignity to which she has been subjected. It keeps him going.

Graham, a white man, is the first to admit that Sears pursues what is probably the most aggressive affirmative action program for sound business reasons. Of course, it does not want to get into trouble with the EEOC. But beyond that it sees its future market growth among blacks. "There's greater purchasing power there than in all of Canada," he says. "How can we ignore this green power?"

Sears is careful not to put black executives only in the black community. One black store manager was sent into a city that Graham calls "the northern outpost of the K.K.K." Graham was not sure of the assignment, but the man wanted to go and has made a success of it.

Despite its undeniable accomplishment, Sears still has a long way to go. No women or minority group people participate in the high-level supervision of Sears's operations. Because these positions are filled by people who have been at Sears for decades, it will take time for women or minorities to reach this level. One Sears executive estimates that the process will take another 20 years.

Perhaps the most striking change is in the mentality of Sears executives—white men. If you take one aside privately and give him the chance to speak his mind, he will tell you, with all apparent sincerity, that he really believes that affirmative action is good for Sears. Almost invariably, you will find that he has a daughter who thinks so, too.

CHAPTER 15

FROM COUNTY AGENTS
TO MISTER ROGERS

Sears, Roebuck has used some curious ways to make a profit. It has shown farmers how to figure out the corn-hog ratio, given away an amazing 7 million copies of a publication called "Tips to Trappers," tried to run an urban renewal progran, operated a couple of foundations and radio stations, and sponsored "Mister Rogers' Neighborhood." Strange ways to make money? They call it public relations, and it is an art that Sears, Roebuck has been practicing since the early days of Julius Rosenwald.

The view at Sears headquarters has always been simple: If you help improve the lot and lives of people, you will probably turn them into good Sears customers. And if, along the way, you get some favorable notice for your efforts, others are bound to be impressed. This brand of business thinking is far from unique, but when it is actively pursued by a company the size of Sears, the company ends up having a potentially major impact on its society.

Sears's brand of public relations began with the farmers just as did the business itself. Perhaps the first concrete program emerged during congressional consideration of parcel post, when many rural merchants opposed this new system, which could only benefit the mail-order houses. While Sears muted its efforts on behalf of parcel post, Rosenwald made a bald bid for support among the farmers. In 1912, he offered to pay $1000—not an inconsiderable sum at that time—to any county that would add enough money to its budget to hire a trained agricultural expert, the county agent. Farmers, he reasoned, would be grateful for the agent, which might lead them to push for parcel post. In that year and the next, the company spent $110,000 to aid counties in Illinois, Wisconsin, Iowa, Indiana, Ohio, and Michigan, all states that happened to be in its prime marketing area. In 1914, Congress passed a law providing federal funds for this purpose, and Sears bowed out. Of course, Congress had also passed parcel post; so the company came out a double winner. So, it argued, did the farmers.

The recession of 1921 hit Sears customers hard, and Rosenwald determined that the company should do something to help them, not really out of altruism, but because it wanted them again prosperous. In 1923, Sears created the Agricultural Foundation, designed to be a profit-making institution devoted to helping farmers increase their income. At first, the Agricultural Foundation was essentially an educational institution. Should a farmer sell his corn or feed it to his pigs? The answer could be determined mathematically using the so-called corn-hog ratio, and the foundation helped farmers learn how to do it. But it also taught them how to deal with the care of livestock and the maintenance of the family homestead.

Perhaps the most unusual way of assisting farmers was the creation in 1924 of radio station WLS (for "World's Largest Store") in Chicago. This was one of the first stations to provide farmers with weather reports and market information, including timely price quotations. It was not a slick media effort. The station was run with a great deal of corny folksiness, calculated to impress the farmer with its informality. It also refused to sell advertising, which obviously would have brought in significant revenues. The aversion to selling time was not because of any early commitment to public radio. Sears was sure that anybody who wanted to buy time in order to reach farmers would be one of its competitors.

Ultimately, it took $500,000 a year to operate WLS. Because management could not calculate if this sizable expenditure actually brought in more customers, in 1928, Sears decided to sell. Samuel Insull, the Illinois utilities mogul, wanted to buy it. Rosenwald had an unalloyed dislike of Insull whom he had fought in Illinois politics and who, he feared, was trying to run the state. He was sure that Insull had no intention of operating the station, which he would combine with one of his own, for the benefit of the farmer. Eventually, a deal was struck with the *Prairie Farmer,* an Illinois farm magazine. In a short time, the magazine was pulling in a solid profit from the operation because it sold advertising.

In yet another program to help its customers, Sears established the Raw Fur Marketing Service in 1925. Many trappers thought they were not getting a fair price for their pelts, so Sears provided the service, at no cost to them. It promised that the furs would be properly graded and sold, with the trappers getting the full payment. The trappers obviously had more confidence in Sears than in the people with whom they had been dealing. This public service undoubtedly helped the company sell more traps and supplies. It was followed up by a Raw Wool Marketing Service and a Dressed Poultry Marketing Service.

The company also began sponsoring a wide variety of competitions for everything from cotton to canning to quilting. One of these attracted some 150,000 entries, not bad for a company then trying to break into the retail business in a big way. Sears was also interested in strengthening its reputation as a local store in face of the onslaught against chain stores. Through its store managers it started financing small community construction projects, on the condition that local people would contribute some materials, time, and labor.

Sears was concerned about the problems of farming in the South because a decline of income there could affect its sales. The basic problem seemed to be excessive reliance on a single-crop economy, but farmers were unwilling to take on more liverstock in order to run well-balanced farms. The company concluded that more direct action was needed and started the "cow-hog-hen" program operated through county agents. Through it, Sears actually distributed stock to young people. Another aid to farmers was the company's sponsorship of farmers' markets adjacent to Sears stores.

In 1936, Wood began a major program designed to help young people on farms gain a college education. Beyond its obvious benefit to both the company and students, the program brought Sears into close contact with the academic world. As the company biography reported: "The good will won from educators, from the recipients of the grants, and through word-of-mouth publicity has been very nearly incalculable." Yet another way of making contact with rural America while performing a public service was the production and distribution of films about farm safety.

Until the end of World War II, almost all of Sears's public relations activities were devoted to improving the company's image in rural areas. And all of the programs run by the company fell into the pattern of direct and independent action: See a need and do something about it without waiting for other agencies.

All the while Sears ran its agricultural programs, the country was changing, and so was the company's clientele. Although a big volume of sales was still done in rural areas, perhaps the typical Sears retail operation at the end of the war was located in an urban setting. These retail stores had not been "downtown" when they were built, but, just as Wood had foreseen, the center city expanded to include them. Although Wood was again pushing the company into new expansion outside the downtown area, the company had to deal with the city, where so many stores were located. It was simply impossible to make a sudden shift from city to suburb.

With three-quarters of its business now being done in urban retail stores, Sears decided to apply the same approach it had used with farmers. If it could keep the cities economically strong, it would save its market there. As a result, it became a major backer of the idea of urban renewal.

Urban renewal in the 1950s was a massive program because the deterioration of city neighborhoods was already well advanced. Sears was plagued with shoplifting and found it difficult to convince its best sales people to work in decaying neighborhoods. Even steady customers were reluctant to go to some stores. An urban renewal effort might change this situation, protecting the company's sizable investment in retail facilities, and it would also mean increased sales of Sears products to be used in the clean-up campaign.

To educate its own employees about the task at hand, the company produced a booklet called "The ABCs of Urban Renewal." The treatment was so objective and useful that the company was beseiged by requests from the general public for copies. A follow-up publication called "Citizens in Urban Renewal" was printed and provided a guide for setting up councils in which the company would participate to improve local conditions. Beyond that, because it found that it was increasingly being drawn into urban renewal problems, Sears began publishing a periodical called "Urban Renewal Observer," which it used to goad its staff into increasing their efforts, even intimating that their advancement depended on it.

Perhaps on the basis of the impact it had on rural America, Sears expected that it could change the condition of cities; but despite what were generally considered to be laudable efforts, it found that it could have little impact on urban decay. The problems there were a good deal more complex than in rural areas. On the farm, Sears had to contend with matters of education and economics. In the cities, deep-seated social problems were the cause of much of the decay. The company's program seemed to be admirably color blind, but the deterioration was due, in large measure, to the flight of a stable and more affluent white population, which left the center city heavily populated by blacks. Sears and other social planners were unprepared to deal with this kind of situation. In addition, however good the company's intentions, saving its urban market could only be a holding action. Downtown locations could not offer the parking space required for the stores to handle the sales volume that Wood had correctly predicted would be available. Twenty years later, it would be common to speak of the "doughnut" society, in which the center city became the hole, emptied of its economic vitality. Looking back, a company public relations official asserts, "We weren't trying to solve the problems of urban America. We were trying to be the town crier." Even that more modest goal was only partially achieved. As a result, Sears would not in the future pursue a policy of direct and independent action designed to have a major impact on society.

Although Sears could not save its inner-city market through urban renewal, it did not simply board up its stores and leave. In 1977, it began a new experiment in St. Louis. When it closed a store there, it turned the building over to the Urban League. It continues to pay the $52,000 in annual property taxes, and it pays the civil rights organization $70,000 a year under a management contract.

"The last thing the area needed was another vacant building," says an Urban League official. But the group reasoned that if Sears could not make a commercial go of the store, neither could small businesses. It came up with the idea of a "supermarket of services," reasoning that government agencies would take space in the building because Sears's subsidy made low rental rates possible. The experiment seems to be working as many social welfare and educational agencies take space.

"We'd never done anything like this before," says a Sears man in Chicago. "What has happened has encouraged us at headquarters to carry the concept further." Sears may try the same formula in other cities, and other retailers are expected to follow suit.

Ever since its urban renewal campaign, Sears has been more of a conventional corporation in its public relations activities. "More" conventional, not completely conventional; because when Sears does almost anything, it does it big. According to an unpublished study by the Conference Board, a New York–based economic research outfit, Sears is the second largest source of corporate charity in the United States, ranking after Exxon, but ahead of such giants as General Motors and Mobil, which are a good deal larger. Corporations do not publish the figures detailing their gifts. As far back as 1941, the company said in its annual report: "It would certainly be in bad taste for a business firm to proclaim the qualities of its soul, or rhapsodize over how it has squared its conscience with its good deeds. It would be as gauche for a corporation to itemize and publish its real or imagined benefaction as for an individual to post in public places the record of his charities." But a little digging reveals that the company gives away around $19 million a year.

In its 1941 comment on charity, Sears implicitly admitted that contributions by corporations help "square its conscience." Does that mean Sears has something to apologize for? That is probably a matter for each executive to decide, for one person's sharp business practices may be perfectly acceptable to another. But, as a matter of company policy, making contributions is not a matter of salving the corporate conscience. It helps show that Sears is a good citizen and that is good for business.

In the same year during which it made its statement on charity, Sears began phasing out the Agricultural Foundation, some of whose activities were sales-promotional and designed to create profit for the company, and replaced it with the Sears-Roebuck Foundation, a nonprofit organization. All of the company's top officers serve on its board, and its top staff people are in corporate public relations. In recent years, Sears-Roebuck Foundation has concentrated on education and the arts.

The company has long been concerned about the development of American values that would undermine the free enterprise system. To a certain extent, this worry is a reflection of the personal opinions of the company's top management, people who, in general, do not favor increased government regulation or higher taxes for either Sears or its customers. Although one of the company's strengths has been to learn how to live with whatever government adopts, rather than to devote all of its efforts to opposing them, Sears has tried to get its free enterprise case across to the general public. The Sears-Roebuck Foundation is one of its chosen instruments.

Most of its educational programs are heavily influenced by these concerns. For example, elementary school teachers, selected by the Joint Council on Economic Education, are sent to summer workshops to gain a basic knowledge of economics, which they have not previously studied. Under the auspices of the Business and Professional Women's Foundation, the Sears-Roebuck Foundation has financed a program "to provide graduate business education for women so that the number of women in management jobs will be increased." It is even likely that some of those given loans under this program will end up working for Sears. In still another economic education program, the foundation aids full-time faculty members at institutions that are members of the American Assembly of Collegiate Schools of Business. These become fellows under a program developed by The Brookings Institution, allowing them to work in the federal government and to attend seminars on how government operates. Finally, through Purdue University, the foundation supports a kind of crash course on economic education for college faculty. Most participants come from state colleges in the Midwest. Because Sears operates in Latin America, the foundation also helps students from Central and South America participate in a program run by the Fletcher School at Tufts University, combining work as teaching fellows and in American companies.

Not all "charity begins at home" for the Sears-Roebuck Foundation, however. It helps some economically disadvantaged students from urban areas go to college. With the National Endowment for the Arts, it sends young performers into communities across the country, providing the recipients with partial incomes and the localities with exposure to talent that they might otherwise miss. It makes student emergency loans to vocational students in need. The Officer Friendly program, designed to help elementary school children learn about the role of their police departments, is funded by the foundation. It has developed a library of free loan films on everything from art appreciation to the job of the police. A major share of the foundation's spending goes for Individually Guided Education, special teacher-education materials used in a number of states. Another of the foundation's big programs involves making unrestricted grants to colleges and universities across the country. Finally, the foundation financed the production of "Mister Rogers' Neighborhood," a popular children's television program shown on public stations.

In 1976, the Sears, Roebuck Foundation distributed some $2.8 million, hardly on the scale of the mammoth Ford Foundation (which is not company-backed), but still significant. Often the foundation sticks with a program over the years and becomes its principal supporter. For example, between 1967 and 1975, it poured $2.1 million into "Mister Rogers' Neighborhood."

Despite the 1941 statement, Sears gets ample credit for the foundation's gifts. All store managers are also considered to be foundation representatives. They play an active role in looking for worthy projects and in selecting those colleges and universities that will receive grants. Local publicity often features the managers passing a foundation check to a college president or some other local notable.

Yet the gifts of the foundation, financed by annual contributions from the company, represent only 15 percent of what the company spends on what is called "civic affairs." Most of the rest of the multimillion dollar program is operated through the retail stores. Managers are authorized to make small contributions to the United Fund, chambers of commerce, and hospital fund drives. When they see a project in their areas to which they want the company to make a larger donation, the decision is discussed with a special committee at the territorial headquarters.

Because the store managers are given considerable discretion in making company donations, Sears has developed a set of guidelines. They are an interesting manifestation of the corporate approach to giving. The directives provide a general philosophy. "The company does not consider donations as mere charity, but rather as a wise investment of corporate funds in carefully selected charitable, civic, and welfare organizations or projects which improve the communities in which company units are located." More specific guidelines are designed to insure that giving follows local conventions and helps the company. Will the gift benefit the company? Does the program serve an important community need? How many people are reached? Does it discriminate on racial or other grounds? How heavy are its administrative costs? The guidelines also ask the store managers to determine if the amount of the gift is "consistent with the company's place in the community. What are other retailers giving?" Sears also wants the manager to forecast if one donation will lead to a flood of requests later from similar groups, establishing "a precedent impossible to maintain." The rules make it hard for a nonestablishment group to win a Sears gift. "Who are the people heading the organization which asks support? Are they recognized community leaders? What is their primary business or professional connection?"

A company official admits that inevitably Sears gets tied to the establishment in its efforts. The women's club, the symphony, the ballet, and the Boy Scouts are typical recipients. Many of these are groups sponsored by well-heeled members of the community, the kind of people Sears would like to have coming into its stores. In recent years, in part because of its past interest in the inner city, Sears has been drawn less frequently into supporting groups associated with the establishment. Because it has been moving vigorously in the area of employment for women and minorities, its donations have increasingly gone to local groups pushing their causes.

The clear purpose of channeling as much as $15 million through the retail stores is to enhance Sears's image as a local institution. Sears can afford to be on the contributors list of every worthy local cause, and its manager is instantly placed among the civic leaders in his or her market area. The division of funding between the nationally oriented foundation and the locally oriented retail stores shows that the company is still concerned about the competitive battle with local retailers.

One of the most often quoted sayings of Chairman Wood around Sears dates from 1938. "Business must account for its stewardship not only on the balance sheet, but also in matters of social responsibility." What the company's record over the years shows is that being socially responsible can also be a big help on the balance sheet. In fairness, Sears has never really tried to have people believe otherwise. That is why its program of corporate giving is firmly installed as a part of its public relations effort.

Aside from donations, public relations handles more traditonal image-improving activities as well. But Sears draws a very clear line and is somewhat uncharacteristic of business in its reluctance to talk about itself. A staff guide for public relations personnel says: "As one of the country's leading corporations, Sears is the object of interest both on the part of the news media and the general public. It is company policy to present, through the various news outlets, stories and other information that will satisfy the legitimate public interest in Sears and its operations."

Sears does publish brochures, but, like its charity, they are aimed more at improving the market than enhancing the company's image. Its publications are part of what Sears calls its "consumer information" program. They range from "How to Select Young Underfashions," designed to get young girls to start thinking about buying from Sears, to "Our Economic System," a weighty series of essays and teachers' guides to help build appreciation for the free enterprise system. Aside from an obvious effort to promote its own retail and catalog operations, Sears uses its publications and free films to try to stimulate an increased awareness of the role of the consumer and, in a more subtle way, a reduction of government intervention in free enterprise. Implicit in this dual approach is the belief that the consumer can be trained to protect himself and that business will have to respond to consumer pressures. If the consumer calls upon the government too much, he will end up paying the bill in the form of higher taxes.

In pushing this philosophy, Sears attempts to go through the existing educational structure. Its consumer and economic education publications are meant for use by primary and secondary school teachers. Undoubtedly, the attempt to change the public consciousness is viewed as a long-term effort.

In its educational efforts, Sears has become aligned with the Business Roundtable, a group of leaders of the largest corporations who believe that their companies' negative public images must be improved. They argue that people tend to be anti–big business, because they do not have all the facts about how the economy works. In 1975, the Business Roundtable sponsored a series of advertisements in Reader's Digest, its most well-known public campaign. The articles, a kind of "gee-whiz" view of the American economy, have been reprinted by Sears in one of its teacher's aids. What Sears does not tell its readers is that it is one of the backers of the Business Roundtable.

Using the Business Roundtable to make its case is characteristic of Sears's way of protecting its interests. Rarely, at any time in its history, has the company been openly involved in political or publicity efforts to protect its own interests. Although personnel in the public relations offices of each territorial headquarters have the job of keeping tabs on the political moves in the state that may affect the company, they try to avoid open political action. Almost invariably, Sears works through retailers' organizations, even though it may be the most important single member of them. Much the same is true on the national level. Retailers' groups give the desired impression of representing a considerable number of firms, and Sears appears to believe that "in union, there is strength." Also, the company avoids getting burned by any negative public or political reaction to the stands it takes by using the retailing organizations.

On the local level, Sears's store managers are urged to get directly involved in community organizations. The store managers can thus get the chance to press for the kind of local development they see as necessary to improve their market. Perhaps just as important, they are making friends for Sears and increasing its acceptance in the local business community, hence creating possibly valuable assets in times of adversity, such as during unsettled labor conditions.

Sears has the potential for considerable political clout. Although the American political scene has not yet experienced the emergence of the "Sears bloc," with more than 400,000 employees, almost all of them voters, it is a force not to be ignored. Stores are encouraged to sponsor candidates' forums. Politicians are invited to speak to employees on the store's premises during the morning hour when they must be at work to get ready for store opening time. Most candidates jump at the opportunity to address that kind of captive audience. Though this is a laudable civic action program, it also allows the store manager to meet people who will later serve in state legislatures and Congress, as well as in other responsible public posts. Then, later, if Sears wants to present its case to these people, it can do so through its store managers, who are, after all, constituents of these elected officials. This may seem a roundabout method of political action, but, again, Sears finds that if the company is seen as part of a group, in this case its own employees, it will have a better chance of wielding influence than if it represented itself simply as a big business.

There is one cute touch. When a senator or member of Congress has a birthday, employees in a Sears store in the state or district are encouraged to send a birthday card, signed by all of them, or even a cake. The gesture is sure to remind the official's staff, if not the officeholder, that there are a lot of people out there who not only wish the politician well, but who also are watching.

In all the furor over illegal political contributions to American politicians and bribes to foreign officials, Sears has survived unscathed. When the stories broke, top officials made a thorough inquiry into corporate political activity, but the company says it found no skeletons in its closet. It has not been the object of any charges. Actually, despite Julius Rosenwald's futile attempt to buy off a Republican senatorial candidate in the 1920s, such pay-offs would be uncharacteristic of a company full of executives as American as apple pie. In fact, Sears was so worried about the public reaction to the disclosures about other corporations that it delayed setting up a political action committee, a fund-raising operation to back political candidates, which is perfectly legal under the post-Watergate campaign reform laws. Eventually, such a fund could turn out to be a potent political force, given the numbers of Sears executives and stockholders. Sears employees could also create their own committee. In the meantime, in the aftermath of the news about illegal contributions, the company issued a strong reminder to its employees, warning them against such gifts and other unethical business practices. Even in this case, the company noted that the ultimate sanction for corporate misconduct could be a loss of public confidence. As is customary, the words of one of the giants, in this case General Wood, were brought out for their ritual salute. "The confidence of the American people in the values, the fairness and honesty of Sears, Roebuck and Co. is the most precious asset this company has. . . ."

CHAPTER 16

THE ORGANIZATION MEN

Sears was a little company that got big without even really knowing it. At first, organization was the epitome of centralization: Richard Sears made every decision. Even after he had gone and the company had passed through the "golden era" of mail-order sales, the same basic plan prevailed. The mail-order business lent itself to regimentation, and, as a result, Sears, Roebuck and Company could be run by a handful of men in Chicago.

Even when Sears made its first tentative moves into retail, the stores were placed, without much thought, under mail-order plant managers, themselves under tight control by Chicago. Perhaps, as much as anything, this extreme centralization reflected Rosenwald's style of doing business. He felt that Sears was, in a very literal sense, his company and that he should be able to control its direction. He had learned about business in the nineteenth century and would never depart from the idea that control must be centralized.

Once again, it was General Robert Wood who changed the basic mail-order structure to prepare the company for the new American economy he so clearly foresaw and specifically for retail operations. Immediately after he became president, he set up a committee of top executives and hired outside consultants to advise him on restructuring the company.

The key element of the new organizational plan, which was adopted in 1930, was that the single chain of command should be replaced by several. Henceforth, there would be direct communication between the top executive with a given specialty, merchandise for example, and any other management people in the field with responsibilities relating to that specialty. The idea was to get a fast response out to the field. Another essential part of the reorganization was the opening of four territorial offices. The heads of these offices were initially considered to be the "representative of the president," and, in later years, each would become something of a minipresident in his own right, exercising considerable discretionary power in his area.

The purpose of the change was decentralization. Unlike mail order, which could truly be a national operation, Wood believed that each retail store would have to be responsive to local conditions. He openly considered domination by Chicago as "interference," and so long as store managers continued to ring up profits, they were to be given a relatively free hand. In effect, by moving power to the territorial offices and setting up several lines of authority to each store, Wood could ensure greater autonomy for the store managers, the only people, besides himself, who had authority over the full scope of Sears's selling operations. And a natural outgrowth of the reform was to split retailing off from mail order at every level.

From the viewpoint of the store managers, however, the new arrangements were as much of a burden as a boon. They still had to follow directives coming down the various lines of authority and were frequently left with the impossible task of reconciling conflicting orders. Some of the new managers could not figure out to whom to report and about what. The depression served to relieve them of their problems because the company was forced to retrench. The territorial offices were abolished. As one employee recalled about the period of neocentralization, "Chicago praised and Chicago damned." Undoubtedly, there was a lot of "damning" because the object in those days was not making bigger profits, but avoiding losses.

The General had never really changed his views about stripping power from Chicago, and after the worst of the depression, decentralization gradually crept back. The successful store managers were given greater independence, but those whose balance sheets were disappointing were kept on a short rein. The larger stores were made subject only to general direction from headquarters, whereas the smaller ones were put under the supervision of district managers.

Districts were replaced by even larger zones, but Wood tried to limit their powers by restricting the size of their staffs. Just about the only area that was not decentralized in the process was buying.

In 1941, Wood pushed the process forward by appointing a vice-president in charge of the Pacific region. Five years later, Wood pronounced the experiment a major success. "Very great size in business creates what we describe in government as bureaucracy and red tape. . . . As a result of the Pacific experiment, we found that every function of the company except the buying function, could be completely decentralized, and that it was unnecessary except in the very rarest cases to refer anything to the company's headquarters in Chicago." Soon after, Wood divided up the rest of the country by adding four territories. The headquarters became a staff organization, except for merchandising.

Under the territorial headquarters, a new organizational structure gradually developed, designed to handle a rapidly increasing number of stores. Some of the largest stores would report directly to the territorial vice-president, but most would be put under the supervision of smaller headquarters. The large stores located in a relatively compact territory, often a metropolitan area, would be placed under a group, whose head might also be a store manager. Just as the territorial staff kept certain functions at their level, the group would also have a staff for such matters as personnel, advertising, and credit. Smaller stores, more widely spread, would be placed in zones, the reincarnation of the old district manager arrangement. It, too, would have staff functions.

The new territorial system placed both catalog and retail operations under field supervision. Each Catalog Merchandise Distribution Center would be responsible for the catalog sales desks and other catalog outlets within its area. Then, the head of the catalog plant would report directly to the territorial vice-president.

The postwar reform was heavily dependent on the people who filled a whole series of new administrative posts. This meant that even greater emphasis would be placed on developing future leaders within the ranks and then bringing them up to positions of greater responsibility. In fact, it was unlikely that store managers would readily take orders from people who had been brought in from the outside. At the same time, the reform offered the possibility of advancement as a reward for top performance in the stores.

Was Wood throwing away the advantages of centralized operation by spreading responsibility? He recognized the danger, and, in 1948, he wrote a letter of warning to company officers.

> We complain about government in business, we stress the advantages of the free enterprise system, we complain about the totalitarian state, but in our industrial organizations, in our striving for efficiency we have created more or less of a totalitarian organization in industry, particularly in large industry. The problem of retaining our efficiency and discipline in these large organizations and yet allowing our people to express themselves, to exercise initiative and to have some voice in the affairs of the organization is the greatest problem for large industrial organizations to solve.

As Sears expanded and prospered in the post–World War II period, it was easy to believe that the decentralization of the company was responsible. By then, the General had become something of a corporate deity, with a reputation for imperious infallibility. The General had decreed decentralization; so it must be right. The proof was in the profit reports. In fact, despite the serious question raised in the General's own letter, the company regarded the matter as settled. In the company biography, published just a year after Wood's warning, the verdict was delivered. "The Sears principle of decentralized retail administration is now the cornerstone of organization policy, responsible to a great extent for the company's retail success, as well as for some difficulties which occur now and then. . . . But company officers believe strongly that the advantages of decentralization far outweigh its disadvantages."

The problem with such an appraisal is that, unlike a scientific experiment, there is no "control," no way of knowing how things might have been if Sears had used a more centralized approach. What is more, it assigns the success to that part of the structure that had been decentralized rather than to one of those parts, such as buying, personnel, and advertising, that had not.

Toward the end of his long tenure in charge of Sears, General Wood increasingly believed that the key to the company's success was its organization, more then its merchandising, operating, or advertising. It was impossible to challenge him, and the people who advanced were those who had been the most apt students of his theory.

"While Presidents came and presidents went in those years following 1939, Board Chairman R. E. Wood went right on. Wood provided management continuity . . . ," reports the company biography. In fact, it could be reasonably argued that the General dominated management until 1968, when he retired from the company's board of directors.

After Lessing Rosenwald stepped down as chairman in 1939, Wood succeeded him and began to move into the presidency a series of men who were loyal to him and his ideas. The first was Thomas J. Carney, who had joined Sears, Roebuck in 1902 as a temporary employee in the shipping department. He had gone to work for Lessing in Philadelphia as operating manager in 1920 and had remained under the younger Rosenwald's tutelage ever after. By 1930, he was a top official at Chicago headquarters while Lessing kept his base of operations in Philadelphia. He was the logical choice for the presidency, because of both his familiarity with all aspects of the company's operations and his ability to work with Wood. And, for old-time employees who regarded him as one of the few top managers who were genuinely interested in them, he was a perfect transitional figure from the Rosenwalds to Wood.

Carney died in 1942 at the surprisingly young age of 56, considering that he had worked for Sears for 40 years. Wood then picked Arthur S. Barrows, a merchandiser who had followed him from Ward in 1926. When Barrows retired in 1946, he was replaced by Fowler B. McConnell. Although he, too, was an old-timer, having joined Sears in 1916 as a stockman, he had come to prominence as one of the General's top aides in the shift from catalog to retail operations.

A pattern was emerging. After General Wood himself, no man would serve as president or chairman without having been with Sears for decades. The General also wanted them to have had experience in retailing. Most important, the men at the top were always to recognize that there was a higher authority: the General himself.

In 1954, at the age of 75, Wood retired as chairman, the post he had made into the company's chief executive officer, just as had Julius Rosenwald. But his retirement did not mean that he had any less control over the selection of those who would carry on his policies.

The new chairman was Theodore Houser, perhaps Wood's closest associate in the management of the company. Houser had been one of the men responsible for developing Sears's merchandising system. A strong executive, he was also known as an intellectual, in marked contrast with the General, who had no such pretensions. Perhaps Houser's most important decision, while chairman, was to retire when he reached the age of 65 and to suggest that no successor should serve beyond that age. There is little doubt that, if he had wanted to, he could have stayed on longer.

With Houser's departure, McConnell was the logical candidate to move up from president to chairman. But the choice for president was less obvious, and several men hoped for the General's nod. But here an unseemly side of the General manifested itself in his dealings with the company's executives. As much as Wood had kept his personal, political, and social views out of his operation of Sears, he nonetheless allowed his anti-Semitism to rule his personnel policy.

Wood had told Tom Brooker, one of his top retail people, that, one day, he would be president. But after rising to the important post of vice-president in charge of factories, Brooker ran afoul of Wood. The story has it that Brooker had the General's only son, Bob, fired from one of Sears's suppliers. Actually, Brooker later maintained that he had not removed young Wood, but that the son had given the father that false impression. Clearly, the General had hoped for his son and indeed his whole family to succeed in a big way. Although his four daughters were not involved in the business, he set a goal for them by promising each a mink coat when she had her third child. They delivered, and so did he.

In the wake of Bob's controversial separation, Brooker left Sears to take charge of Whirlpool, in which Sears had a major interest. Although he might already have lost his chance to become president, his having joined Whirlpool meant the door was still left open a crack. But while he was at Whirlpool, Brooker gave the General the final excuse the slam it shut.

"To get wholesale distribution, I wanted to bring RCA into it—

it was necessary to bring RCA in," he later explained. "That meant dealing with General David Sarnoff, the head of RCA, and the General [Wood] didn't like Jews. But he saw he had to go along, and he did," said Brooker, who was not himself Jewish. Although Wood was forced to recognize that RCA's participation was vital to Whirlpool, he held Brooker responsible for bringing in Sarnoff's firm. Brooker's fate was sealed. He went to Montgomery Ward, which he eventually headed, and his record there indicated that his departure was a real loss to Sears.

Ed Gudeman had avoided any such conflict with Wood, who had originally hired him. Gudeman had risen to the post of vice-president in charge of merchandising, one of the top three or four jobs at Sears, and expected he would get his turn as president. He had more seniority than Austin Cushman, vice-president in Los Angeles, who also aspired to the position. But Wood made it clear that he did not want a Jewish president and thus that he could not accept Gudeman. It was one of those curious quirks of circumstance that Wood had received his job at the hands of Julius Rosenwald, a Jew, but refused to let a Jew succeed him. Some who knew Rosenwald suggest that he had thought that his own religious beliefs had been a detriment to the company's progress and specifically wanted to be replaced by a Christian. Even so, conditions had changed 30 years later. The General's actions were not motivated by such commercial calculations, but by his own views, developed in childhood and nourished by his belief that the Jews were among those who had been out to "get" him for his leadership of America First.

Because rejecting Gudeman in favor of Cushman would have divided the directors, Wood chose Charles Kellstadt, the man in charge of the Southern Territory. That spurred a round of resignations both of Gudeman's supporters and Cushman's, and Gudeman himself left in disappointment and disgust, after having helped create a merchandising operation without equal.

Brooker offered his former colleague a spot at Ward. "You be chairman, and I'll be president or I'll be chairman and you be president. It doesn't make any difference," Brooker told Gudeman. But Ed Gudeman would do no more than become a director and consultant to Ward. He turned his energies first to a partnership in Lehman Brothers, the New York investment house, and then to public service as under secretary of commerce in the Kennedy administration. Until the end of his life, he remained bitterly disappointed by his treatment at the hands of the General.

Kellstadt, appointed at the age of 61, obviously held only an interim appointment. As *Newsweek* wrote in 1961, "While no one will ever outrank the General in the Sears hierarchy, Charlie Kellstadt is doing his best to make a mark in the brief time allotted him." It was tough, because, even in his eighties, Wood was dropping into his office almost every day.

In 1962, Kellstadt, who had become chairman two years earlier, retired. He was replaced by Austin Cushman, who had been biding his time in Los Angeles. In the end, the General had his way.

The power struggle at the top had at last opened the way for some younger men. The combination of the General's having stayed as chairman until he was 75 and Houser's retirement policy had meant that none of the older executives would be able to head the corporation for more than four years. But, in 1960, the disruption of the chain of succession caused by the Gudeman affair led to the elevation of Crowdus Baker, a mail-order specialist, to the presidency at the tender age of 54. Baker would go no higher, in part because he lacked retail experience and had never headed a territory. In fact, some people at Sears wondered how he had ever reached the presidency because of his obvious "deficiencies." Baker would be the only Sears president to serve under three chairmen and would eventually be made vice-chairman, an honorific title designed to get him out of the chief operating officer's slot. Gordon Metcalf, brought in from the Mid-West territory, succeeded Cushman as chairman. With his appointment, the last of the Gudeman affair was liquidated.

The men who occupied the two top positions in the company in the quarter century after Wood formally resigned as chairman toiled in his shadow. They would actually represent an extension of his administration. Speaking of Sears, Rosenwald, and Wood, Cushman had said, "The rest of us who followed had the guts and the ability to work on their legacy." Little happened in that period to call the General's judgment into doubt because, thanks to his early decision to expand in the postwar period, Sears had far outdistanced its rivals.

But the world was changing, and Sears was slow to adjust to new competitive conditions. If anything, decentralization was allowed to

increase, with groups and zones proliferating all over the map. More
and more power came into the hands of the store managers, who had
the right to refuse to sell what the merchandising department had
selected.

Another problem was the direct result of the company's success.
It grew too big to be commanded by any one person with less
authority than the General. In effect, as the General grew older,
Sears had to admit that he could not be replaced.

The year after Metcalf became chairman was the turning point.
General Wood, at 89, retired from the board. (He died the next year.)
And a new president was appointed, representing as sharp a break
with the past as Sears would allow itself.

The new man was Arthur M. Wood, who, though no relation to
the General, had joined the company while the General was still
chairman. Arthur Wood was unlike his predecessors in not having
worked his way up through the ranks as a merchandiser. A graduate
of Harvard Law School, he had been in private practice in Chicago
when Thomas Carney had invited him to set up an in-house legal
department for Sears. He had not started at the bottom, and his
career was mostly as an administrator, first as counsel, then as comp-
troller. When it became clear that he might have a shot at the
company's top posts, he was sent to the field to learn the retail
business firsthand. Just as Cushman and Metcalf, he was put in
charge of the Far West Territory and then was briefly the head of
the Midwestern Territory, headquartered in Chicago.

Several factors appear to underlie Wood's grooming for the presidency and ultimately the chairmanship. He showed himself to be a
man of considerable executive ability. For a company in need of
organizational reform, he brought a different approach because of his
prime experience as an administrator rather than as a retailer. Yet
he was "safe" because of his long tenure with the company. (More
security for Sears came in the appointment of A. Dean Swift, a
retailer, as Arthur Wood's president. Although some years younger
than Wood, he had been with the company six years longer.) And
Wood would never be quoted as saying anything particularly witty
or revolutionary. Like J. Pierrepont Finch in *How to Succeed in
Business Without Really Trying,* he "played it the company way."
Said Arthur Wood, "I don't have a philosophy that differs from the

company's." Said one official who knew him, "Wood was, is, and always will be a very careful lawyer."

Not only did Arthur Wood face the problem of a company whose organizational structure was increasingly outdated and the difficulty of the succession to the General, but he also had to recognize that Sears was confronting strong, new competition. First had come a rash of discount houses, many of which failed. But they had an idea that was, after all, the basic Sears idea: If a company could buy in big enough lots, it should be able to pass on considerable savings of scale to customers. Ultimately, the best company at this kind of retailing emerged: S. S. Kresge Company's K marts. K mart had no frills, especially in the administrative realm. Store managers were given little discretion, and each store was a carbon copy of all the others. *The Wall Street Journal* concluded, "One plan of operation is obviously cheaper than 1,213 of them, and that is undoubtedly one reason for the K marts' huge success." The outside observer could not help but again be impressed by the analysts' instant ability to attribute retail success to how a company is organized.

Sears's management itself was impressed. K mart clearly had the key to rapidly expanding sales and had moved into second place, passing J. C. Penney and Montgomery Ward. It was time to look at what K mart was doing right.

In July 1976, all Sears management personnel received a letter from Arthur Wood, who had become board chairman in 1973. To an outsider, the letter might have seemed to be a bit of dry corporate prose, but to Sears executives, it was nothing short of a revolution. The company had reached one of those corporate turning points about which most people are completely unaware. So long as the goods are on the shelves and the prices are right, nobody much cares.

The letter mandated a reorganization of Sears's top executive staff, which would lead to increased centralization in the entire organization. In his cautious and methodical way, Arthur Wood had been planning and considering his move for several years. By the curious coincidence of names, it was possible to sum up the 1976 organizational reform in this way: "Chairman Wood is dead. Long live Chairman Wood."

The first and most obvious change was for Arthur Wood to share some of his responsibilities with three other people: the president; the

senior vice-president–merchandising; and the senior vice-president–
field. Just as the General's structure had come as the result of a
suggestion from an outside consultant, so, too, McKinsey and Company and Hay Associates had given the new Wood his cues. These
three executives and finance, operation, and planning people would
report to Wood. Though some might suggest that such a change was
only a way of dealing with personnel matters involving the people
affected, it seemed, in fact, to represent the first major change in the
way the company had been run since Julius Rosenwald had taken
over.

Perhaps, with no dominant personality like Richard Sears, J. R.,
or the General, it was time to do away with the "cult of the personality," and accept "collective leadership." The new Office of the Chairman was going to make decisions that had been left to the field, but
a council of four men would now make them, not just one.

On the selling side, the field vice-president was, according to
Wood's letter, given "responsibility for approving and issuing the
retail selling plan and for determining basic assortments and pricing
of price-impression and key promotional items." Behind this verbi-
age tolled the death knell of the independence of the store manager.

Now a retail selling plan would have to be followed. In that way
Sears hoped to realize the same economies of scale as discounters.
All stores already had had to accept a basic assortment of goods,
representing about 40 percent of their sales, and this selection would
now be determined centrally for the country as a whole. Pricing on
goods that represented 15 to 20 percent of sales would also be decided within the Office of the Chairman. That meant the store
managers would still have some price discretion, as indeed they do
at K marts, but in those stores where Sears wanted to push its price
advantage the most, the decisions made in Chicago would have to
be followed.

To accomplish this kind of control, nine merchandising groups
were created under the senior vice-president–merchandising, one of
the inner circle in Chicago. These groups supposedly reflect current
consumer buying habits: home appliances and home entertainment,
home improvements, home fashions, recreation and leisure, automotive accessories, women's apparel, women's accessories and speciali-
ties, men's apparel and furnishings, and children's and youth ap-

parel. If there was to be any real autonomy left, it would be among these groups, each of which would operate as something of an independent business. Structurally, the major change was that this same division along merchandising lines went right down through the administrative organization to the retail stores. By reporting from store to zone or group to territory to headquarters according to product line, store personnel would obviously be removed from the total control that had been exercised by store managers.

Store managers were supposed to help Sears meet local conditions, and, even under the 1976 reforms, that remains true. But the new structure is supposed to permit the stores to tell headquarters what works and what does not by an advisory method that stops short of allowing them to refuse to carry merchandise. The corporate programs are supposed to be designed to meet the needs of individual stores, but it is an open question whether Sears will end up like K mart, with most decisions requiring uniform response by the managers. One obvious reason why discretion at the local level must be limited is the national advertising campaigns that central price and marketing decisions require.

The General was worried that Sears, as a giant, would be too powerful. He could not prevent the company from becoming a giant and, of course, did not want to hamper its growth; so he spread power to all members. The result was a weak organization with slow reflexes. More then 20 years later, that approach is simply not good enough. K mart is not Montgomery Ward, which was so easily vanquished. It feels free to play by a different set of rules than the older chains. The kid is fast on his feet. As a result, the champion has been forced to trim down to meet his challenge.

Perhaps, because he lacked their colorful personalities, Arthur Wood will never be rated with Sears, Rosenwald, and the General. But his quiet revolution might prove to be as important to the company as some of their most vaunted innovations.

CHAPTER 17

WHERE AMERICA SHOPS?

"After decades of dominance, Sears, Roebuck and Co. is now just one of the boys," wrote *Forbes* magazine in October 1974. Sears was in trouble, and some economic newsmen pounced on the story the way vultures swoop down on a carcass. Bad news about Sears is big news.

The news reports were both right and wrong. Right, in that Sears, which had for so long seemed immune to the problems faced by other retailers, thanks to the foresight of General Wood, now had to deal with the same frustrations and setbacks as Ward or Penney. Wrong, because Sears was hardly "just one of the boys." Ever since Sears passed Ward at the turn of the century, its dominance has never been in doubt. In 1977, writing about the new challenger, K mart, *The Wall Street Journal* said, "It probably will never catch first-place Sears, Roebuck and Co., whose $16.36 billion in sales last year nearly doubled Kresge's, but Kresge officials don't say it's impossible." K mart (soon after this article appeared, Kresge changed its name to K Mart) officials gave themselves five years to catch up to where Sears already was. It would be a statistic worth going back and checking later.

If reports of Sears's difficulties seemed to be exaggerated in the interests of writing a good story, the company's serious problems were undeniable. While its momentum would assure its continued dominance, this time, the world had changed faster than Sears. As *Business Week* wrote a year after the *Forbes* piece, Sears had an "identity crisis."

Of course, some of the company's woes in the early 1970s were due to economic conditions beyond its control. The nation had plunged into the most serious economic slowdown since the depression. Inflation devoured purchasing dollars, and unemployment sent added millions to collect government subsistence stipends. Sears, like other retailers, lost customers and their dollars. But the company was even harder hit than most because of its ownership of Allstate Insurance, which sustained whopping underwriting losses.

But bad times went even deeper. The General had foreseen the rise of the automobile and the great push to the suburbs and had recognized the economic potential of both, long before the competition. In the 1970s, the country was changing again, but the transformation was more difficult to perceive. And now, there was no Richard Sears or Julius Rosenwald or Robert Wood to come up with an appreciation of what was happening or a formula to deal with it. Sears had clearly lost one of its most valuable assets: its initiative.

The most fundamental of the changes was in American society itself. If you ask most Americans to which economic class they belong, about four-fifths will say they are "middle class." The remainder will rate themselves as "poor." The self-perception of the poor is accurate. The federal government's 1974 estimate, based on family income, found that 11 million families, about one-fifth of all American families, qualified as poor.

But what about the other 80 percent? This is the broad and mythical middle class that Sears and its competitors consider their market. As long as you believe that there is but one major economic class and its average income level is gradually rising, all you have to do is concentrate on that class and keep trying to pull your customers from families with incomes at or above the average. That has been the avowed policy of Sears.

Economist Robert L. Heilbroner has pretty well destroyed the myth of the middle class, at the same time as Sears has been operating as if it were a reality. Heilbroner, who teaches at the New School in New York, makes a good case for the existence of not one, but four, economic classes above the poor.

At the top, according to Heilbroner, are the rich. You are rich if your annual income is at least $100,000 a year. Even more important, he says, is how much you are worth. Heilbroner finds that, at most, far less than 1 percent of all families qualify as rich. These people constitute a generally unreachable market for Sears, Roebuck and Company.

Below the rich comes the upper class, one in which some Americans would be surprised to find themselves. About 5 percent, or 2.75 million families, fall into this category, based on an annual income of more than $32,000 in 1974. One reason why many in this category still think of themselves as middle class is that their standing is based on income, not wealth. "The true upper-class family stays there after retirement," says Heilbroner, "because it has dividends and interest to supplement its retirement pay." Those who do not, drop to the next lower class when they retire. However you define this class, it is of considerable interest to Sears. These are people in middle management or professional work, and they have large disposable incomes that make them prime customers for the big-ticket items on which Sears makes the biggest profit.

Then, at last comes the middle class. But it is a lot smaller than generally believed, says the professor. Still, it represents about 35 percent of all the families in the United States. Its income limits are $15,000 up to $32,000.

This is the primary class at which Sears aims. Heilbroner notes that this class is both smaller and less wealthy than is generally believed. Sears wants these customers because it has assumed, like most of the rest of us, that, most people are actually members of this class. But we are wrong. What we may be overlooking is the largest single group of all.

Perhaps about 40 percent of the population belong to what Heilbroner labels the working class. These are the people "on the make," that traditional economic class that is striving to move up the economic ladder. Family incomes fall between the $6,500 that marks the top income of the poor and the $15,000 that is the start of the middle class. These are the families of so-called blue collar workers—factory people, bus drivers, and maintenance men. People in this group have to watch their spending carefully because they have little disposable income after taking care of the essentials of food, shelter, and transportation. They look for low prices and no frills. In fact, the growth of discount stores is a recognition of the growth of a class with limited buying power.

This working class is the same group that was the basic foundation of the Sears market. The company biography, published in 1949, states it clearly. "Throughout its history the fundamental appeal the company has had for buyers has been standard-quality goods at low prices. . . . it does seem clear that the customers of Sears, Roebuck and Company were convinced that Sears sold for less."

Over the years, Sears stayed with those customers who had been attracted by its low prices. They went to the cities and so did Sears. Their income levels rose in suburbia, and Sears upgraded the quality and cost of its products. Many of the original Sears families rose to the middle class, and Sears went right along with them.

There was a sound, economic philosophy behind this policy of "trading up." By the 1960s, however, it had become obvious to management that there were no new frontiers for the company to cross as a stimulus to sales. The catalog remained a major part of the business, but other companies were entering the field, often using Sears's own techniques. At one time Sears had represented more than half of all catalog sales, but the rise of the specialty firms was eating into its domination. In fact, their challenge, more than any other factor, led to the proliferation of Sears's own specialty catalogs.

Sears could not rely on adding more big stores as a way of promoting growth. After 50 years in the retail business, it had stores just about everywhere they would be profitable. To push expansion much further would have meant putting stores into marginal markets.

That left Sears with its merchandise. How could the company make the goods sold in its stores bring in a higher profit? The answer was to move gradually up to higher-priced items. As prices go higher, if volume remains the same, profits will climb. Besides, there is usually a bigger profit on more expensive items. To *Forbes,* the strategy looked like this: "Imagine McDonald's introducing a sirloin steak, raising the price of its Big Mac and withdrawing its plain hamburger. That was Sears' growth strategy, namely, to 'trade up America,' as some insiders put it."

It is hard to know if Sears actually thought that it was merely sticking with its core clientele or if "trading up" was the only way to keep profits growing. In either case, the company's customers ran into trouble with the stagflation of the 1970s, and suddenly "trading up" was not a wholly workable idea. The disposable income of Sears customers simply did not allow for "trading up." Instead, they were looking for bargains that Sears no longer offered.

If Heilbroner's analysis is right, then Sears was gradually deserting the economic class that had made the company for one that had barely existed when Sears had started out in business.

Not only was Sears a "traitor" to its class, but it also suffered because of a fundamental change in the attitude of many American consumers. In the immediate postwar period, people eagerly splurged their disposable income in a rash of consumer purchases. This buying did not represent merely pent-up demand after the sacrifices of the war years but was a sure sign of emergence from the working class by millions of people. Educated under the G.I. Bill, young men, children of factory workers, were able to achieve managerial and professional positions. With their new-found income, they set out to buy the luxuries of life about which their families had always dreamed.

But their children had a different viewpoint. They had never been "have-nots," and so mere material possessions were not as important. Of course, they still sought the good life in a material sense, but they began to think more about what they were buying. Whether they knew it or not, Ralph Nader and his cohorts were affecting their consumer behavior. Add to this the energy crisis, and a new consumer mentality was becoming evident. People became more conservative customers, and they recognized that there must be limits to their acquisitiveness, simply because the supply of raw materials was finite. This recognition reinforced the experience of inflation, leading people to be more careful shoppers. Inflation alone might have been just a passing phase, one from which the big-spending consumer would emerge unchanged. But something more fundamental had happened. As one investment house wrote in its analysis of Sears's prospects: "We believe that demand and supply factors have changed for retailers. We expect that the 'tougher,' value-oriented consumer will be with us through the 1970s and was not just a cyclical phenomenon."

There was a hard reality behind this appraisal. The cost of food and energy had risen to take a bigger share of family income, and that was unlikely to change. So there was less left to spend at Sears and other retailers.

These developments put Sears at a competitive disadvantage. Other retailers could increase their sales by opening more stores. Unlike Sears, they had not yet covered all the good markets. Their expansion inevitably brought them into more direct competition with Sears, a situation that no longer discouraged them if they were able to sell at a lower price. At the same time, local merchants, even in Sears's prized appliance market, were able to compete on the basis of lower prices, thanks to improved distribution, which allowed them to benefit from economies of scale. Suppliers came increasingly to treat them as though they were outlets of a single chain.

If Sears had failed to perceive that economic conditions and changes in the consumer mentality would put it in a difficult competitive position, it was not insensitive to the need for action once problems began appearing in the balance sheet. The first apparent measures were designed to meet the discounters on their own grounds by cutting prices and frills. The secret of K mart's success is its ability to appeal to the working class. Contrast these two remarks. Said a woman in a Sears store in Connecticut, "An average-income family can't afford to shop here anymore." Meanwhile, a man in an Illinois K mart explained, "Things are a few pennies cheaper here. Do I need any other reason?"

Budget shops have been introduced into some Sears stores, but without the kind of fanfare that might have been expected. Some store managers were openly reluctant to give much space to these departments, whose merchandise would earn only low profits, and some Sears competitors claimed that the giant retailer was using its budget stores as dumping grounds for merchandise it was having a hard time selling. Clearly, the budget store experiment would need more impetus from headquarters if it were to have a major impact on the company's fortunes.

Another move was to test ministores in small towns. These stores would stock only the most popular lines. And Sears would borrow heavily from the discounters in operating them.

K mart showed just how far this kind of trend might go. It has shopping carts, check-out counters, few sales people. *Business and Society Review* rated it as one of the worst American firms, when it comes to social responsibility. "K mart doesn't have to be community minded, because it's not really part of any community," it said.

That was one of the results of having free-standing stores, far from the madding mall, in sharp contrast to Sears.

The reason for keeping these initial efforts to deal with the inroads made by discounters and other retailers relatively quiet was that Sears did not want to abandon its effort to upgrade. The real challenge would be to find a way of holding on to its middle-class customers while trying to make contact again with working class people. And, even if it were going to take on the discounters, it would have to avoid selling discounters' goods. A large part of the company's good image derives from its reputation for the durability and soundness of its products. A study by the Council on Economic Priorities, a private group, rated K mart last in product safety in three major categories. Although K mart officials challenged the findings, Sears could never afford even to be suspected of such a fall from its own standards.

In 1976, Sears undertook a structural reform that was designed to allow it to adjust to the challenge of the discounters, and K mart in particular. At the heart of the reform was increased centralization, with a consequent reduction in the autonomy of local store managers. That was entirely characteristic of K mart, which allows its local people little discretion and designs all of its stores according to the same basic pattern. Prices on key Sears goods would henceforth be set nationally in order to give the company sufficient flexibility to compete with K mart.

But the fallout of the 1976 reform went much further. Traditionally, each store manager had been judged on his monthly profit-and-loss statement. As a result, the pressure was on the managers to ring up as impressive a profit as possible, and selling more big ticket items, with higher profit per item, was the accepted way to accomplish this goal. Volume might be sacrificed as long as a manager could achieve an impressive performance in sales as against costs. Yet this approach conflicted with the objectives of merchandisers, who were given the job of realizing purchase savings through volume buying. In short, store managers were interested in profit margins, not volume, while merchandisers were shooting for increased profit through increased volume. Obviously, there was an inherent conflict. What is more, store managers were loath to go along with company directives to cut prices, and they had the discretionary authority to refuse to follow such orders. If they lowered prices, their profit-and-loss statements would suffer, they reasoned.

The store managers' approach undermined the Sears tradition of offering given lines at three price levels. Generally, they chose to carry Sears's own brand-name, quality lines to the detriment or outright exclusion of lower-priced lines. For example, you could find high-quality Craftsman tools, but no inexpensive tools.

Freewheeling managers could disrupt the company's inventory planning in another way. They could obtain from suppliers items to be placed on sale at special reduced prices. Instead of ordering just what they needed for the sale period, they would build up their stocks for selling even after the promotional drive. These goods then crowded out other, less profitable items, which were then not available to budget-minded customers.

Beginning in early 1977, Sears began compensating managers on a basis different from the traditional approach, which had emphasized keeping the margin between operating costs and sales as large as possible. That approach was based on keeping each store as far in the black as possible, but it was not in the best interest of the company as a whole because it sacrificed sales volume. In short, for the first time, Sears recognized that the whole was more than the sum of its parts. Now compensation is based more on overall sales volume. Obviously, the managers must still turn a profit, but with sales volume as the measuring rod, they can afford to push items with a lower profit margin, those very items that tend to appeal to working-class customers. At the same time, there should remain little incentive for store managers to fix selling prices above those intended by the company. If the laws of supply and demand still apply, lowering prices should help increase volume. Sears store managers know how to promote sales, and the most dynamic salesmen among them were licking their chops in anticipation of the marketing challenge when the new system began. From the point of view of the aerie in the Sears Tower, the new system had another obvious advantage. For the first time, store managers and merchandisers, the key people in the retail operation, would both be after the same goal: increasing sales volume.

The overall strategy, of which the change in compensating store managers was a major part, has gradually emerged. The company wants to hold on to the markets it has acquired among the middle class. Because it does not want suddenly to begin transmitting a new message to them, that it is merely another discounter, it will certainly not pull back from what it has been doing. Instead, the new strategy is based on adding another facet to Sears's operations.

Where can Sears increase its share of the market? It will first take on the discounters, by stocking lower-priced merchandise. Certainly, the company has a great deal of experience in attempting to undersell the market. To some extent, it must recapture the spirit of Richard Sears in conveying to its traditional market, one that may have felt deserted by Sears, that it is again offering good-quality items at low prices. The puffery will be absent, but Richard Sears's aggressivensss should be felt again.

Of course, Sears is not actually a discounter and does not see itself becoming one. The low-priced lines will not be as extensive as those in chain stores that carry nothing other than discount goods. But the change means the reappearance of distinct price levels for certain key items, those that are in big demand and through which Sears can rather rapidly acquire an image as a provider of low-priced goods. The orders coming from the new Office of the Chairman on price relate as much to the tickets at the bottom of the line as to those at the top. Store managers will be expected to toe the line on these directives. And Sears will make a major effort to advertise certain goods selling at the bottom of the line.

Keeping inventories at about the right level has always been one of the strong points for retailers and catalog houses. When they guess wrong, they risk either losing customers or losing profits. Understocking costs customers, and overstocking means that, later, prices will have to be cut deeply to move the merchandise. Part of the new strategy will be to keep inventories of lower-priced goods sufficiently large. Store managers still have the right to determine the inventory of their outlets, but their discretion will be limited by the increased use of basic merchandise lists, representing products that they must always have available for sale. And they will be under new rules designed to prevent them from overstocking big-ticket items during promotional campaigns. The idea is to come closer to the discounters, which behave more like supermarkets than department stores. Stores will have to carry a wider variety of goods, which will prevent managers from devoting space to big inventories in specific items. As a result, just as in the supermarkets, inventories will have to be turned over more frequently. At the same time, this practice will allow top management to give orders to respond to competition from discounters and to see a fast response to those orders.

In another move designed to reach into the discounters' market, Sears is pushing budget departments selling women's apparel. By giving more space to budget stores and stocking them properly, the company can expand both sales and merchandising efforts in this area. One investment research department estimates that Sears is aiming for 10 percent of the $5 billion national market in budget women's wear.

Sears is trying to hold on to its "upgraded" middle-class customers while returning to a major effort to sell to its traditional working-class clientele. Even beyond upgrading, Sears wants to increase its higher-priced lines, an effort that would probably have to be made no matter what else had happened. Sears had come to view this market as the one where it could expand. The critical *Forbes* article had quoted one competitor as saying: "I keep asking myself: 'What is Sears' next growth kicker?' I can't think of anything." Sears could, and it was a push into this higher-priced market—the upper class and the rich. In its staple items, like appliances and tools, the company had already succeeded in establishing itself as providing the top of the line. Even in other areas, where it had not been known for being the quality leader, it had scored notable successes. It had brought premium radial tires to a broad market, as well as the Die-Hard battery, Weatherbeater paint, Toughskins jeans, and even furniture, an area where it had had little reputation for quality.

It is no happenstance that these products have all been associated with specific brand names that have been heavily promoted. Sears sees the use of its own proprietary names as the way of selling better-quality goods. It has put substantial resources into research and development of its own products in recent years. One example is the dual-action washing machine agitator, which it thinks will help sell a lot more top-quality appliances. Whirlpool will make the new machines for Sears, but because Sears paid for the research, Whirlpool will not be able to introduce the new feature into its own machine.

The initiative in this drive rests with the merchandisers, who are to watch for new developments and products. Sears does not want to wait until others have moved heavily into the markets for better products because the biggest profits are to be made in skimming the cream. Merchandisers can now be more confident that the Office of the Chairman will oblige store managers to carry the new products they develop and that the company will also back them up with increased promotion.

The biggest opportunities, or the greatest problems, depending on how you look at it, have been in selling clothing. Here, at least, Sears has been successful in sticking with its traditional customers, the people who buy work clothes and simple dresses. Most of its sales of clothing are at an average well below the industry averages. For example, its average selling price for a dress is $25. The company would like to keep its average low, even as it sells more apparel at higher prices. Sears lacks the fashion image that its competitors— department and speciality stores—have already developed. You can ask any male executive at Sears where he gets his suits, and he will display a Sears label. But many will admit that they are wearing a special order item that is not generally available in the stores. Sears wants to introduce such apparel to its racks and thereby encourage men to accept the Sears label on the lining in the same way that they accept those of more prestigious stores.

In women's clothing, the company is trying mightily to gain a fashion image. Never particularly subtle in its advertising, it is calling its women's departments the Fashion Place. It has added big-name designer collections and even hired a fashion coordinator away from Bloomingdales. And it is displaying fashion merchandise better than ever before.

In short, Sears, the retailer, is trying to do two things at once. It wants to recapture its traditional market by offering them goods in direct competition with the discounteres. At the same time, it wants to increase sales to more affluent customers both through upgrading and opening new markets. To some this might appear contradictory and even self-defeating. But, at least one investment house research department takes a differing view. "In fact, it appears to position Sears strongly in the role of a promotional department store, a retailer sector that was virtually abandoned as traditional department stores upgraded earlier." Perhaps the most important reason why Sears thinks it can pull off its plan to be all things to all men —and, more importantly, women—is its sheer size. At various times, large segments of the American population have thought of Sears as the place that carries just about everything they might want. What Sears is trying to accomplish is the creation of that image for both the working class and the middle class.

Traditionally, both the store manager and the merchandiser have been the keys to Sears's success. Given the freedom to act as they thought best and stimulated by a bigger paycheck if they helped rack up more profits, they became the symbols of the company's way of doing business. Although there will still be plenty of room for store managers to ring up handsome incomes, the reform at Sears means that the merchandisers alone will be dominant.

Because of the enormous size of their orders, merchandisers have to be able to commit the company well in advance. Now, under the new system, when the Office of the Chairman approves a merchandising program, they will be assured that their selections will be sold in Sears stores. This is vital if the company is to be able to offer goods at lower prices. Bigger orders have always meant lower costs for each item, and the system that allows Chicago to dictate to store managers means that Sears will be asking for longer production runs. If all goes well, not all of the savings will be passed on to customers. Some will go toward increasing profits.

Each of the nine new merchandising groups is run like a separate business. Merchandisers are expected to develop formal, written marketing plans for lines under their control. The commercial life cycle of each product will be outlined and analyzed in such plans. The life cycle of a product begins with its development, continues through its commercial exploitation, and ends when the product is replaced by something new. With projections for each product, top management is aiming to be in a position to judge the company's needs and its promotional requirements well in advance. For those goods that reach a stage of "maturity," or relative market saturation, Sears will have to try to bring prices down. That, in turn, will be possible because store managers will have to follow instructions on selling and pricing such goods. For products at an early stage in their life cycles, Sears should be in an especially good position because it develops its own brand-name goods.

But trying to build up Sears's own brand-name items will not be good enough. The company has traditionally been reluctant to stock goods closely associated with other manufacturers because top management has worried that they do not reflect Sears's own characteristics and style and, hence, dissipate the company's marketing advantage. But, in some areas at least, this advantage has been more apparent than real. Customers are doubtful about Sears electronic equipment and photographic supplies, for example, which are in direct competition with heavily promoted goods enjoying a sound reputation. The demise of fair trade laws, which set minimum selling prices, was something of a blow to Sears, which had originally opposed them. When they were removed by a combination of nonobservance and legal repeal, Sears found that it could be undercut by many competitors. Now, it has decided to sell others' goods under their own names. You simply cannot "out-Kodak" Kodak, and there is no way to compete with top-quality Fisher tape decks; so Sears sells them. Thus, Sears can be expected to maintain its brand-name products as its ultimate source of retailing strength while adding other lines that already have a strong and unbeatable public identity.

Sears may also get into other kinds of business. For example, it has given some space in an El Monte, California, store to a dental clinic. When asked the reason for this move, the company's Western Territory concessions manager said, "We're always interested in expanding the number of services we offer in the hope that customers will think of additional reasons to come to our stores and shop."

This effort to convert the company's considerable "drawing power" into "selling power" is a vital part of the effort to compete with the discounters. K mart claims to have reached three-quarters of the American population, just as has Sears. So simply getting people into the store does not assure Sears of a competitive advantage. If this effort to turn browsers into purchasers is to be successful, a lot depends on how merchandise is displayed. So Sears may look a lot different over the coming years as Chicago issues even more explicit instructions to the retail stores on how they should display merchandise to attract customer interest.

Surprising as it may seem, Sears has always lacked a long-range plan of operations. The entire reform represents an attempt to get the company's destiny more nearly under control. In 1972, Arthur Wood established a planning group with the job of looking at the kind of business the company should be doing ten years down the road. If it is successful, Sears should be able to avoid the kind of crisis caused in the 1970s by the combined impact of stagflation and the discounters.

The changes at Sears in the mid 1970s represent a big change for the company. Even a conservative investment advisory report hazards this conclusion: "While it is too soon to make definitive optimistic estimates of Sears' sales and profits over the next few years, we believe that it is not premature to identify the current period as a crucial turning point." The first indications were encouraging. In 1976, Sears resumed its impressive sales and profits performance.

What seems to be lacking in the reforms of Sears is the dash, the flair, and even the romance of the earlier days. Sears, Roebuck and Company, for all its size, is a company that was created by its three "greats": Sears, Rosenwald, and Wood. Obviously, their brilliance and foresight imparted to the company a momentum that has carried it forward long after they have gone. Because the company has relied so heavily on people brought up through the ranks, the heads of the company who succeeded the "greats" embodied the same values and the same way of looking at the business.

These were grey people. None of them could aspire to the eminence, not only in Sears but in American business, that had been achieved by the legendary three. Unlike the men who made Sears, whose tenures were long, they have passed through the executive suite in rapid succession. General Wood once admitted that perhaps he had been at fault for not grooming people who had a better chance of remaining at the helm for a long period.

The grey people followed grey policies. It was as if the company's motto was "When in doubt, find out what Wood or Rosenwald did." This approach worked only as long as Wood's policies remained valid. But the world eventually moved out from under Sears, and the absence of the strong leader, the person who regarded Sears, Roebuck and Company as his personal fiefdom, was felt. In short, Sears became a company like other companies, run by the same kind of corporate management technicians.

It was this fall from grace that led to the exaggerated reports of its woes in the financial press. The business world had accepted Sears's special place, its ability to succeed by almost miraculous good judgment. But when the "greats" were gone and the company was run by mere mortals, it suddenly appeared vulnerable.

No corporate reform can guarantee the emergence of another great business leader. But it can remedy some of the most obvious problems resulting from the void left by the "greats." The Office of the Chairman, with four people sharing top policy positions, allows for future chief executives to be groomed at the highest level. In that way, the company may avoid the rapid turnover of the past two decades. And this new institution of collegiate corporate management, if it really works and if it is more than a way to solve transitory personnel problems, can be the structural way of compensating for the lack of a distinguished leader. In effect, the reform says that it now takes four people to replace J. R. or the General.

Of course, not everything that Sears and Rosenwald and Wood left to the company is outmoded. The essence of their lasting contribution was in making Sears an integral part of American life, a commercial reflection of solid, middle-class values. If Sears sells shoddy goods, fails to honor its guarantee, and overcharges its customers, it betrays all that remains of value in their legacy.

To be sure, these values are not pursued out of a spirit of patriotism or altruism. They represent sound business practices, whether the company is faced with the competitive challenge of Bloomindales or K mart.

In the end, the continued success of Sears depends on its ability to change the way it does business to meet changing tastes and demands and its fidelity to certain enduring characteristics that are its strength.

The 1976 reforms represent the company's bid to keep pace with the country and perhaps again to get the jump on change. Says Bert C. McCammon, professor of business administration at the University of Oklahoma, "I just can't think of another organization that has a more extraordinary track record in reprogramming itself to adapt to change."

Couple with this a commitment to Sears, Roebuck and Company. Each new generation of executives senses an obligation to keep the company growing. One Sears executive used to keep four frames on his office wall. Three held the portraits of the "greats." The fourth was kept empty—a constant challenge to each succeeding chairman to join the pantheon.

Index